AFRICAN POVERTY AT THE MILLENNIUM

Causes, Complexities, and Challenges

Howard White and Tony Killick
in collaboration with
Steve Kayizzi-Mugerwa and Marie-Angelique Savane

THE WORLD BANK
WASHINGTON, D.C.

Cover design by UltraDesigns.

ISBN: 0-8213-4867-1

Library of Congress Cataloging-in-Publication Data:
White, Howard, 1960-
    African poverty at the millennium : causes, complexities, and challenges / Howard White, Tony Killick.
        p. cm
    Includes bibliographical references.
    ISBN 0-8213-4867-1
    1. Poverty—Africa. 2. Africa—Economic conditions. I. Killick, Tony. II. Title.
    HC800.Z9 P684 2001
    339.4'6'096—dc21

Print on demand - LSI

Contents

Foreword

This report was prepared for the Strategic Partnership with Africa (SPA) by a team from the Institute of Development Studies, University of Sussex, U.K., in association with Save the Children Fund, U.K., Laval University, Canada, and the Overseas Development Institute, U.K. The team has been supported financially and technically by a Reference Group of SPA donors made up of Norway, Sweden, Switzerland, the United Kingdom, the United States, and the World Bank. The enthusiasm and commitment of this support is acknowledged with great appreciation.

According to the recent World Development Report, *Attacking Poverty,* the number of poor people (those consuming less than $1 a day) in Sub-Sahara Africa "increased from an already high 217 million (in 1987) to 291 million (in 1998) . . . leaving almost half the residents of that continent poor." (World Bank 2000) Africa's share in global income poverty has risen. And as more dimensions are added in any assessment of human suffering (incorporating also ill health, illiteracy, isolation, and insecurity), the more challenging Africa's plight appears to be. The multifaceted nature of the poverty problem and the widening gap between the levels of human well-being in Africa compared with the other developing regions are the central themes of this report.

These then are the "sobering implications" of the complexity of the poverty problem in Africa. There are no simple solutions to deal with the kaleidoscope of interlocking factors that keep many Africans in poverty. But what are the key elements of poverty reduction strategies in the region? The report rightly points to the need for accelerated economic growth if living standards are to improve for the majority of Africans. For this to occur, there obviously has to be peace, stability, and political commitment. It is also important that growth is broad based, and that rural livelihoods are fostered. And for many poor Africans, it is vital that their human capabilities are strengthened, through better access to health care and education services. This, in turn, calls for more effective delivery of public services and a strengthened, more accountable public administration. The report also warns against the dangers of overgeneralizing. Each country faces it own particular difficulties and challenges. And whatever solutions are to be applied, they must be developed and implemented by Africans in Africa.

Alan Gelb
Chief Economist, Africa Region
The World Bank

Acknowledgments

This report was prepared by Howard White and Tony Killick in collaboration with Steve Kayizzi-Mugerwa and Marie-Angelique Savane on behalf of the Strategic Partnership with Africa (SPA) under the guidance of the World Bank. Thanks are due to the members of SPA for both their financial and intellectual support to the production of this report. Considerable assistance has been provided by Nicola Desmond and inputs provided by the project advisors, Robert Chambers and Simon Maxwell.

Thanks also to Reg Green for comments on an earlier draft. Some of the ideas have been discussed at seminars at the African Development Bank, Abidjan, and the Overseas Development Institute, London. Useful comments on earlier drafts have been received from staff in several agencies, authors of the background papers, and various others. The contents of this report cannot be taken to represent the views of the SPA, World Bank, nor any member of the SPA.

Acronyms and Abbreviations

ANC	African National Congress
CDF	Comprehensive Development Framework
CFA	Communauté Financière Africaine
CGAP	Coalition for the Global Abolition of Poverty
CPR	Contraceptive Prevalence Rates
CWIQ	Core Welfare Indicators Questionnaire
DAC	Development Assistance Committee
DALY	Disability Adjusted Life Year
DFID	Department for International Development
DHS	Demographic Health Survey
EC	European Commission
EPI	Expanded Program of Immunization
EWS	Early Warning System
FDI	Foreign Direct Investment
GAPVU	*Gabinte de Apoio à População Vulnerável*
GDP	Gross Domestic Product
GWE	Growth with equity
HDI	Human Development index
HIPC	Highly Indebted Poor Country
IDA	International Development Association
ILO	International Labor Organization
IMF	International Monetary Fund
MAP	Monitoring the AIDS Pandemic
MIS	Management Information System
NGO	Nongovernmental Organization
OECD	Organization for Economic Co-operation and Development
PA	Poverty Assessment
PC	Private Consumption
PPA	Participatory Poverty Assessment
PR	Poverty Reduction
PRSP	Poverty Reduction Strategy Paper
PSR	Poverty Status Report
RDP	Reconstruction and Development Program
SME	Small and medium enterprise
SP	Sector Program
UNDP	United Nations Development Program
UNESCO	United Nations
UNIP	United National Independence Party for Zambia
UPE	Universal Primary Education
WDR	World Development Report

Executive Summary

The Nature of Poverty

Two principles must underpin poverty analysis. First, we should never forget the hardship and tragedy that lie behind the figures. Each year two million African children die before their first birthday. Virtually every one of these leaves a grieving family. Second, we must grasp the meaning of the multidimensionality of poverty. We do not mean merely that poverty has many dimensions: that dignity and autonomy are every bit as important to well-being as income, although this is true. The different dimensions of poverty interact in ways that reinforce each other; this point is the crucial insight from social exclusion. The poverty trap is as much a social phenomenon as an economic one, in many cases more so. The poor can become outcasts, whose very poverty removes them from the social

Table 1 The harsh face of poverty in Sub-Saharan Africa (approximate estimates)

The estimated total population of Africa in 1995 was 580 million. Of these:

- 291 million people had average incomes of below one dollar per day in 1998.
- 124 million of those up to age 39 years were at risk of dying before 40.
- 43 million children were stunted as a result of malnutrition in 1995.
- 205 million were estimated to be without access to health services in 1990–95.
- 249 million were without safe drinking water in 1990–95.
- More than 2 million infants die annually before reaching their first birthday.
- 139 million youths and adults were illiterate in 1995.

Sources: Word Bank, *World Development Indicators 1998*; *Human Development Report 1998*; World Bank Web site.

support systems that may have allowed them to recover their position. These two qualitative points lie behind our description of poverty in Africa, which is necessarily oriented toward more quantitative material. Table 1 provides a quantitative overview of the extent of deprivation and hardship experienced by Africans.

Two caveats cannot be repeated frequently enough. First, developing country data are of poor quality, and this point applies particularly to Africa and, specifically, to many of the indicators relating to poverty. Second, there is considerable variability in the data. But even taking these reservations into account, there has been an Africanization of global poverty. Data on income poverty since the late 1980s show Africa's share of those living on less than a dollar a day to have risen: the absolute number of poor in Africa has grown five times more than the figure for Latin America, and twice that for South Asia (table 2). Although data are not available over a longer time period, the poor economic performance of many African countries for the last two decades implies that these recent changes reflect a long-run trend. Social indicators have improved but more slowly in Africa than elsewhere. Twenty years ago infant mortality was lower in Africa than South Asia; today it is substantially higher (table 2). Primary school enrollments in South Asia have risen from just over 70 percent in the early 1980s to 100 percent. In Africa, they stand at the same level as over 20 years ago, having deteriorated in the 1980s, at under 80 percent.

The variability in African performance provides some grounds for optimism. Botswana has been one of the fastest growing economies in the world and is one of the two countries (the other is Cape Verde) in which the elimination of poverty in the near future is a real possibility. Other countries have made notable achievements in some

Table 2 Africa lags behind and the gap is widening

	Infant mortality (per 000 live births)			Primary enrollment (net)			Income poverty (absolute no. below poverty line, millions)		
	1980	*1997*	*Change*	*1980*	*1997*	*Change*	*1987*	*1998*	*Change*
Sub–Saharan Africa	115	91	–26	78	77	–1	217	291	74
East Asia and Pacific	56	37	–51	111	118	6	415	278	–137
Latin America and Caribbean	60	32	–88	105	113	7	64	78	14
Middle East and North Africa	95	49	–94	87	96	9	25	21	–4
South Asia	119	77	–55	73	100	27	474	522	48

Note: Change is percentage change.
Source: World Bank, *World Development Indicators.*

important aspects: 15 out of 46 African countries have primary gross enrolment rates in excess of 100 percent, although some have struggled to maintain such levels in the face of economic decline and the quality of education is a major concern. But there are also many grounds for pessimism. The last three decades have seen the weakening of economic and political systems. In the last two decades 28 countries have been involved in conflict: in the mid-1990s close to 4 percent of Africa's population were displaced persons. The devastating effects of HIV/AIDS are far from having worked through, robbing families of their livelihood, draining family and health service resources and leaving children orphaned. Finally, many African economies are faced with a fragile environment, with poor soils and frequent drought.

Who are the poor?

Categorizing and characterizing the poor is not an atheoretical activity. It defines the understanding of poverty, and directs us to its causes. Three overlapping categorizations are important in the African context: chronic versus transitory poverty, poor versus destitute, and the dependent versus the economically active poor. The destitute, many of whom are dependents such as elderly (particularly women whose assets are taken when they become widowed) and disabled, count amongst the chronically poor. But many of the economically active may move in and out of poverty, being vulnerable to spells of poverty on account of either personally specific (idiosyncratic) shocks such as illness or theft or more general (structural) shocks such as conflict, drought, or economic crisis. Households are also more likely to be poor at certain stages of the household life cycle, when there are many young children (being partly responsible for the link between large household size and poverty), or once children have

moved away to establish their own households. Analysis of the dynamics of poverty is constrained by the limited availability of panel data, but the available evidence shows that less than one-quarter of the population in a range of African countries are always poor, with up to 60 percent of the population (but more usually around one-quarter) moving in and out of poverty (table 3). This pattern confirms what data from other developing countries has shown—that transitory poverty is a common phenomenon, pointing to the importance of vulnerability and of securing livelihoods as an antipoverty strategy. However, how people survive moves into poverty, why it happens and how they escape again (and the implications of this phenomenon for poverty measurement) remains one of the key gaps in our knowledge.

But these results should not lead us to ignore the importance of poverty traps: mechanisms by which once people become poor they cannot escape it. The poor, of course, have fewer assets and are less able to accumulate either physical or human capital, and may also be excluded from their community's social capital. More graphically, the children of the poor are more likely to be malnourished, illiterate, and landless (table 4). The poor can ill-afford the complementary inputs to enhance the productivity of the assets they have, be it fertilizer or new technology for land, or school equipment for their children, or allowing them time to study. Those with few assets are also the most vulnerable. A period without income caused, for example, by illness can lead them to sell off even the few assets they have. Inability to afford treatment during illness can leave someone permanently debilitated or disabled. And they are less likely to have the resources to either cope with or recover from large-scale shocks such as displacement or the loss of family members through violence or HIV/AIDS. Poverty traps may also be termed "irreversibilities," where a period of hardship results in

Table 3 Proportion of households always poor, sometimes poor, and never poor

		Always poor	Sometimes poor	Never poor
Africa				
Côte d'Ivoire	1985–86	14.5	20.2	65.3
Côte d'Ivoire	1986–87	13.0	22.9	64.1
Côte d'Ivoire	1987–88	25.0	22.0	53.0
Ethiopia	1994–95	24.8	30.1	45.1
South Africa	1993–98	22.7	31.5	45.8
Zimbabwe	1992–95	10.6	59.6	29.8
Other				
Chile	1967–85	54.1	31.5	29.8
China	1985–90	6.2	47.8	46.0
India	1968–70	33.3	36.7	30.0
India	1975–83	21.8	65.8	12.4
Pakistan	1986–91	3.0	55.3	57.2
Russia	1992–93	12.6	30.2	14.4

Source: Baulch and Hoddinot (1999).

permanent deprivation. The ultimate irreversibility is premature death, which affects millions of Africans each year. For children who do not die, their physical and intellectual development can be permanently impaired by periods of malnutrition.

Key characteristics of the poor lead to the identification of several groups of the poor. Lack of able-bodied adult male labor is the key characteristic of many of the traditional poor: the elderly (particularly widows), female-headed households, disabled, and orphaned. Conflict and HIV/AIDS are giving rise to an increasing number of street children and child-headed households, who are marginalized from many productive opportunities. Analysis of household survey data from several countries suggests that female-headed households are not necessarily poorer than those with male heads. But this view is at odds with the results from qualitative studies, and is explained by the tendency to classify as female-headed those households with no currently resident male, thereby including in this group those with a male relative who has migrated

and is remitting income. Closer analysis of Tanzanian survey data reveals that, although female-headed houses have approximately the same per capita consumption as male-headed ones, female-headed households with no supporting male (widowed and divorced) have mean consumption barely more than one-half that of other female-headed households

Analysis of the same data set shows households with a disabled member to have mean consumption of less than 60 percent of the average (and a headcount 20 percent greater than average). Disability is a hidden face of African poverty. It is not a residual category, unamenable to policy intervention. The poor are more likely to suffer as the physical burden of their labor makes them more exposed to injury and causes them to be disabled by illness or injury that would not be a great affliction for a more sedentary worker. Limited access to health care is likely to turn a minor ailment or injury into a permanent disability, illustrating another irreversibility faced by the poor.

These averages do not tell us about intrahousehold allocation, which further reinforces the patterns already described. Women work longer hours than men (in Ghana and Tanzania women spend nearly three times as much time on transport, and transport four times as much as men), consume less of household income, and are less likely to resort to medical treatment for illness. Women's freedom continues to be restricted, female enrollment rates are lower than those for boys, and they are subject to high rates of domestic violence: poverty has a double negative impact on women. Within a household, it breeds violence against women and children. Redistributive social structures may provide some relief to the poor but does not bring them to equal status. Orphans and "poor cousins" are often less well fed and clothed and have heavier workloads: once again child poverty emerges as a critical feature of African poverty requiring direct attention. A Bemba man commented that "no one would know the difference between a slave and a poor relative," a quote that points to the position of slaves. Despite laws to the contrary,

Table 4 Characteristics of poverty (selected countries)[a]

	Guinea–Bissau	Lesotho	Malawi	Uganda	Zambia
Household size (avg. for poor/avg. for nonpoor) (%)	116	97	123	127	124
Location in poorest region (% poor relative to national average)	130	163	129	147	138
Literacy (% poor relative to national average)	73	84	94	96[b]	92

a. Countries selected on basis of data availability. Data mainly relate to late 1980s or early 1990s.
b. A later estimate for Uganda yields a ratio of 78 percent.
Source: Hanmer, Pyatt, and White 1997, tables A3.1 and A3.2.

slavery, or conditions of servitude sufficiently close to slavery as to make no difference, continue in several countries.

The economically active poor are characterized by their lack of assets and lack of access to services and to markets. This lack is conditional on various factors such as remoteness, gender, and ethnicity. In most countries 90 percent or more of the poor are rural, many living away from roads. Women lack access to institutions to increase the productivity of their labor. Other important groups of the poor, both estimated at around 10 percent of Africa's rural population, are the landless and pastoralists. Landlessness appears to have declined following independence, but has reemerged in the last two decades, a process that will probably be accelerated by the privatization of land. Pastoralists tend to be illiterate and both geographically and politically remote. They are often not covered by household surveys (for instance, in Mauritania) but are clearly among the poor. Other groups, usually different ethnically but also in their means of livelihood, which have been historically marginalized, continue to be so. The San in Botswana are one example, accounting for the high degree of inequality in that otherwise successful country.

Related to the effects of remoteness is the fact that there are very large intranational variations in well-being. For example, although Ghana's infant mortality rate is only 75 compared to Nigeria's 91, infants in Ghana's northern region face a higher probability of premature death (with a rate of 114) than those born in any of Nigeria's four regions (table 5). With a variation in rates between regions from 49 to 1,994, Ghana is an extreme case, but significant variability is also found in other countries, for example, a low of 56 in Tanzania compared to a maximum of 128.

The nature of poverty is changing. The catastrophic effects of conflict undermine the livelihoods of whole communities. The estimated 20 million refugees across the continent constitute a growing share of the poor. Refugees often lack access to food and long periods without access to services. In refugee camps, immunization rates are low and malnourishment and infant mortality high. HIV/AIDS has also played an important part in reversing the downward trend in infant and child mortality and strikes at families who might otherwise have been expected to be safe from poverty. In consequence, life expectancy has been falling in the worst hit countries; for Botswana life expectancy will have fallen to 40 during the next decade, whereas if there had been no AIDS epidemic it would have been approaching 70. Both conflict and AIDS have severe implications for children, who may be forced to join the swelling ranks of street children, child prostitutes, or child soldiers. Less dramatically, urbanization is proceeding— the share of urban areas in total population doubling to 30 percent since 1960—and, with it, urban poverty has become increasingly important. Formal-sector employment has failed to keep pace, and in some countries even fallen; this trend has typically put the burden on women to become breadwinners. The urban poor are rather different than those in rural areas, living in slum conditions and increasing insecurity being major aspects of their poverty.

These changes make the already scanty data on income poverty difficult to interpret (table 6). There has been a sharp rise in the percentage of the population below the poverty line in Nigeria, little change in Zambia, but a substantial fall in rural Ethiopia, Mauritania, and Uganda. As may be expected in at least some cases, trends for urban

Table 5 There is substantial intranational variation in well-being: infant mortality rates by region in selected countries

	Region									National
	1	*2*	*3*	*4*	*5*	*6*	*7*	*8*	*9*	
Tanzania (1996)	128	108	107	99	80	56	...	...	...	97
Sudan (1990)	77	71	97	62	75	91	...	...	...	79
Nigeria (1990)	88	110	83	85	...	...	...	...	...	91
Malawi (1992)	121	130	144	...	...	...	...	...	...	132
Namibia (1992)	56	84	56	...	...	...	...	...	...	65
Ghana (1993)	76	72	58	78	56	65	49	114	105	75
Eritrea (1995)	107	93	70	87	71	57	...	...	...	81
Zambia (1992)	69	114	77	149	71	132	...	...	...	102
Zimbabwe (1994)	44	54	...	...	...	...	...	...	...	49
Uganda (1995)	77	98	99	75	...	...	...	...	...	87

... Not applicable.
Source: Demographic Health Surveys (various years).

Table 6 Consumption poverty trends (selected African countries)

		Headcount		Squared poverty gap[a]	
		Year 1	Year 2	Year 1	Year 2
Burkina Faso	Rural	51.1	50.7		
1994–1998	Urban	10.4	15.8		
	Total	44.5	45.3		
Ethiopia					
1989–1995	Rural	61.3	45.9	17.4	9.9
1994–1997	Urban	40.9	38.7	8.3	7.8
Ghana	Rural	37.5	30.2		
1989–1992	Urban	19.0	20.6		
	Total	31.9	27.4		
Mauritania	Rural	72.1	58.9	27.4	11.9
1987–96	Urban	43.5	19.0	9.7	2.1
	Total	59.5	41.3	17.5	7.5
Nigeria	Rural	45.1	67.8	15.9	25.6
1992–96	Urban	29.6	57.5	12.4	24.9
	Total	42.8	65.6	14.2	25.1
Uganda	Rural	59.4	48.2	10.9	6.56
1992–1997	Urban	29.4	16.3	3.5	1.65
	Total	55.6	44.0	9.9	5.9
Zambia	Rural	79.6	74.9	39.1	23.2
1991–1996	Urban	31.0	34.0	9.7	5.4
	Total	57.0	60.0	25.5	16.6
Zimbabwe	Rural	51.5	62.8	10.2	13.0
1991–1996	Urban	6.2	14.9	0.5	1.4
	Total	37.5	47.2	7.2	9.3

a. Poverty gap measures the average distance below the poverty line, and the severity measure gives more weight to the poorest.
Source: Data provided by the World Bank.

poverty are less favorable than those for rural areas (Ethiopia, Ghana, and Zambia). Similar observations apply with respect to the squared poverty gap, which captures how far below the line people are with greatest weight to the poorest, with the exception of Uganda where this measure has risen despite the fall in the poverty headcount.

This review of the nature of poverty highlights some important and sobering facts. First is the scale of the problem, and that it is in some respects worsening. The pessimism arises from the fact that political instability continues unabated, and that many politically stable countries continue to have poor economic performance. But a second key finding is the variability in both the experiences of a specific country and in the nature of poverty between countries. First some countries have made, and continue to make, substantial progress in tackling various aspects of poverty. Second, the poor are far from undifferentiated, and different groups are poor for different reasons and will require different interventions. But there are substantial numbers of both the dependent and economically active poor who cannot be automatically assumed to benefit from growth where this does occur. Conflict, HIV/AIDS, and the impact they have on traditional safety nets all point to the fact that poverty reduction is about far more than the pursuit of growth.

The Causes of Poverty

There is no established theory of poverty, a conceptual framework that allows the identification of the major causal factors in a particular setting. However, the causes may be classified in various ways, three of which appear particularly helpful. First, they may be classified by social process: economic, political, social/demographic, and situational (for example, remoteness). Second, they may be classified by level: international, national (macro), and household (micro). One set of factors (for instance, poor economic performance) determines the overall level of poverty in a country, and another, such as lack of education, determines which households are poor. Finally, causes may be identified as being either primary or proximate. It is also worth noting that many causes interact, so that cause and effect are not always easy to determine.

Political and social causes are identified as primary causes of poverty, with a poor environmental base and demographic factors also listed as such. Low rates of economic growth, clearly a key factor in discussing African poverty, are identified as a proximate causes, an outcome of political systems unfavorable to growth.

Economic stagnation has caused much poverty, and worsening distribution has exacerbated the situation

There is no denying the link between growth and poverty reduction: the incomes of the poor rise with overall growth (figure 1). Countries with large numbers of poor need growth to reduce these numbers. The causes of poverty are thus to be found partly in the causes for the relative, and in many cases absolute, decline in African economic performance that began in the mid-1970s (figure 2).

Figure 1 The income of the poor grows with overall growth

Income growth of bottom 20 percent (percent per year)

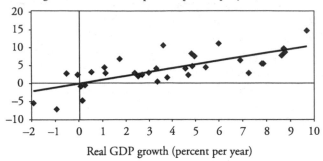

Real GDP growth (percent per year)

Source: Roemer and Gugerty (1997, table 4)

Figure 2 Income and consumption show long-term decline

Percent

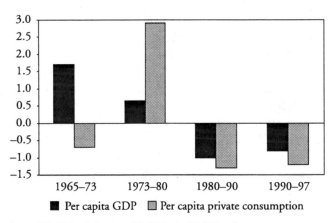

■ Per capita GDP ▨ Per capita private consumption

Source: World Bank database; World Bank, *World Development Indicators 1999.*

Performance in the 1990s has been mixed. Countries in conflict have recorded falls in output, and most others averaged rates below population growth. A handful has achieved average rates close to or above 5 percent, but the weakness of many fundamentals is not encouraging. A more positive note is that the demographic transition has begun in the majority of cases, which, as discussed below, can help usher in higher growth.

The extent to which higher growth, where achieved, reduces poverty depends on both the initial distribution and subsequent changes in distribution. Much is said about the need for pro-poor growth, that is, growth from which the poor receive a disproportionate share of the benefits.

But the evidence that what growth there is constitutes this kind is not encouraging. The macro level evidence shows Africa to have high levels of income inequality, and it has worsened in the last decade. Gender inequalities persist in access to physical, human, and social capital, and are argued by many to result in inefficiencies in resource allocation that undermine productivity. At the sectoral level, the continuing poor performance of African agriculture suggests a pessimistic picture with respect to the spread of the benefits of growth. And poorer regions, which are usually the more remote, often seem too disconnected from macroeconomic developments to join in increases in prosperity. While rapid gains in yield in other developing areas may hint at the potential to be realized in Africa, the constraints appear formidable. The analysis of who the poor are suggests several groups who may well not benefit from growth: the dependent poor, the landless, smallholders producing for subsistence (particularly those in remote areas), pastoralists, the unemployed, and many in the informal sector.

What are the causes of this low growth? This poor performance cannot be blamed on external factors: world trade has been booming and Africa received record aid inflows until very recently. For many countries political instability and outright conflict have undermined economic performance. But in others, in which a measure of stability has been preserved, the fundamentals of economic growth—investment in both physical and human capital—has remained weak. As described below, the initial postindependence drive to higher service provision soon faltered. Investment was propped up by capital inflows in the 1970s, but efficiency was low and declined as the capital stock rapidly depreciated (resulting, of course, in the debt problem that persists to this day): infrastructure crumbled and capacity utilization was low. The external environment is not in itself the problem. African economies have responded weakly to the possibilities offered by globalization, as a result of the inadequate role accorded market signals. The export record and export diversification have been poor, and the continent has failed to attract private investment on a significant scale. But the reasons for "bad policies" need to be sought in the political situation.

This story of the reasons for low growth is repeated looking at the most important sector for poverty reduction: agriculture. As shown in table 7, African agricultural performance lags behind that of other regions, and the level of inputs is much lower. Rural households have increasingly diversified their income sources to nonagricultural

Table 7 Indicators of agricultural change (1979–81 to 1995–97)

		Sub–Saharan Africa		Latin America & Caribbean		South Asia	
		1979–81	1995–97	1979–81	1995–97	1979–81	1995–97
1.	Irrigated land (% of cropland)	3.6	3.8	9.8	11.2	27.8	37.2
2.	Fertilizer consumption (kg. per arable ha.)	419	576	786	931	918	1370
3.	Food production index (1989–91 = 100)	79.5	108.3	80.4	118.9	70.3	119.2
4.	Cereal yield (kg. per ha.)	1089	1050	1840	2576	1410	2197

Source: World Bank, *World Development Indicators 1999*, tables 3.2 and 3.3.

activities. But thin rural labor markets and increased competition in the informal sector mean that income from these sources is often very insubstantial (for instance, making small margins on trading single items).

The facts presented here allow us to answer the central questions in "the debate that won't go away" concerning the impact of economic reform ("structural adjustment") on the poor. Against the view that, where properly implemented, reform policies have resulted in higher growth, others continue to argue that the poor suffer. This issue is best approached by considering two questions: (i) whether adjustment has caused increases or reductions in poverty and (ii) whether the poor have been adequately protected during adjustment. The main link between most economic reforms and poverty is growth. While some policies, such as macroeconomic stability, have a well-demonstrated positive impact of growth, the same is not true of all liberalization measures. The correct balance between state and market remains a matter of considerable debate, with a shift back in the 1990s toward an increased role for the state. Furthermore, the distributional impact of reforms is at best unclear, but early claims that policy change would improve distribution appear to have been unfounded. There are also reasons to believe that women's burden has been increased by some policies, although there are also cases of gain, such as the role of women traders in West Africa.

With respect to the second question—have the poor been protected?—the answer must be no. The picture with respect to social spending is mixed, and, despite efforts to build safety nets these have remained largely limited in both scope and effectiveness. There is no indication that attention has been paid to the distributional impact of policies to be implemented let alone redesign of policies to improve that impact. Policy management under adjustment has thus continued a tradition of neglect of

poverty reduction, which brings us to the issue of government failure.

Both states and markets have failed the poor

The political context has held back poverty reduction in four ways: (i) the absence of a stable framework for growth, including the collapse of the state into conflict; (ii) poor service delivery and skewed distribution of services; (iii) the absence of a poverty reduction strategy; and (iv) the inability to target. Underlying each of these four points is the nature of the African state. Newly independent governments inherited colonial state structures with few roots in local society, and politically motivated support during the Cold War reinforced this lack of accountability, though governments frequently resorted to repressive means to suppress political activity. Both formal and informal political structures developed along parasitic lines, distributing benefits through systems of patronage. Economic performance weakened as the state sector was increasingly plagued by inefficiency and corruption. The private sector was preyed upon for what it could offer, or suppressed altogether.

Such state structures should not be expected to direct scarce state resources to the poor, and that they did not is evident from both inter- and intrasectoral spending patterns. Lacking political voice of their own, the introduction of antipoverty measures usually requires support from the middle classes, either from enlightened self-interest or to reduce the threat they perceive from the poor. There is little evidence of such tendencies emerging in Africa, which may be partly attributed to growth failure. These factors also underlie the difficulty of targeting, where political support is needed to avoid elite capture of benefits.

Governments have acted to restrict economic activity in ways that have harmed the poor. But this is not to say that removing such restrictions, that is, liberalization, may be expected to automatically result in pro-poor growth. Knowledge of the working of critical markets, such as rural labor markets and the effect of land market liberalization, is an area in which our understanding urgently needs to be improved. However, it seems likely that market failures are an important impediment to poverty reduction. There are positive externalities to investment in health, education, water, and rural infrastructure. In Africa nearly three-quarters the burden of illness is from communicable diseases, far more than the rate in other developing countries, making these externalities particularly strong. Infrastructural investments may also be justified using public goods arguments. Markets important for rural development, such as credit and extension services, also fail owing to asymmetric information and uncertainty. Marketing channels for both inputs and outputs seem not to function well in many countries, or at least regions of countries. Markets are not gender blind; barriers to access are typically greater for poor men than they are poor women, and power structures mediate the market mechanism in ways that favor men (for example, with respect to access to land).

These market failures call for action by the state to redress them, but it has also been argued that the state has failed at poverty reduction. This sobering state of affairs must temper any optimism about the rapid reduction of poverty in many countries. The empowerment of the poor is part of the way out of this double bind, but cannot substitute for the role the state must play if development and poverty reduction are to proceed. Thus empowerment must be accompanied by building coalitions for poverty reduction and extending state responsiveness beyond the central level.

The poor have inadequate capital

Africa has a weak asset base, and the poor have limited access to what assets exist. This comment applies to all kinds of capital: physical, environmental, human (discussed below), and social. Infrastructure is low, with, for example, fewer and worse roads than other regions. And these facilities are less accessible to the poor who are more likely to live in remote regions (table 8). Women are further disadvantaged, with less access to land and credit, and so able to command fewer inputs (table 9).

While social capital can protect the vulnerable and support the poor, there are limits to it. In particular, at times of general crisis in a community (as with conflict, famine or AIDS) support systems may break down. Secondly, some of the poor may fall outside the system.

Those excluded from the family support system will typically be among the poorest of the poor. In many African languages the word for poor means literally the lack of support: *umphawi* in the Chewa language of modern Malawi means one without kin or friends. But social exclusion can extend to those with relatives nearby: a recent study among the Chagga in Tanzania records how a child may die of malnutrition while living in the compound of a wealthy relative if the mother is considered an outcast.

Table 8 People in poorer regions have less access to transport and education: the case of Ghana (early 1990s)

| | | | Percentage of communities with: | | | | |
| | Mean expenditure | Access to drivable road | Access to public transport | Primary school | Primary enrollments at least 50 percent | | Time spent fetching water (minutes per day) |
					Male	Female	
Greater Accra	234	100	57	100	57	58	15
Ashanti	191	100	89	100	93	93	28
Central	181	100	76	94	67	67	21
Eastern	164	59	48	59	94	90	30
Volta	160	78	39	78	73	70	40
Western	146	100	85	96	100	100	24
Upper East	145	78	0	78	55	23	71
Brong Ahafo	136	78	28	78	87	81	38
Northern	133	63	19	63	44	19	37
Upper West	104	60	40	60	30	30	37

Sources: Ghana Statistical Service, *Ghana Living Standards Survey: Report on the Third Round; Rural Communities in Ghana.*

Table 9 Male-headed households have more resources than female-headed ones: ownership of equipment in Senegal (percentage)

	Tractor	Plough	Cart
Male-headed household	2.0	36.1	23.2
Female-headed household	0.6	9.5	5.1

Source: World Bank (1995b).

Or social safety nets may fall apart when communities are under stress, as in the case of the Ik, described in Colin Turnball's (1973) *The Mountain People*, where family members no longer felt any obligation to feed one another. More generally, social change will slowly realign traditional support systems, so that the poor will rely more on the state for support. More generally, there is a concern that traditional social safety nets are eroding. While it is true that government systems are not emerging to take their place, communities are adapting by investing in new forms of social capital, so any simple generalization will not suffice.

Sustaining improvements in social indicators requires growing income and better state service provision

Improving social indicators requires economic growth to allow higher private consumption of welfare-increasing items and to provide the tax base to finance state provision. Hence social indicators, such as life expectancy, improve with income (figure 3). However, the figure shows not only that lower income in Africa means lower life expectancy, but that Africa underperforms in turning income into other welfare measures.

The African poor are triply disadvantaged: first by the widening international gap as African social indicators lag behind those in the rest of the world, partly as a result of poor growth; second, by Africa's relative poor performance in turning income to social welfare; and, third, by national disparities in health and education between the poor

Figure 3 Social indicators improve with income but Africa underperforms (scatter plot of life expectancy against income per capita)

Life expectancy

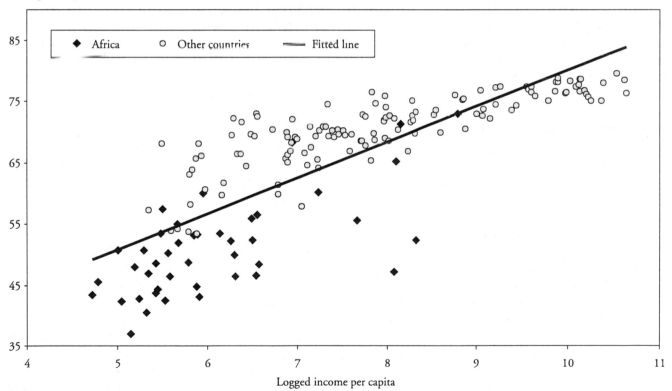

Logged income per capita

Source: World Bank, *World Development Indicators 1999.*

and the nonpoor. Improving social indicators requires growth, both to increase private consumption and to finance better state provision. Improvements in health, education, and water supply all have an enormous potential contribution to make in reducing poverty, both directly by improving the well-being of the poor and indirectly by supporting growth. This potential is far from realized in Africa, where human development indicators lag behind other regions of the world, and in many cases the gap is widening.

The drive to higher service provision that followed independence faltered in the 1970s. Economic decline hit many countries so that real spending fell. Both quality and quantity suffered, with some countries, such as Ghana, experiencing declines in primary enrollment rates of 10 percent or more. In no country outside Africa are gross enrollments below 70 percent, but it is below this level for 19 out of 46 African countries. In Somalia the figure is less than 10 percent, and only 29 percent in Niger. Accurate measures of quality are not available, but parents regularly complain of lower standards; in the words of one Nigerian parent, "In our days, I started writing letters to my parents from the time I was in Primary 3. Nowadays, many Primary 6 pupils cannot even spell their own names properly."

Where sickness prevails, or children go uneducated, it is the poor who bear a disproportionate share of the burden. Mortality rates are typically twice as high for poor men as they are for nonpoor and three times as high for poor women as nonpoor ones; rates for poor children are three to five times those of the children of the nonpoor, and again the ratio is higher for girls than boys. Tuberculosis prevalence is twice as high among the poor. Primary school enrollment rates are lower for lower income groups than higher ones, and higher for boys than for girls (figure 4), and secondary enrollment among the poor is negligible (often around 1 or 2 percent or even less).

Health and education spending is in principle a way of targeting the poor. But, in reality, social spending remains misdirected, with state subsidies disproportionately benefiting the nonpoor. On average, public spending on a university student is 20 times that of a primary pupil, although this figure exceeds 100 in Malawi. Data from a number of African countries show that the bottom 20 percent receive between 5 and 17 percent of public spending on education, whereas the top 20 percent get between 21 and 44 percent.

A range of factors—financial, physical, cultural, political, and low quality—interact to restrict the access of the poor. Yet universal primary education and greatly improved

health status are achievable goals. To attain these targets, social service reform must overcome the constraints the poor face in accessing services, rather than reinforce them. The 1990s have seen a more nuanced approach to user charges emerge in many countries, with a growing recognition that exemption schemes intended for the poor frequently did not work. Despite falling expenditure in the 1980s, Africa devotes a higher share of its gross domestic product to health and education than do other regions, and there is much scope for improved quality through greater efficiency, introducing measures such as double-shifting and turning educational administrators into teachers. Yet once again both conflict and HIV/AIDS pose substantial challenges to these possibilities.

Household and population dynamics

The changing nature of social relations embodied in the household is central to an understanding of African poverty. Household members are more likely to be poor at some stages of the household life cycle than at others. An agriculture-based household with many young children will have low mean consumption, but this will increase as the children can be productively employed in household production or in the period in which they migrate but have no family of their own. The parents' consumption will be maintained if grown children successfully establish their own production. For an urban household children may be a burden on the household for longer, unless this burden can be spread among relatives so that young children are sent to live with grandparents, or others may go to another relative nearer school.

Third, while household size is typically taken as a correlate of poverty, it is household composition—as reflected in the child/adult ratio, the female/male one, and the overall dependency ratio—that matters for household welfare. Female-headed households are often, although not always, disproportionately poor; but if such households include those with an absent male who is remitting income, then they can be among the better off. But if the household lacks an able-bodied male, it is disadvantaged by a female/male imbalance, and perhaps doubly so if the child/adult ratio is also high; as already noted, lack of able-bodied (male) labor is the key characteristic of the poorest African households. Families with high child/adult ratios are more likely to be poor, but it is also the poor who are likely to have such ratios. Among better-off families, the woman is more likely to be educated and have access to paid employment, so that the opportunity cost of her time is higher. Moreover, richer families may

Figure 4 Enrollment rates are higher for the non-poor than the poor, for urban residents than for those in rural areas, and for men than women

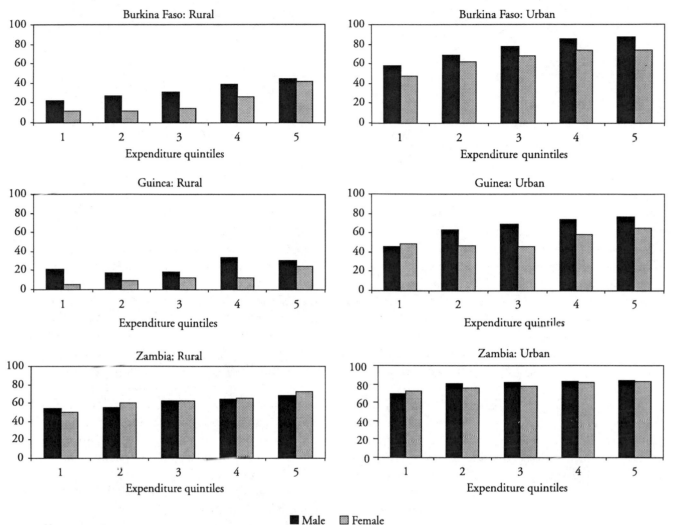

Note: The graph shows net primary enrollment rates for selected countries in the mid-1990s
Source: Appiah (1999, Table 4).

"substitute child quality for child quantity," this decision underlying the demographic transition that is starting to take place.

The demographic transition is the change from high levels of fertility and mortality to low ones, so that population growth tends to low levels, or even to zero, as fertility rates approach the replacement rate. Typically people start to live longer, and infant and child mortality drop before any decline in fertility, so that a period of rapid population growth is experienced. Socioeconomic development, and lower under-five mortality itself, then set in train a trend toward lower fertility. While there has been speculation about a "delayed demographic transition" in Africa, the most recent evidence, mainly collected in the

three rounds of Demographic Health Surveys, shows large falls in fertility in some countries over the last two decades and modest falls in several more. The data are clear: the demographic transition has begun. Mortality, fertility, and population growth are all falling in Africa (table 10).

The demographic transition has typically been led by socioeconomic development, particularly rising incomes. But many countries in Africa have experience prolonged economic decline, so that the source of the African transition has been factors other than growth. The most likely causes are lower under-five mortality and female education. Associated with these two factors are later age at marriage and increased contraceptive use. However, contraceptive use is less than 10 percent in many countries

Table 10 The demographic transition: birth and death rates by region

	Crude birth rate		Crude death rate		Population growth	
	1980	1996	1980	1996	1980–96	1996–2010
East Asia and Pacific	22	19	8	7	1.5	0.9
Europe and Central Asia	19	13	10	11	0.7	0.2
Latin America and Caribbean	31	23	8	7	1.9	1.4
Middle East and North Africa	41	29	11	7	2.9	2.1
South Asia	37	27	14	9	2.1	1.5
Sub-Saharan Africa	47	41	18	14	2.8	2.5

Source: World Bank, *World Development Indicators 1998*, tables 2.1 and 2.2.

and under 20 percent in most. There is a large, unmet demand for contraception, and the meeting of that demand is an essential part of a successful poverty-reduction strategy. Successful reproductive health programs, of course, require more than the provision of contraceptives and must take account of the social context. Government and donors would do well to learn from past mistakes.

Poverty and demographics are linked at both the macroeconomic and microeconomic levels. There are many convincing arguments at the macroeconomic level as to why lower fertility will boost growth and improve income distribution. For example, lower dependency ratios will increase savings, and reduced labor supply will increase real wages. Econometric analysis supports such theories: in Africa a reduction in the total fertility rate of 4 per 1,000 may be expected to reduce the incidence of income poverty by more than 7 percent. These macroeconomic benefits will be felt by poor families even if their own fertility levels are not falling, but many of the household level gains depend on fertility decline among the poor themselves. At the microeconomic level larger families tend to be poorer, and family size has a strong inverse relationship with child welfare. Poor households with many children cannot afford to adequately clothe and feed them let alone send them to school. Child mortality is higher among larger families, as is maternal mortality, especially for older mothers giving birth to high birth-order children. Reducing fertility will thus decrease mortality, which in turn will further reduce fertility.

Poverty Reduction Policies

Two important caveats must be placed on the discussion of poverty-reduction policies. First, one must be realistic about what is feasible, and more specifically about iden-

tifying the limitations on what can be achieved through the state. Second, one must recognize how policies in practice frequently depart from what has been planned.

Nonetheless, some basic principles to guide policies for poverty reduction can be established. These principles stem in the first instance from the social and political embedment of African poverty, and thus the need for social and political change to achieve lasting poverty reduction. First, policy initiatives should be homegrown out of a broadly based consensus: these conditions are critical not only as ownership is a prerequisite for success, but as strategies must be designed to fit country-specific circumstances. The key changes needed are government commitment to reducing poverty and structures to hold them accountable to such targets as they adopt. Second, there is a need to know more about the causes of poverty, particularly about how different policies can affect the different groups of the poor. Such analysis will require an understanding of how policy effects are mediated through inequalities between and within households. There is also a related need to collect more and better data, and in a form that can be analyzed in relevant groupings, for example, men versus women. Third, there is the need for a comprehensive approach, since undue focus on one element of a poverty-reduction strategy will not work. Finally, government institutional capacity to design and implement programs is often too weak to seriously tackle the causes of poverty.

Moving beyond these principles, some guidelines (or a checklist) can be established. First is the requirement for a stable political and economic environment. Conflict prevention and resolution are a key part of a poverty-reduction strategy. Beyond that, growth is necessary but also requires attention to distribution. There are doubly blessed, or win-win, policies that improve both growth and distribution, and these include basic social services, including family planning and rural infrastructure (which should usually be labor intensive). These policies will help reinforce or promote the coping strategies of the poor, as will limiting state encroachment on their livelihoods by, for example, restrictions on formal sector activity. Poverty-monitoring systems remain rudimentary and are yet to be developed. But there is no grand big idea that is going to solve Africa's poverty problem. And each country's strategy needs to be rooted in the country-specific causes of poverty and be appropriate to reach those most in need. For example, the economically dependent poor cannot benefit directly from public works, and neither can the time-constrained economically active poor. But time is required to build up economic, political, and institutional capacity and commitment to poverty reduction. The international community can be supportive of these efforts, but it cannot lead them.

Box 1 The many dimensions of poverty

There are many manifestations of poverty in the African context, each reinforcing the other. Africa is falling behind on all fronts, leading to an Africanization of global poverty. This message is illustrated by the development cobweb: the nearer the center you are the worse off you are with respect to eight dimensions of human well-being. The cobweb compares levels of well-being in Africa with the standards achieved in the rest of the developing world. We have the following well-being dimensions:

- Proportion of the population living above the consumption poverty line
- Gross primary enrollment rate
- Life expectancy at birth
- Adult literacy rate

- Income equality (as measured by one minus the Gini ratio)
- Proportion of the adult population not living with HIV-AIDS
- Probability of survival to age five
- Proportion of children (under five years of age) not malnourished

The distance between the dotted line (for other developing regions) and the solid line (for Africa) measures the *relative* gap between Africa and the rest of the developing world. Well-being outcomes in Africa are inferior for all dimensions. For some, the gap is significant (income poverty and primary enrollment); for others less so (female-male primary enrollment gap, for example).

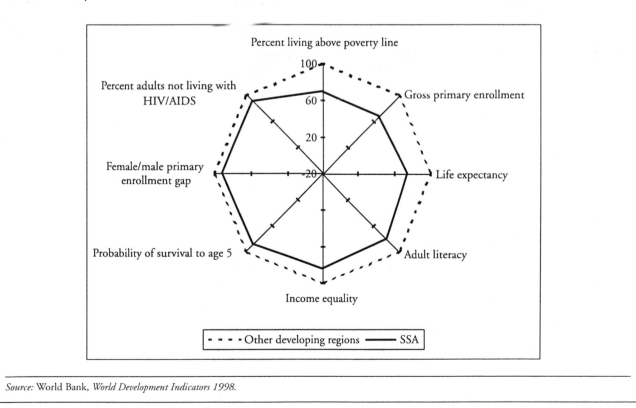

Source: World Bank, *World Development Indicators 1998.*

Poverty-monitoring systems can play a valuable role in the fight against poverty. Such systems have three functions: recording, research, and response. The first of these is the recording of progress toward meeting agreed upon targets, which is a part of the process of government accountability for poverty reduction. Research includes both academic study of issues such as the determinants of poverty but also more policy-oriented analysis, including evaluation of the impact of government policies. Finally, there is response: collecting information in a way that allows government response so as to best address the poverty problem. The latter is perhaps the most important function, requiring close cooperation between producers and users of data.

The donor community also needs to redefine and refocus its work if they are to support Africa's efforts at poverty reduction. Much of the aid spent in Africa in the last three decades has not demonstrably reduced poverty. Although poverty reduction is at the core of most donors' policy statements, the evidence is that the reality remains somewhat divorced from the rhetoric. This rhetoric has increased in recent years, with the promotion of the Comprehensive Development Framework and now the adoption of Poverty Reduction Strategy Papers as central to donors' partnership with developing country governments. While these new steps are welcome, there are reasons for making a more decisive break with the past, and for learning from it. There is a large degree of inertia in most aid programs, so it remains true that still only a small, but increasing, share of aid goes to direct poverty reduction (but this is in the context of declining aid budgets).

As a starting point donors could address the antipoor biases in their own aid programs (urban bias, road bias, and so on), but more deep-seated systemic changes are needed in the ways donors work. One direction for these changes is to be more selective allocating aid, including debt relief, in accordance with government commitment to reducing poverty and the openness of domestic debate on policy issues. Another aspect of selectivity is to pay greater attention to the political context, and direct explicit attention to conflict prevention and resolution. While donors appear to be moving down this path, there remain great dangers that aid-supported programs will remain "donor driven," as has been the experience of many sector programs despite a large part of the rationale for sector programs to let government be in the driver's seat. Donors need to accept the time needed for both a learning process and to build the support required for constructing a domestically owned Poverty Reduction Strategy Paper, and not provide "assistance" that ends up controlling the process. The recent pilot in Burkina Faso in which local officials developed a system of performance-based monitoring provides an example of how external assistance can guide without dictating.

Are the International Development Targets for poverty reduction achievable? Previous international targets have come and gone, and much academic analysis suggests a similar fate awaits these new targets. The impossibility of achieving these goals is not, however, our message. Rather, it is that, if they are to be achieved, something different, something more, needs to be done than at present.

PART I: *Africa's Poverty Problem*

In this analysis of the nature of Africa's poverty problem, chapter 1 offers a first account while being wary of the dangers of overgeneralizing about a complex and interacting condition, both between and within the countries. There are various conceptualizations of poverty, and how it is understood and measured can influence the choice of policy responses. Chapter 2 confronts these issues as an introduction to an attempt in chapter 3 to discover the dimensions of poverty in Africa and describe the ways in which they are changing.

CHAPTER 1

A First View

The Growth of African Poverty

Out of a population of 580 million in the mid-1990s, more than 270 million Africans were living on daily incomes equivalent to less than a dollar a day, 250 million Africans did not have access to safe drinking water, and over 200 million had no access to health services. About 140 million youths were illiterate. More than two million children die each year before reaching their first birthday. The scale of poverty in Africa is staggering and behind it lies an immense scale of individual tragedy and suffering. Every dead child is mourned. A father from Tanzania who lost two sons through malnutrition asked, "Can you tell me why this had to happen?"

The *World Development Report 1990* (WDR 1990) showed not only the large extent of poverty in Africa but also that this problem increased markedly during the 1980s, both absolutely and relative to other developing regions. Already, in the "lost decade" of the 1980s, some Africanization of global poverty was under way. What of the 1990s?

Improved data that have become available over the last decade both validate the conclusions of the *World Development Report 1990* and point to a continuation, perhaps acceleration, of the same trends. Table 1.1 and figure 1.1 present data on social indicators and their changes between 1980–97, and table 1.2 presents international comparisons of income (dollar-a-day) poverty. The

Table 1.1 International comparisons of social indicators, 1980–97

	East Asia and Pacific		Latin America and Caribbean		Middle East and North Africa		South Asia		Sub-Saharan Africa	
	1980	1997	1980	1997	1980	1997	1980	1997	1980	1997
Life expectancy at birth (years)	65	69	65	70	59	67	54	62	48	51
Infant mortality (per 1000 births)	56	37	60	32	95	49	119	77	115	91
Under five mortality (per 1000)	83	47	...	41	137	63	180	100	189	147
Child malnutrition (stunting)[a]	52[b]	38[b]	25[c]	13[c]	31	22[a]	66	54	37	39
Undernourishment (% population)[d]	27[b]	13[b]	13	11	9	9	38	23	37	33
Primary school enrollment rate[e]	111	118	105	113	87	96	73	100	78	77
Youth illiteracy: male	5	2	11	7	2b	14	36	25	34	20
Youth illiteracy: female	15	4	11	6	52	27	64	48	55	29

... Not available.
a. Second column is 1995.
b. Southeast Asia.
c. South America.
d. First column is 1979/81.
e. Second column is 1996 and second 1995/97.
Sources: World Bank, *World Development Indicators 1999* (World Bank 1999); for child malnutrition, see World Health Organization (WHO), *Third Report on the World Nutrition Situation*, table 3 (Geneva: WHO 1997); for undernourishment, see Food and Agriculture Organization of the United Nations (FAO), *State of Food Insecurity in the World 1999*, table 1.

Figure 1.1 Changes in social indicators, 1980–1997 (percentage)

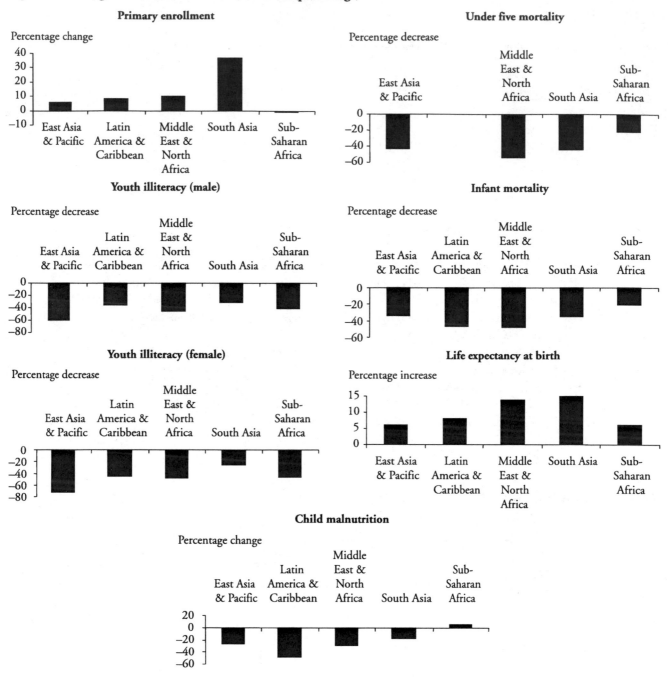

Sources: *World Development Indicators 1999; Third Report on World Nutrition Situation.*

reliability of *all* these data is suspect, particularly for Sub-Saharan Africa, so it is important not to overinterpret the results. However, broad trends emerge that are likely to be outside the error margins of the data.

The social indicators in table 1.1 show immediately that Africa's comparative record is poor in almost all respects,

particularly regarding life expectancy (still a mere 51 years of age and barely improved since the beginning of the 1980s), infant and child mortality, and general malnutrition. Figures are much higher for all these variables than for the rest of the developing world, although significantly down from the 1980 levels. Primary school enrollment rates are also severely to the disadvantage of Africa, where there has been no improvement over the period covered.[2] In other respects—child malnutrition and illiteracy among youths—the African figures are more in the middle range: a lot worse than the best but well below the worst (South Asia).

By examining changes from 1980 to 1997, the full gravity of the situation becomes evident. Along with South Asia, Africa started the period with a very adverse situation. Since it should be easier to improve on a bad situation than on a good one, Africa's results over these two decades might have been expected to be better than average, as was the case in South Asia for most indicators. But Africa did not realize this catching-up potential (figure 1.1). Only in the case of youth illiteracy did progress in Africa keep pace with the rest of the developing world. In all other respects, the continent's record is clearly weaker than the rest, and in two areas (child malnutrition and primary school enrollment) there was actually a minor deterioration.[3] Figure 1.1 leaves little doubt that, overall, Africa's relative position has deteriorated.

Of course, with the noted exceptions, the indicators have improved in absolute terms, so the trend has been in the right direction even if Africa's relative standing has deteriorated. There are, however, three important caveats. First, the data in table 1.1 are mostly shares, so the absolute number of children not going to school has dramatically increased. Similarly, the figure of more than two million infants dying each year has not changed greatly in the last three decades, despite declining mortality rates. Second, social indicators have a distributional component, so that observed gains may benefit those already doing well rather than the disadvantaged. Finally, in several countries of eastern and southern Africa, there are now dramatically deteriorating mortality and health indicators, in substantial part due to the spread of the HIV/AIDS pandemic (see chapter 3, table 3.3).

Table 1.2 presents major developing regions' estimates of the number of people with incomes equivalent to less than US$1 a day (adjusted for international differences in currency purchasing powers) in 1987 and 1998.[4] Nearly 300 million Africans—almost half of Africa's total population—were below this poverty line in 1998. Poverty has increased in three of the five regions shown, but most rapidly in Africa, causing its share of total income poverty to rise sharply over the period. In many countries in Africa, it is not hard to find the opinion that life is in many respects harder now than 20 or 30 years ago, a view borne out by longitudinal studies in Tanzania (see, for instance, Howard and Millard 1997) that document a long-run decline in nutrition. An insight into this general decline is offered by the comment of a woman from Sukumaland (Tanzania): "In the 1970s bicycles disappeared" (Drangert 1993, p. 230).[5]

Echoing the conclusion of the *World Development Report 1990* concerning the 1980s, it can truly be said that the Africanization of world poverty has continued in the 1990s, and has probably accelerated. And, as will become clear later in this report, there is every prospect of a continuation of this trend. Projections on plausible assumptions about future trends in output growth and income inequality indicate clearly that Africa will have the greatest difficulty in reducing the incidence of poverty, by comparison with other regions (Hanmer and Naschold 1999).

International comparisons, which are standardized into ratios and indices, cannot fully catch the scale of the

Table 1.2 Population living on less than US$1 per day, 1987–98 (millions of people)

	1987	1998	Absolute change	Percentage change	Headcount 1998 (%) (estimated)
East Asia	418	278	−140	−33	15
Latin America	64	78	14	22	16
Middle East and North Africa	9	5	−4	−44	2
South Asia	474	522	48	10	40
Sub-Saharan Africa	217	291	74	34	46
Memo item					
SSA as a % of above regions	22	33			

Note: The headcount is the percentage of the population below the poverty line. Figures for 1998 are preliminary estimates but are consistent with firmer figures for 1996. Incomes are calculated at constant international prices adjusted for purchasing power parity.
Source: World Bank (2001), *World Development Report*, table 1.1.

Box 1.1 The harsh face of poverty in Sub-Saharan Africa (approximate estimates)

- The estimated total population of Africa in 1995 was 580 million. Of these
- 291 million people had average incomes of below US$1 per day in 1998.
- 124 million of those up to age 39 years were at risk of dying before 40.
- 43 million children were stunted as a result of malnutrition in 1995.
- 205 million were estimated to be without access to health services in 1990–95.
- 249 million were without safe drinking water in 1990–95.
- More than two million infants die annually before reaching their first birthday.
- 139 million youths and adults were illiterate in 1995.

Sources: World Bank (1998) and other World Bank sources; United Nations Development Program, *Human Development Report 1998* (UNDP 1998); FAO, *State of Food Insecurity in the World, 1999,* table 1.

---

poverty faced by the people of Africa. Box 1.1 expresses the problem in terms of the number of people affected. These data speak for themselves. Note, however, the poor condition of the social infrastructure and of the state's ability to provide basic services.

The Danger of Overgeneralizing

Africa is a vast continent and care must be taken not to overgeneralize. There is much variation between countries, both as regards their current situations and trends over time. Some of this variation reflects regional differences, such as higher levels of infant and child mortality in West Africa, although this gap is narrowing, partly because the prevalence of HIV/AIDS is higher in eastern and southern Africa (for infant mortality rate/child mortality rate [IMR/CMR] data, see Hanmer and White 1999; for data on HIV/AIDS, see MAP (Monitoring the AIDS Pandemic) 1998).

Table 1.3 presents data for 12 countries (selected on the basis of data availability and representativeness). There is clearly a wide range of values across countries for each indicator. It is also evident that there is no great consistency between the measures of income poverty and the other indicators. Nigeria and Zimbabwe have substantial income poverty but relatively favorable social indicators,

Table 1.3 Poverty indicators for selected countries

	$1 a day poverty measures		Child welfare		Social infrastructure	
	Headcount[a] (percent)	Poverty gap[2]	Stunting[b] (percent)	Infant mortality[c] (per 1000)	Access to water[c] (percent)	Access to health[d] (percent)
Côte d'Ivoire	18	14	24	85	82	...
Dem. Rep. of Congo	...	...	45	85	25	26
Ethiopia	46	12	64	107	27	46
Kenya	50	22	34	59	49	77
Madagascar	72	33	50	102	32	38
Malawi	...	...	48	132	54	35
Mali	...	...	30	149	44	40
Mozambique	...	...	36	133	28	39
Nigeria	31	13	38	87	43	51
South Africa	24	7	23	48	...	...
Uganda	69	29	38	96	42	49
Zimbabwe	41	14	21	56	74	85

... Not available.

Note: Countries are selected on basis of data availability, population size, and geographical spread.

a. Most data relate to late 1980s and early 1990s, although the Ethiopian figures are for 1981–82. The headcount figure shows the percentage of populations with incomes of less than US$1 per day. The poverty gap is the shortfall of income/consumption below US$1/day, expressed as a percentage of the poverty line and per capita of the total population.

b. A measure of height-for-age relative to the norm for a standard international reference population. Data are drawn from the period 1992–97.

c. 1995 data.

d. Data from 1990–95. Measures population within one hour travelling time to local health services.

Sources: For dollar per day and stunting data, see World Bank, *World Development Indicators 1999.* For other items, see (ADB [African Development Bank] 1999), *African Development Report 1999.*

and the same is true to a lesser extent of Kenya. Madagascar, Uganda, and Ethiopia (for which, however, the income estimates relate to the early 1980s, when Ethiopia was in steep economic decline) combine severe income poverty and adverse social indicators (Malawi would almost certainly be added to this list were income poverty data available), whereas Côte d'Ivoire and South Africa are fairly consistently at the less unfavorable end of the spectrum.

There is also considerable variability *within* countries. Demographic health surveys provide data on infant and child mortality by region or province. Table 1.4 shows data from selected countries, giving the various regional rates reported and the national rate. Only in the case of Zimbabwe is the maximum rate below the minimum rate of some other countries. In all other cases, infants in some regions of relatively low mortality countries have a higher probability of early death than those resident in certain regions of countries with higher overall mortality. For example, at 114, infant mortality in northern Ghana is higher than the national rate for Nigeria of over 90, indeed higher than that in all regions of Nigeria, though Ghana's overall rate is just 75. At an even greater extreme, the low rates achieved in Zimbabwe contrast with those in excess of 300 in some refugee camps, or the 80 percent probability of dying before age five for children born with AIDS.

Table 1.3 provides only snapshot information, but some evidence is available on trends over time. Data on changes in access to social infrastructure between 1985 and 1995 show a mixed picture across the countries listed in table 1.3 (data from ADB 1999, table 3.5). The Democratic Republic of Congo (formerly Zaire) experienced an unam-

biguous deterioration, and Uganda saw a clear improvement (both these trends probably being war-related), while there was little change in Malawi. In the other countries the data were either incomplete or showed differing trends between water and health services. World Bank data on infant mortality in 1980–97 show improvements, some quite large, for all 12 countries except Kenya, where there was no change (see table A.3 in the appendix).

Examination of data from demographic health surveys for nine countries similarly reveals a complex picture, with substantial variations between countries and also with alternative indicators pointing in different directions (Sahn, Stifel, and Younger 1999). Analysis of an asset index encompassing ownership of consumer durables, housing characteristics, and education shows significant decline in poverty in seven out of the nine countries (Sahn, Stifel, and Younger 1999, table 2). But data on malnutrition (reported in table A.5 in the appendix) suggest a more nuanced picture. Three nutritional indicators are commonly used: height-for-age (stunting) is a measure of long-run nutritional status, weight-for-height (wasting) is a short-term indicator, and the two are combined in weight-for-age, which is a good measure of nutritional status in very small children. The figures show the percentage of children under the age of three falling below an internationally defined standard for each of these three measures. The picture emerging is that, first, malnutrition levels are very high, with stunting barely dropping below one-quarter at the minimum and approaching half of all children at the maximum. Second, malnutrition is worst in rural areas—with a few exceptions for weight-for-height, rural rates exceed urban ones, being on average about 50

Table 1.4 Substantial intranational variation in well-being: infant mortality rates by region in selected countries

| | Region | | | | | | | | | |
	1	2	3	4	5	6	7	8	9	*National*
Tanzania (1996)	128	108	107	99	80	56	...	...	...	97
Sudan (1990)	77	71	97	62	75	91	...	...	...	79
Nigeria (1990)	88	110	83	85	...	...	...	...	...	91
Malawi (1992)	121	130	144	...	...	...	...	...	...	132
Namibia (1992)	56	84	56	...	...	...	...	...	...	65
Ghana (1993)	76	72	58	78	56	65	49	114	105	75
Eritrea (1995)	107	93	70	87	71	57	...	...	...	81
Zambia (1992)	69	114	77	149	71	132	...	...	...	102
Zimbabwe (1994)	44	54	...	...	...	...	...	...	...	49
Uganda (1995)	77	98	99	75	...	...	...	...	...	87

... Not available.
Source: Authors' calculations from *Demographic Health Surveys* (various years).

percent higher. As regards change over time, the clearest pattern is the increase in short-run malnutrition, which has risen in all countries except Zambia. Paradoxically, stunting (long-run malnutrition) has decreased over the same period in some countries. There are some differences with respect to rural and urban performance over time. Most notably, the percentage of underweight children has significantly increased in rural areas in five out of eight countries, whereas it has done so in urban areas in only one case (and with significant declines in two countries).

As regards income poverty, no directly comparable country trends are available, but there is World Bank information on trends in *consumption* poverty for six African countries, broken down as between urban and rural areas. These data are presented in table 1.5. The squared poverty gap columns provide a measure of the size of the gap between the poverty line and the mean consumption lev-

els of those below it in a way that gives greater weight to the consumption of the poorest.

Once again, a mixed record is revealed. In Ethiopia, Mauritania, and Uganda the trend is unambiguously toward less poverty, with substantial reductions in both measures. The Nigerian and Zimbabwean results are equally unambiguous but in the opposite direction. In Burkina Faso and Zambia the trend appears to be toward less rural and more urban poverty, although in both countries the changes in headcount numbers may well be small enough to fall within the error margins of the estimates.

Conclusion

Overall, then, Africa as a whole is falling behind the rest of the world in the prevention of poverty, and in some respects the problem is getting worse, but indicators point

Table 1.5 Consumption poverty trends in selected African countries

		Headcount		Squared poverty gap	
		Year 1	Year 2	Year 1	Year 2
Burkina Faso	Rural	51.1	50.7	...	...
1994–98	Urban	10.4	15.8	...	...
	Total	44.5	45.3	...	...
Ethiopia					
1989–95	Rural	61.3	45.9	17.4	9.9
1994–97	Urban	40.9	38.7	8.3	7.8
Ghana	Rural	37.5	30.2	...	...
1989–92	Urban	19.0	20.6	...	...
	Total	31.9	27.4	...	...
Mauritania	Rural	72.1	58.9	27.4	11.9
1987–96	Urban	43.5	19.0	9.7	2.1
	Total	59.5	41.3	17.5	7.5
Nigeria	Rural	45.1	67.8	15.9	25.6
1992–96	Urban	29.6	57.5	12.4	24.9
	Total	42.8	65.6	14.2	25.1
Uganda	Rural	59.4	48.2	10.9	6.6
1992–96	Urban	29.4	16.3	3.5	1.7
	Total	55.6	44.0	9.9	5.9
Zambia	Rural	79.6	74.9	39.1	23.2
1991–96	Urban	31.0	34.0	9.7	5.4
	Total	57.0	60.0	25.5	16.6
Zimbabwe	Rural	51.5	62.8	10.2	13.0
1991–96	Urban	6.2	14.9	0.5	1.4
	Total	37.5	47.2	7.2	9.3

... Not available.
Source: Demery (1999), table 5; based on World Bank data.

in different directions. The proportion of global poverty attributable to Africa is rising and the likelihood is this will continue unless there are radical changes to policies and performance. The manifestations of poverty blight the lives of ever more millions of Africans, causing huge suffering and diminishing the possibilities of progress. At the same time, however, the situation on the continent is complex, and there is much variation in the positions of individual African states. The temptation to overgeneralize is large but should be avoided. This temptation should be avoided partly because the diversity of experience reflects diversity in the meaning and nature of poverty. Underlying this is the issue of whether poverty is an appropriate phenomenon to seek to measure. Following this introduction to the African situation, chapter 2 explores more conceptual issues as a prelude to a fuller discussion of the many dimensions and changing nature of the poverty problem in chapter 3.

Notes

1. This report is confined to Sub-Saharan Africa, and use of the term *Africa* refers to Africa south of the Sahara.

2. As documented in chapter 9, enrollment rates deteriorated in the 1980s but picked up again in several countries in the 1990s, showing no change over the period shown in table 1.1.

3. These changes are small enough to be within the error margins of the data.

4. The weaknesses of such poverty measures are discussed later, and the difficulties of drawing strong inferences about changes over an 11-year period, given the large error margins of the data, must be borne in mind.

5. As documented by the same source, bicycles have made a comeback in the 1990s, although they remain scarcer than before (see chapter 8).

CHAPTER 2

Different Poverty Concepts Can Point in Different Directions

Different Poverty Concepts

Material deprivation is at the core of poverty: low income and consumption levels, resulting in poor nutrition, inadequate clothing, and low-quality housing. But poverty is not just about income or consumption. It also includes deficient command over productive assets and access to key public services. Vulnerability and its resulting insecurity are further characteristics, aggravated by an inability to make provisions for emergencies: vulnerability to droughts, floods, and other natural disasters; to human disasters such as the death or illness of a breadwinner, as well as war and civil disturbance; and to economic phenomena such as inflation or market collapses.

Poverty has important less materialistic aspects, too. Among these is dependency arising, for example, from unequal relationships between landlord and tenant, debtor and creditor, worker and employer, man and woman. Both encompassing and going beyond these various aspects is social exclusion, referring to the inferior access of the poor to state services and other collective provisions, and to the labor market; inferior opportunities for participation in social life and collective decisionmaking; and a lack of decisionmaking power. Hopelessness, alienation, and passivity are thus common among those living in poverty. Finally, poverty is also relative: people can be said to be poor when they are unable to attain a level of well-being regarded by their society as meeting a reasonable minimum standard.

Poverty can thus be viewed narrowly or broadly: the broader the view, the more encompassing it is but the harder to measure. There is therefore a trade-off between relatively narrow income- or consumption-based definitions that, however, lend themselves to aggregated measurement and comparability, and broader but more elusive

conceptualizations. The range of possibilities is illustrated in figure 2.1, where band 1 represents a purely income-based view and band 6 the most inclusive approach.

In this scheme, "PC" stands for private consumption (or income); "S" refers to services normally provided by the state (although occasionally by the private sector) such as schooling, health services, and treated water; "assets" refers to such items as land, equipment, and other productive inputs; "SEC" refers to the extent of vulnerability and insecurity already mentioned; and "dignity" and "autonomy" relate to the degree of dependency and social exclusion.

What should be the balance between different approaches? Much of the choice is about the tension between functionally useful categories and the extent of social contextualization. Measures based on income or consumption—the most commonly used for international

Figure 2.1 A pyramid of poverty concepts

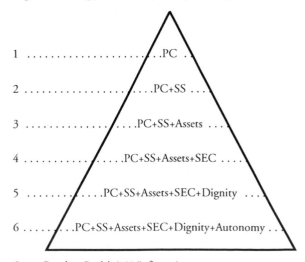

Source: Based on Baulch (1996), figure 1.

comparisons—have the advantage that the required data are often available. Moreover, the simple headcount indices (of the type reported in table 1.2 in chapter 1) can be easily augmented by measures using the same data to indicate the severity of the poverty by giving more weight to observations far below the poverty line than to those just below it (table 1.5 in chapter 1).

Despite these substantial merits, income-poverty measures also have important limitations. It is difficult to ensure comparability across countries and to establish an objectively robust definition of a poverty line. Individuals should preferably be the unit of analysis, but in practice surveys invariably take the household as their unit of analysis. They thus abstract from the position of individuals in the distribution of household consumption and raise difficult issues about what constitutes a household (what to do about males who have migrated to the towns and who send remittances back home, and how young children should be treated in measuring household size).[1] Furthermore, a focus on income poverty may miss important dimensions of poverty and thus fail to capture crucial aspects of the processes of causation. An obvious example is that of vulnerability, for which some indication of assets is necessary.

Asset-based approaches highlight the paucity of various kinds of capital as a major source of deprivation and as an indicator of vulnerability, since assets provide a buffer against adverse shocks. There are measurement problems here, too, of course, and the approach retains some of the materialism of income-based measures. At present, there are little systematic data presenting asset-based measurements, but the data from Sahn, Stifel, and Younger (1999) discussed at the end of chapter 1 begin to fill this gap.

Another approach for which a good deal of (not always trustworthy) data are available is to augment income with basic-needs indicators, such as mortality and literacy. These can throw important light on aspects of the human condition and are less narrowly economic in their approach. They can draw greater attention to individual, as opposed to household, well-being and to the centrality of the opportunities and choices open to people. However, the combination of social indicators into composite indices, such as the United Nations Development Program's (UNDP) Human Development and Human Poverty Indices, have elicited criticism and are essentially arbitrary in their weighting systems. There are also doubts about the accuracy of some of the data employed (see chapter 14).

At the opposite end of the spectrum from income-based measures is an approach based on community-level dis-

cussions intended to elucidate local perceptions of the nature of poverty, the assets of the poor, the constraints they face, and the influence of household dynamics. Practitioners of such "participatory poverty assessments" (PPAs) stress the importance of the social context and some are dubious about the usefulness of national-level aggregates, and perhaps of the very idea of measurement. In practice, poor people largely report their condition in terms of material deprivation: not enough money, employment, food, clothing, and housing, combined with inadequate access to health services and clean water, although they are also liable to stress such nonmaterial factors as security, peace, and power over decisions affecting their lives. It can be difficult to ensure representativeness in participatory assessments, however, with an ever-present danger that the voices heard will be mainly those of local elites, the well-to-do, and men.

The various poverty concepts, however, should not be seen as competing with each other. The different dimensions of poverty interact in various ways. Poor education and ill health, which are most common among the children of parents with low income, restrict earning potential. Income poverty has been shown to be one of the factors that explains intercountry variations in health outcomes in addition to a country's overall level of economic development (see Carrin and Politi 1995). Greater stocks of assets make the nonpoor less vulnerable to external shocks than the poor, and the need of the poor to hold assets as a hedge against shocks means that they cannot use them to accumulate further wealth as can their better-off neighbors.[2] With high direct costs on top of high indirect opportunity costs, and nothing to fall back on, the poor literally cannot afford to get ill. This problem is particularly severe for the growing numbers of urban poor who have a narrower range of survival strategies to call upon. What may be a mild illness or injury for a salaried person in a sedentary occupation may deprive a poor person, engaged in hard manual labor, of her or his livelihood. The poor can be socially stigmatized by their poverty, reinforcing the barriers that make it impossible for them to climb out of poverty: the poverty trap can be as much, or more, a social phenomenon as an economic one—this is the point of social exclusion. Human rights are thus not only one aspect of poverty but, as suggested in box 2.1 below, the poor are more vulnerable to human rights abuses.

Table 2.1 presents some of the ways in which the different dimensions of poverty may interact with one another. Each cell represents how the dimension listed at the

---

Box 2.1   Human rights and poverty

Practices persist throughout Africa that are incompatible with the achievement of poverty reduction. All of these practices restrict the dignity of affected individuals, but several, such as debt bondage and slavery, have an important economic dimension. Though only one example is given here, many more could be added.

Although slavery has been outlawed in all countries, there is incontrovertible evidence that the practice persists. Lack of education and restricted access to the outside world are the instruments by which this is maintained, as slaves may be ignorant of their legal position and unable to seek alternative employment in any case. An escaped slave explained:

> I have never heard the abolition discussed in my master's house. . . . All the ones I have met who have heard of it learned from other black communities, which is why masters are so sensitive to any contact between slaves on the one hand, and free haratines [freed slaves] and other blacks, on the other hand.

In West Africa, there are 30,000 or more *trokosi*, young girls given to priests by families guilty of some offence. To atone for their crime, the family gives a virgin daughter to a priest, making her subject to economic and sexual exploitation.

Another widespread practice has been for children to be placed in the households of other family members. Where the exchange is from a poor family to a rich one, these arrangements may be only a short step from slavery. As has been documented in several West African countries, the custom has evolved so that parents are paid for the children to be placed in a family of strangers. All ties with the family are cut. This type of arrangement is a growing trade in Benin and Togo, with the children ending up in oil-rich countries such as Nigeria and Gabon.

Poverty forces parents to sell their children, and they may be forced into similar arrangements for themselves. Debt bondage is thus both a cause and consequence of poverty. Poverty drives people into entering debt bondage arrangements from which they cannot then escape.

Sources: Anti-slavery International; Aird (1999).

---

top of the column may reinforce the dimension in the corresponding row. For example, human capital can increase income/expenditure through its productivity effects.

The table is not intended to be exhaustive either in terms of cell contents or in the rows and columns. For example, the devastating effects of conflict are not captured

Table 2.1   Interactive effects from column heading to row

	Income/expenditure	*Physical assets*	*Human capital*	*Social capital*	*Political rights*
Income/expenditure	…	Asset availability allows h/h to withstand shocks	Increased productivity	Provide access to income opportunities and social protection	Protection against arbitrary disruptive interventions
Physical assets	Allows asset accumulation	…	Education improves access to some assets	Social networks can provide access to assets (including common property)	Preferential access to assets
Human capital	Can afford health and education	Can afford period of inactivity	…	Can rely on social protection in times of need	Benefit from biases in resource allocation
Social capital	Able to meet social obligations to access social networks	Asset holdings guarantee social standing	Weak human capital may mean unable to operate with social network	…	Can provide basis for rights to level of social protection
Political rights	Economic presence provides basis for political influence		Less educated less able to articulate demands or participate in political system	Can protect basic political rights	…

… Not applicable.

here. Many of the interactions mentioned here will recur in this report, as will the strong implication that the war against poverty is a battle to be fought on many fronts.

Why Conceptualizations Matter

Being clear about the meaning and nature of poverty is important because the definitions used and the measurements applied shape how the problem is viewed and the choice of policies to combat it. But who will decide, and on what basis, between objective indicators and the more subjective PPA outcomes? Are individual voices to be accepted uncritically or is knowledge mediated by statisticians to be preferred? There are different value systems at work here (see box 2.2), so much depends on the importance attached to social context. Objective indicators are decontextualized, whereas in PPA all depends on context, with poverty related to the ability of individuals to live decently within their society.

At the policy level, income-poverty measures of course draw attention to economic concerns. If the poverty line is set so that around half the population (or more) are poor, as is the case in much of Africa, then the focus is likely to be at the macroeconomic level and on measures to influence the pace and nature of gross domestic product (GDP) growth. In contrast, concentration on basic needs indicators points in a more interventionist direction, for example, toward targeted provision of essential services. PPA assessments, in turn, point more toward the coping strategies of the poor and grass-roots actions, and can be sceptical about the potential of national-level measures. Others argue that political rights are the prerequisite for sustained improvements in the well-being of the poor.

Box 2.2 A pastoralist view of poverty

Broch-Due (1995, p. 3) contrasts perceptions of poverty among savannah dwellers with that of the pastoralists of East Africa. Groups like the Turkana conceive of wealth largely in terms of cattle, and "contrast the prosperous life of their nomadic camps with the 'poor' life of foragers, farmers, fisher folks and others who they conceive of as existing on the fringes of society. Irrespective of income or nutrition, the cultural constructions surrounding cattle herders place them at the 'centre' of society and portray them as 'rich' while others who are at the periphery, in the 'bush,' are regarded as poor."

Source: Broch-Due (1995).

To what extent are these visions competitive rather than complementary? Do those identified as poor differ appreciably according to the definition used? A study of Côte d'Ivoire applied varying definitions, confined to material and other objective indicators, to the same set of data and found that they did not choose the same people (Glewwe and Van der Gaag 1990). The disparities would surely have been greater had the range of definitions employed included more subjective indicators. This presumption is strengthened by "Jodha's paradox," derived from a study of two Indian villages between 1964 and 1984. Villagers whose real incomes had declined during these 20 years reported their situation as having improved, citing decreased dependence on low-pay jobs and on patrons and landlords, improved mobility, and better consumption patterns (Jodha 1988). At a much more aggregate level, there are divergences for Africa between performance in social indicators (for example, as summarised in the UNDP's Human Development Index) and in headcount measures, as seen in the discussion of table 1.3 in chapter 1. The analysis by Sahn, Stifel, and Younger (1999) of demographic health survey data shows similar discrepancies, with rises in the asset index but deterioration in nutrition indicators in several cases.

At the same time, one should not exaggerate the extent of the differences. Other evidence, for example on Kenya and Ghana, shows rather close correlation between the extent of poverty revealed by headcount and PPA methods. And, although the Côte d'Ivoire study referred to above did identify materially different poverty groups, most definitions used were quite strongly correlated with each other. More generally, the subjectively based participatory approaches produce results consistent with those of household expenditure surveys, with the poor stressing the importance of access to money, jobs, and assets such as land and education—all income-related—although food security also emerges as a preoccupation. Similarly, there is broad correlation between the cross-country results of income-based poverty line measures and the Human Poverty Index developed by the UNDP that excludes income variables, although there are also important differences, partly because some of the measures used are not sensitive to short-term changes in well-being.

In any case, there is more to this issue than correlation. Each approach yields its own unique type of information, so that the appropriateness of the method depends on the nature of the information required. The various approaches to aggregation have their value, just as the PPA approach yields insights that cannot readily be obtained from statistical surveys, such as the importance people attach to how they are valued by their peers, and draw attention to such aspects as whether individuals have to undertake demeaning types of work, whether they can feed their children properly, bury their dead decently, and live securely. PPA studies also draw attention to the important category of the "dependent poor"—the abandoned elderly, orphaned, handicapped, and displaced. They may also highlight the position of those missed by more formal techniques, such as the homeless, including street children and street elderly.

Finally, the view offered here is consistent with one stressing capabilities, opportunity, security, and empowerment. To a large extent these are the positive sides of the various dimensions identified in this chapter. This overlap reinforces the messages that the different dimensions interact, but that they are different and complementary. Indeed, there is growing interest in the potential of research that, for example, combines headcount, asset-based, and PPA approaches: difficult but methodologically feasible and potentially very rich.

Notes

1. In practice, children are usually counted as equivalent to half an adult, a pragmatic solution but one that raises many questions. Women are also often counted as less than men, which has given rise to criticisms (Nelson 1996).

2. For an application of this argument, see Dercon's (1997) discussion of cattle in western Tanzania.

CHAPTER 3

African Poverty Has Many Dimensions

Categories and Characteristics

It is already evident that poverty in Africa, as elsewhere, is a complex phenomenon and takes many forms. Various categorizations are useful in analyzing Africa's poor and in designing poverty-reducing interventions. Some of the most relevant categories are described in this chapter.

Chronic and transitory, or permanent and temporary, poverty

The relative importance of these two categories is an empirical matter on which few good data exist for developing countries, particularly for Africa. There are substantial measurement problems here, with statistics usually based on occasional surveys rather than continuous observation, and with abnormal events liable to produce untypically large results. However, available evidence suggests that shocks of various kinds cause many Africans to move in and out of poverty, often over surprisingly short time spans.

Table 3.1 presents data based on year-to-year observations from a recent review of available panel data series. The proportions of poor cannot be compared across countries, and the extent of mobility across the line is sensitive to the number of years in the panel and may be expected to be correlated to the location of the line. The data show a sizeable proportion of the population—generally between about one-quarter and one-third, but more in Zimbabwe[1]—move in and out of poverty. These figures appear slightly lower than those for the non-African countries recorded but are still considerable. There are indications that there are also substantial within-year, seasonally based movements, as illustrated for Ethiopia in box 3.1. It is very probable that the measured degree of volatility is highly sensitive to the measure of poverty chosen: basic

needs indicators would almost certainly reveal substantially less mobility. And of course the presence of volatility has implications for poverty measurement, making it sensitive to the time at which the data are collected.

This phenomenon has great potential policy relevance. The chronically poor are those trapped in poverty from some mix of poverty causes, such as absence of political influence, few assets, and lack of market access. Removing poverty among them requires building their social, physical, human, and political capital. Transitory poverty, by contrast, directs governments to measures that will reduce the incidence of, or vulnerability to, shocks such as harvest failures, fluctuations in prices (and perhaps in policies), and ill health, and offer temporary safety nets (see box 3.1). Of course, the distinction between these two

Table 3.1 Proportion of households always poor, sometimes poor, and never poor

		Always poor	Sometimes poor	Never poor
Africa				
Côte d'Ivoire	1985–86	14.5	20.2	65.3
Côte d'Ivoire	1986–87	13.0	22.9	64.1
Côte d'Ivoire	1987–88	25.0	22.0	53.0
Ethiopia	1994–95	24.8	30.1	45.1
South Africa	1993–98	22.7	31.5	45.8
Zimbabwe	1992–95	10.6	59.6	29.8
Other				
Chile	1967–85	54.1	31.5	29.8
China	1985–90	6.2	47.8	46.0
India	1968–70	33.3	36.7	30.0
India	1975–83	21.8	65.8	12.4
Pakistan	1986–91	3.0	55.3	57.2
Russia	1992–93	12.6	30.2	14.4

Source: Baulch and Hoddinot (1999).

Box 3.1 Insecurity and poverty mobility in Ethiopia

Table 3.1 shows that, even over a two-year period, more Ethiopians were poor in one of those years than in both (with less than half remaining above the poverty line in both years), and other data for that country confirm the importance of temporary episodes of poverty. In addition, there is evidence of considerable within-year fluctuations in the numbers in poverty, especially due to seasonal fluctuations in the availability and price of grains and other foodstuffs. For example, the estimated headcount of consumption poverty fell from 34 percent to 27 percent during two periods of 1994.

In order to identify the types of shock that cause such marked fluctuations in the numbers below the poverty line, participants in a rural household survey of 15 Ethiopian villages during 1989–95 were asked to identify events over the previous 20 years that had caused them particularly severe losses, with the following cited as the most serious (percent of all respondents):

Harvest failures	78
Policy failures	42
Labor shortages	40
Problems with oxen	39
Problems with other livestock	35

Not surprisingly, Participatory Poverty Assessment (PPA) studies in Ethiopia record that villagers are much concerned with issues of security: food security but also (reflecting the recent history of Ethiopia) freedom from conflict.

Source: Unpublished World Bank papers, largely based on work by Dercon and Krishnan.

---

categories is not rigid. For example, for households chronically on the margins of poverty, a shock may be the last straw, making it desperately hard for them to claw their way back up. Transitory shocks may lead to irreversible poverty situations. Death is the ultimate irreversibility, claiming many children, but there are also premature deaths of the elderly and, at times of famine, among the population at large. Such large shocks feature as the next category. Moreover, the "transitorily poor" is a portmanteau category that includes those only occasionally pushed below the poverty line and those who spend most, but not all, of their time below it (Baulch and Hoddinot 1999). Obviously, it is important for policy purposes to distinguish between these cases.

Catastrophic poverty

This category of poverty results from a severe shock such as famine, HIV/AIDS, or conflict. Such shocks need not be entirely exogenous: both famine and conflict (which are themselves related) are born out of poverty as is, to some extent, the rapid spread of HIV/AIDS.

The poor and the destitute, or the poor and the poorest

Policymakers find it easier to assist the poor than the destitute. The former have the capacity and resources to function in a sustainable way, albeit at a low level, thus providing a basis for enhancing their livelihoods. By contrast the destitute have no means of support, so that this distinction blends into the next category.

Dependent and economically active poor

The literature on poverty in Africa has largely concentrated on the active poor, and there is a particularly serious lack of hard information on this aspect. But the indirect evidence is strong that dependants—handicapped people, the aged with no immediate family to help them, orphans, refugees and other displaced people, female-headed households reliant on remittances from men in the towns, child-headed households where the eldest of the children take care of their siblings following the loss of their parents—are numerous and particularly likely to be impoverished. The need for further research into this aspect is urgent because it too has potentially large policy implications.

Among economic dependants, child poverty is particularly serious, both because the incidence is particularly high and because Africa's long-term future lies in the well-being of its children. An estimated 40–50 percent of children in most African countries live below the poverty line—some 100 to 150 million children (Harper and Marcus 1999). The World Health Organization (WHO 1997) estimates that two-fifths of all children are malnourished (a figure broadly supported by the data in table 1.1, chapter 1), and the stunting of children as a result of malnutrition may actually be worsening (see figure 1.1, chapter 1). According to the 1997 *Status of Poverty Report,* in every African country analyzed the children were more likely to be poor than adults, in both urban and rural communities. When livelihoods fail, children suffer neglect in health and nutrition and have to give up school in order to work, either for low wages or unpaid at home, in order to replace parents seeking to augment household earnings outside the home. As a result of alcoholism, depression, and violence, they also absorb many of the social and psychological costs of poverty within households. Finally, the scourge of AIDS is resulting in large increases in the number of orphans in the worst-affected countries, as is conflict, which children are drawn into as combatants. Accompanying this is the emergence of child-headed households—not captured in many statistics—living on the margins of society and certainly among the poorest.

Urban and rural poverty

These types of poverty take different forms: access to jobs and to cultivable land are the crucial elements in the two respective cases. A high proportion of poverty in Africa occurs in the rural economy. This includes many of the working poor, although that category straddles both urban and rural communities. The urban working poor have earnings (usually within the informal sector) below the poverty line.[2] The real value of formal-sector earnings has been in secular decline in most African countries over a long period and, although firm data are absent, the same is almost certainly true in the informal sector, too, where they started at lower levels in any case. The function of this sector as an employer of last resort makes it intrinsically likely to generate low earnings, in the face of labor forces growing far more rapidly than formal-sector employment. The rural analogy to this (especially in eastern and southern Africa) is the pressure of population increasingly pushing farmers onto the extensive margin of semiarid land with highly unreliable rainfall, and/or resulting in the fragmentation of land holdings into ever smaller plots.

Gender-based poverty

This category of poverty is a major feature of the African scene. This is strongly connected to the high incidence of child poverty and has adverse implications for the care of the elderly. The special disadvantages of women, and the economic inefficiencies arising from these, were the subject of the 1998 Status Report entitled *Gender, Growth and Poverty Reduction*. Income-poverty measurements show a mixed picture for female-versus-male headed households, probably because there may be an absent male supporting the household. Analysis of Tanzanian survey data reveals that, although female-headed houses have approximately the same per capita consumption as male-headed ones, female-headed households with no supporting male (widowed and divorced) have mean consumption barely over one-half that of other female-headed households (Cortijo and LeBrun 1999). It is also unambiguously clear that there are gender disparities in access to, and control of, directly productive assets such as land and credit, human capital in the form of education and health (chapters 8 and 9), in participation in household and community decisions (chapter 11), and that women suffer in particular from "time poverty," that is, the absence of leisure time, or even time to perform all the tasks expected of them.

Introduction of the gender element draws attention to a further characteristic of Africa's poverty, how deeply it is embedded in social attitudes and structures. Kabeer and Whitehead (1999, p. 19) put it well:

> The form in which women's poverty manifests itself depends on cultural context far more than it does for men, suggesting that it cannot be understood through the same conceptual lens as men. Women are generally poorer than men are because they lack the range of endowments and exchange entitlements which male members of their households tend to enjoy. They are less able than men to translate labour into income, income into choice and choice into personal well-being.

One specific way in which disadvantage is built into the social fabric in many African societies is the inferior rights of women to arable land, which are generally restricted to user rights rather than ownership. Even more serious is women's poor access to cash, that is, to the market; their frequent exclusion from cultivation of cash crops; their especially limited access to credit; and the acute pressures on their time, having also to look after the family. Another example of the interaction between social structures and poverty is in the particularly high incidence in West Africa of poverty in polygamous households, especially among junior wives (Iliffe 1987). A further aspect relates to situations in which "strangers" (recent immigrants) suffer from inferior rights and are substantially confined to (often poorly paid) agricultural labor, or situations in which members of particular ethnic groups are discriminated against. The ethnic basis of much poverty provides yet another example of social embeddedness, of which the recent history of South Africa provides an extreme example.

Some further common characteristics can also be mentioned. One is the strong association that exists between income poverty and large numbers of dependent children, which helps explain the seriousness of child poverty already described. In most countries for which data are available the average size of households classified as poor is substantially larger than other households (table 3.2 and chapter 9). The link between poverty and household size is a fairly universal characteristic of poverty, as is a negative correlation between poverty and education, particularly the education of the household head. Table 3.2 shows that illiterates are more likely to be poor than the educated. Similarly, those with only limited primary education are likely to be poorer than secondary school or college graduates.

A correlate of poverty attracting less attention is remoteness or residence in a disadvantaged region. Iliffe (1987, p. 235) writes of "destitute areas . . . remote from transport, bereft of services, unable to market crops or secure local employment, obliged to export labourers, victimised more by neglect than exploitation." For example, average rural incomes in Zambia in regions close to the railway in 1980 were six times as large as those far away; expectations of life at birth in Tanzania's capital city, Dar es Salaam, were one-and-a-half times as long as those born in the most remote region. Remoteness raises transaction costs, reducing farm-gate prices and returns to labor and capital, and weakening incentives to participate in the monetized economy. The connection between this condition and the underdeveloped, sometimes deteriorating, condition of transport and other infrastructural services needs no elaboration. This factor is related to one of the other correlates of African poverty: a tendency for it to be concentrated in one or more geographical regions within a country, which is also illustrated in table 3.2.

A further characteristic is that a high proportion of the poor suffer from food insecurity. In rural areas such insecurity is heightened by land fragmentation and forced movements into remote areas. It is worsened too by the unmodernised, rain-fed nature of much smallholder agriculture, combined with an apparent long-term deterioration in the quantity and reliability of rainfall in many regions.[3] It is also common for the rural poor not to be able to meet their own food needs and to be reliant, therefore, on uncertain sources of money income to make good the deficiency. At the extreme, rural food insecurity results in famine. Although largely conquered in all other regions of the world, famine persists in Africa. One study lists 15 African countries which have been affected by famine since 1968 (other sources add further countries or regions), and speaks of the "militarization of famine" because it is increasingly conflict-related.[4]

In the towns, food insecurity is almost certainly growing as poverty becomes progressively urbanized and where the poor spend up to three-quarters of their incomes on food. It is exacerbated by the rapid rise of the labor force relative to the expansion of formal-sector employment and declining real earnings already mentioned. Publicly provided safety net programs have provided only a very limited safeguard, with the coping strategies of the poor themselves providing the main buffer (Maxwell 1999).

To summarize, it emerges that a number of threads run through the various categories of the poor described above. The factor of time is one of these, most obviously in the discussion of chronic versus transitory poverty but also as it relates to the position of children and to what is described as catastrophic poverty. Social position is another recurring factor, for example, as it relates to the distinction between economically active and dependent poor and to gender-related poverty. Location, or economic distance, should also be mentioned, as it relates, for example, to the urban-rural distinction and to the influence of remoteness and regional differences. The disparate nature of these influences—time, social position, and location—underlines the complexity of the phenomenon under examination.

Table 3.2 Characteristics of poverty (selected countries)

	Guinea–Bissau	Lesotho	Malawi	Uganda	Zambia
Household size (average for poor/average for nonpoor, percent)	116	97	123	127	124
Location in poorest region (percent poor relative to national average)	130	163	129	147	138
Literacy (percent poor relative to national average)	73	84	94	9[a]	92

Note: Countries selected on basis of data availability. Data mainly relate to the late 1980s or early 1990s.
a. A later estimate for Uganda yields a ratio of 78 percent.
Source: Hanmer, Pyatt, and White (1997), tables A3.1 and A3.2.

Profiles of African Poverty

From these and other generalizations a picture emerges of the nature of poverty in Africa, albeit one that inevitably cannot do justice to the complexities or to the differences across geographical regions. Most poverty remains rural, and the rural poor are the starting point for the discussion. But there are some who are at risk wherever they live: the handicapped, abandoned aged, orphaned, refugees. And, remembering the probably large importance of transitory poverty, those living not far above the poverty line and vulnerable to adverse shocks of various kinds are always at risk, at least temporarily—many farmers, those in insecure employment, and those in conflict-prone areas.

Who are the rural poor? Most are eking out an existence on smallholdings. These farms are typically very small or in low-fertility regions, or both, dependent upon an uncertain rainfall and cultivated with only basic implements by methods little different from those of 50 years ago. The land will be sown largely to subsistence crops, augmented by a few chickens, goats, or other small animals. There is a well-above-average chance that the de facto household head will be a woman—either a widow, a woman who has been left by her husband or, most frequently, with a husband who works in a town and who struggles to send some of his earnings back to his family. Whether woman or man, the chief breadwinner is likely to be illiterate or to have had only the most rudimentary primary schooling. There are apt to be an above-average number of children, often (particularly the girls) themselves prevented from attending school by shortages of money and the need to work on the farm or in the house. If they live in remote areas, far from a paved road and modern services, or in a disadvantaged region, neglected for geographical, ethnic, or political reasons, there is an even greater likelihood that they will live below the poverty line, and the depth of their condition is likely to be more severe.

Frequently, the landless (many of them "strangers") are another important category of rural poor, estimated with their dependants to represent about 10 percent of the continent's total rural population. They rely upon selling their labor but, except during seasonal peaks, the opportunities may be few and the rewards slight. They may be able to augment their earnings by cultivation of small subsistence plots. Pastoralists are a further important category, at least by objective criteria (but see box 2.2, chapter 2). Well over one-tenth of Africa's rural population is estimated to be pastoralist. Because of their lifestyle, as

well as official neglect, they are especially likely to be uneducated and to have little access to other services, having been called by one commentator "the most strikingly excluded peoples throughout the continent" (Clapham 1991, p. 99). Such is their exclusion that they are often omitted from income and expenditure surveys, as in Mauritania, despite being a significant part of the population (Cherel-Robson and Baulch 1999). The land over which they graze their livestock is likely to be under pressure, from encroachment by settled farming communities and through (a partly consequential) degradation caused by overgrazing. Certain fishing communities have also been identified as particularly prone to poverty, chiefly due to declining catches and increased commercial competition (UNDP 1998).

The economically active urban poor can be divided into the unemployed and the working poor, although in practice these groups blend into each other, for most of those with no job per se help to sustain themselves by casual work, or low-level self-employment, such as petty trading or waste recycling, so that the genuinely unemployed are only those who can afford to be so. The urban poor are more likely to be adult males and relatively young, and many are recent immigrants from villages. Like their rural counterparts, they probably have had little or no schooling and have few other relevant skills to offer. Unlike the rural poor, the costs of housing and transport are likely to be major items in their budgets. More generally, their cost of living will be a good deal higher than in the villages from which many of them have come, and they will be more vulnerable to the effects of inflation. They are likely to live in slum conditions: unhealthy, overcrowded, insecure, and neglected. Crime, violence, mental disturbance, and alcoholism are common among those around them.

New poor

Finally, mention can be made of the new poor—those who have previously been among the relatively well-to-do who now find themselves in straitened circumstances, typically as a result of economic recession and structural change. Classic examples are former junior-level civil servants, such as clerks, secretaries, or public enterprise workers, who have lost their jobs and the indirect income-generating opportunities their work made possible, as a result of measures introduced under programs of structural adjustment. In objective terms, their condition is likely to be less severe than the cases described so far because they will have more resources to fall back on, more alternative opportunities. But if poverty is also about felt ill-being, about the shock of adverse change and loss of self-esteem, their position can be adverse indeed.

The Nature of African Poverty Is Changing

The above provides a snapshot of the present poverty situation in Africa. But such portraits can mislead if they freeze what is actually a fluid situation. Such is the case here. Important changes are occurring.

First, poverty is becoming gradually urbanized. While straightforward comparisons of urban versus rural poverty can be misleading, since the cost of living is higher in urban areas, meaning that a higher poverty line should be used. If it is not, then the number of urban poor will be underestimated. The variation in nutrition is higher in urban than rural areas, so that a comparison of mean nutrition levels will also hide the extent of deprivation. Nonetheless, a review of high-quality data on poverty and nutrition shows that the number of urban poor and underweight and children is increasing, as is their share in the national total (Haddad, Ruel, and Garrett 1998). Hence while African poverty still occurs disproportionately in the rural economy, it is clear that urban poverty is claiming a rising share of the total. This phenomenon is partly a consequence of a general urbanization. Africa's towns are expanding about twice as fast as the total population, and the proportion of the population living in urban communities has more than doubled since 1960, from about 15 percent to well over 30 percent today. The failure of amenities, such as water and sanitation, to keep pace with population growth is one of the factors behind the reemergence of malaria in cities such as Nairobi and Harare, from which it was thought eradicated.

While the urban population is expanding, the growth in formal-sector jobs has everywhere fallen far below the pace of urban labor force expansion (and in some countries has actually fallen in recent decades), placing large downward pressures on real earnings, creating more open unemployment and, above all, pushing ever increasing numbers into the informal sector, with inevitably depressing effects on earnings there too. Much of the rise in "employment" in urban informal sectors really signifies growing underemployment—more part of the problem than the solution. These trends are eroding the ability of urban workers to save and remit part of their earnings to their families in the villages, which also aggravates rural poverty.

Recently, AIDS has had devastating effects in the most badly affected countries of eastern and southern Africa, with two million deaths a day across the continent. In just the first seven years of this decade the long-term rise in life expectancies has been drastically reversed in a number of countries (table 3.3). UNAIDS has estimated that in Botswana life expectancy will fall to 40 during the next decade, whereas if there were no AIDS epidemic, it would approach 70 (UNAIDS 1998).

The impact of this catastrophe has fallen particularly hard on children, with rising infant and child mortality rates in several countries. But it has hit their parents hard, too, particularly in the economically most active age groups, with severe consequences for household incomes, nutritional standards, and health and well-being. There has been a huge rise in the number of orphans, with an estimated eight million children having already been orphaned by HIV/AIDS in Africa (MAP 1998, p. 20), and that number will continue to grow.

A further—but disputed—deterioration that most observers believe is under way is an erosion of traditional safety nets that in the past have helped to limit the scale of poverty in Africa: family, community, and ethnically based sharing mechanisms that care for the dependent, avoid some of the worst inequalities in access to communal assets like land, and help to smooth fluctuations in livelihoods. It is important to be realistic about the limitations of such mechanisms at the best of times. The extent and effectiveness of such provisions have always varied a good deal across different social structures, and it has always been the case that many of the poor have had to rely for their survival mainly on their own efforts. Descriptions above have made it clear that groups such as the handicapped, strangers, widows, and the abandoned elderly

Table 3.3 AIDS is reducing life expectancy: life expectancy at birth in selected countries (years)

	Botswana	Kenya	Malawi	Rwanda	Uganda	Zambia	Zimbabwe
1990	60	60	48	49	52	53	60
1997	51	54	41	40	41	43	49

Source: World Development Indicators 1999.

number prominently among the poor, and that is a sufficient caution to those tempted to take an idealized view of traditional arrangements. Without doubt, these have mitigated the worst inequalities, have been particularly good at caring for the young, and have minimized the most extreme manifestations of poverty, such as starvation.

These arrangements are coming under great pressure, however. This is due partly to the growth of poverty itself—the more poor there are the harder it is for the rest of the community to look after them. The rapid spread of HIV/AIDS, particularly in eastern and southern Africa, is another obvious source of extreme stress. The high incidence of violent conflict similarly erodes the ability of traditional safety nets to cope. Large numbers of people have been displaced, putting them gravely at risk, eroding social organization, and creating many more orphans. Furthermore, growing population pressures are squeezing the traditional access of poor people to cultivable land, or pushing them onto the low-yielding margins, swampland, and forests, a process similar to the pressures on pastoralists noted earlier. Indeed, landlessness and the associated feature of increasing fragmentation of land holdings are growing features of rural poverty. More generally, the gradual commercialization of economic life is replacing traditional obligations with more contractual relationships, a process accelerated by the rapid pace of urbanization.

At the same time, however, public provision has generally been uncertain at best. Thus Maxwell (1999, p. 1,950), writing about the urban poor, argues the following:

[I]n contemporary urban Africa . . . the individual and the household, and sometimes the extended family—but not the state—are the locus of efforts to combat poverty and food insecurity. People are not passive victims —within the constraints they face, people do their best to cope, to make ends meet, to protect their livelihoods, and meet their basic requirements. To a small extent, these efforts may have the support or financial backing of the state or local government, but by and large they are the efforts of the individuals and households, and may be misunderstood, neglected, or suppressed by governments.

The poor have always had a wide range of coping strategies (see box 3.2) for periods of stress, to diversify sources of income and consumption. Reliance upon traditional social safety nets has been central to these strategies but

so has the search for alternative livelihoods. Indeed, diversifying livelihoods became a commonplace activity for all strata of society in the 1970s and 1980s as crises deepened. Consumption patterns are adapted by substituting inferior meals, eating less (skipping meals), and eating "wild foods."

The intensifying link between poverty and environmental degradation is another aspect of the changing African scene. Starting with an unusually high proportion of arid and semiarid land, Africa faces growing problems of deforestation, desertification, water shortages, and soil erosion. The International Food Policy Research Institute estimates that land degradation is affecting two-thirds of total cropland and one-third of the area under pasture. Much of this is due to a combination of overgrazing and agricultural overexploitation, as well as to adverse trends in rainfall. The marginal land on which many of the poor rely is highly vulnerable to soil erosion, leading to a vicious circle of falling yields, increased exploitation, and further erosion. This situation imposes a growing constraint on poverty reduction at both the macro and the micro levels. However, given the right conditions, such as access to capital, poor people have shown themselves able to improve their environments, and that increased land use can be accompanied by environmental improvement rather than degradation (Tiffen, Mortimore, and Gichuki 1994).

Finally, there are the disastrous effects of warfare and civil conflict. While conflict is far from a new phenomenon and is not obviously on a rising trend (the Nigerian civil war of the late 1960s was among the most severe episodes), it is beyond dispute that conflict is a major feature of postindependence Africa, creating new multitudes of poor. More than half (28) of all African states have been embroiled in conflict during the 1980s and 1990s, and relative to the population affected, Africa was by a considerable margin the most conflict-affected region during these decades (Luckham, Ahmed, and Muggah 1999). It is estimated that in 1996 3 to 4 percent of the total population—17 to 23 million people—were international refugees or internally displaced, although most were concentrated in a few countries. In several affected countries (Liberia, Rwanda, Sierra Leone, Somalia) the institutions of state have been almost completely incapacitated for shorter or longer periods.

The connections between this situation and poverty are not hard to understand. Large numbers of the orphaned, widowed, and disabled have been created. The vulnerability of the poor has also been increased by breakdowns in the rule of law, seizures of assets, heightened tribal

---

Box 3.2 How Do They Manage? The Survival Strategies of the Rural Poor

The poor of rural Africa, victims of an uncertain climate as well as of the natural rhythm of the seasons, are well accustomed to the need to cope with periods of hardship. But what once were occasional measures have increasingly become the norm. In the Mopti region of Mali, for instance, certain wild foods, formerly gathered only in a difficult year, are now regularly consumed by some groups, particularly in areas of increasing drought (Lambert 1994). Coping strategies are thus changing into adaptive strategies throughout the seasons and in every year. But some traditional coping strategies (for instance, securing assistance from neighbors or kin in times of crisis) are coming under threat. This is often due to worsening ecological conditions and rising living costs, although it is also partly caused by changing relationships and weakening obligations of mutual assistance, due to generally worsening levels of poverty.

Rural dwellers' survival strategies are diverse. Off-farm sources of income are extremely important. While such activities depend upon social and gender differences, informal activities include hawking, load carrying, wood collecting, weaving, and hairdressing services, while richer farmers tend to focus on activities such as repair work, tailoring, cross-border trade, and medium-level commerce. Within the rural economy, measures include changes in cropping patterns,

migration in search of employment, collection of wild foods, reductions in consumption, and sale of possessions or productive assets. Women are worse off in terms of diversification strategies because of traditional household responsibilities, and inequalities in land ownership and rights.

A participatory living conditions survey in Zambia asked farmers about their coping strategies, and this provided a rather vivid picture of how they coped (World Bank 1997a, in percentages of respondents mentioning):

Reducing food intake/meals	67
Substituting ordinary meals with poorer food	54
Reducing other household consumption	51
Piecework on other farms	40
Food for work	39
Begging from friends	34
Other piecework	25
Substitution of wild food	19
Informal borrowing	16
Sales of assets	12
Relief food	11
Petty vending	9
Taking children out of school	5

---

tensions, and growth of insecurity. Conflict has led to the destruction of infrastructure and jobs. It has also been associated with rapid inflation, against which many of the poor—particularly in the towns—are unable to protect their living standards. State services have collapsed, or their quality has deteriorated as resources are siphoned into the war effort.

The Sobering Implications of Complexity

The analysis of part I has several lessons for the examination of the causes of poverty that follows in part II. First, there can be no disputing the gravity and widespread nature of the problem, both on the basis of comparisons with other developing regions and when looking at the absolute extent of poverty. Moreover, and despite the manifold weakness of data in this area, the emerging picture of a poverty crisis does not rest upon any one measurement. Rather, it is validated by a wide range of indicators approaching the topic from various directions. However, there are two important qualifications, the first of which identifies an urgent need for additional research. This first relates

to indications that, at any one time, a large share of total poverty may be transitory and that chronic, long-term poverty is quantitatively smaller. Evidently, the amount and nature of desirable corrective actions will differ markedly according to the relative importance of these two categories. Ignorance of the situations of the economically dependent poor, and of how their welfare if affected by the overall performance of the economy, as well as by specific policy interventions, identifies a further major gap. The second major qualification relates to the wide variation in individual country situations established in connection with tables 1.4 and 1.6 of chapter 1. It is extremely important for aid donors and other external actors not to apply blanket judgements and solutions to what is in fact a kaleidoscopic situation.

A further corollary from the evidence is that it is unhelpful to think in an undifferentiated way about "the poor." For the purposes of understanding their condition and how it might be addressed, it is essential to recognize the many faces of poverty in Africa. The various categories of the poor identified above, as well as the changing nature of the poverty situation, rules out any simplistic single-cause-single-solution approach. Careful, discriminating diagnosis is called for.

More particularly, an implication of the description in this chapter is that poverty cannot be banished simply by actions confined to improving economic performance and raising incomes. This follows from the socially embedded nature of the problem, pointing to the necessity also for consultation and action at the societal level (particularly in order to tackle the disadvantages of women), and from our identification of various groups of economic dependants as large components of the complete poverty picture, particularly the scourge of child poverty. Action, then, is needed on a wide front, not least to compensate for the increasing pressures on traditional safety nets and to respond to the terrible scourge of HIV/AIDS. Actions for the avoidance or resolution of violent conflicts also emerge as going beyond their own obvious intrinsic merits to address major aspects of Africa's poverty.

Notes

1. The higher figure for Zimbabwe partly reflects the longer panel, which has four years of poverty estimates.

2. In other regions of the developing world, formal-sector workers may well receive a wage below the poverty line; this has not as yet been a problem in Africa given the relative underdevelopment of formal private sector activity.

3. Thus for the 89 years for which data are available for the Sahel, rainfall has been below the long-term mean in 52 of those years.

4. From von Braun, Teklu, and Webb (1999). The countries identified were Angola, Burundi, Chad, Ethiopia, Eritrea, Madagascar, Malawi, Mali, Mauritania, Mozambique, Niger, Somalia, Sudan, Uganda, and Democratic Republic of Congo.

PART II: *The Causes of Poverty*

The causes of poverty in Africa are multifaceted: economic, social, and political; international, national (macro), and micro. Part II examines these causes, beginning with an overview in chapter 4. Chapter 5 examines the influence of domestic economic performance, specifically the record on overall and agricultural growth, as well as the evidence on income distribution. Given the slowness of past economic growth in Africa, chapter 6 examines potential reasons for this, including the influence of weak policies, the effectiveness of policy reform programs, and the influence of the outside world: trading conditions, capital movements, and the debt overhang. The political context is explored in chapter 7, which reexamines the desirable role of the state in the presence of large-scale failures of both states and markets. With a particular focus on rural issues, chapter 8 considers how the poor lack access to capital, which is pursued further in chapter 9 in the analysis of weak social capital (poor social outcomes) among the poor and the related issue of social sector development. Chapter 10 explores the evidence for a demographic transition and its links to poverty. Finally, chapter 11 draws together the various strands of the analysis relating to the important gender dimension of Africa's poverty.

CHAPTER 4

Overview of the Proximate and Primary Causes of Poverty

The Danger and Value of Generalization

It is both easy and hard to write about the causes of poverty in Africa. The easy part is to identify candidates. The multifaceted nature of the poverty problem, the heterogeneity of the poor, and the variety of country situations all mean that it is easy enough to recognize factors contributing to these situations. The hard parts are to avoid overgeneralization or the creation of mere shopping lists, within which it is hard to discriminate. The purpose of this chapter is to present a comprehensive overview while avoiding these pitfalls.

The danger of overgeneralizing was made clear in part I. For example, chapter 3 delineated various categories of the poor and their condition: transitory and chronic poverty, the poor and the destitute, the economically dependent and economically active, urban and rural poverty, gender-based poverty, and poverty resulting from catastrophic shocks. There are also variations in country experience, for example, the particular concentration of the effects of HIV/AIDS in eastern and southern Africa, and the devastating but geographically specific effects of conflict situations. Finally, the nature of social and political organization and dominant livelihood strategies vary across the continent.

The validity of generalized explanations is also limited by the different conceptualizations of poverty discussed in chapter 2. Thus economic approaches point to different possible causes than, say, an approach that starts from social exclusion. An eclectic approach must be followed that takes advantage of the specific insights offered by each of the approaches.

At the same time, this variety can lead to obfuscation. While it is not sensible to search for single-cause, single-solution answers, it is highly desirable to get as far as possible with an analysis that recognizes that not all candidate causes have equal status, and so lay bare the most fundamental factors at work.

There are two ways in which the "causes of poverty" can be classified. The first is to distinguish between the international/macro factors that determine the overall level of poverty in a country from the micro (household) factors that determine who is poor. A second distinction is that between primary and proximate causes, which is presented in table 4.1 and will be discussed in the remainder of this chapter.

Columns 2 and 3 of table 4.1 go beyond an undiscriminating shopping list of causal factors to suggest a hierarchy among them. The table classifies the identified causes of poverty in three ways:

- Interactive factors, which may be both cause and consequence of poverty
- Primary causes, being the deep-seated underlying factors causing African poverty
- Proximate causes: causes of poverty that are themselves outcomes of deeper sources

This classification is not without problems. There is no accepted theory of poverty that establishes a hierarchy of causes, nor is there any widely adopted empirical model that might serve the same purpose. Indeed, it is doubtful whether any single theory or model could adequately cover the complexities of the African situation. In the absence of a generally accepted theory, the approach here can be criticized as relying excessively on the judgement of the authors. Moreover, what should count as primary or proximate depends on the time horizon adopted: the idea of a "primary" factor is closely related to, if not synonymous with, the notion of a long-term cause. However, the classification offered is also open to the objection that it is

Table 4.1 The causes of poverty are numerous

	Interactive	Primary	Proximate
	(1)	*(2)*	*(3)*
A. Economic			
1. Low growth/productivity	→←		√√√
2. Slow job creation/capital intensity			√√
3. Inadequate productive assets			√√
4. Macro and market instability			√
5. Market failures	→←		√
6. Inequalities of income and wealth			√√√
7. "Globalization," adjustment			√√
B. Situational			
1. Location (remoteness, poor-region, etc.)			√√
2. Environmental degradation	→←	√	
3. Proneness to shocks (disasters, AIDS)	→←		√√
C. Social and demographic			
1. Household composition	→←	√	
2. Poor human capital; weak social services	→←		√√
3. Personal dependence (disablement, etc.) plus weak traditional safety nets	→←		√√
4. Gender biases	→←		√√
5. Poverty-inducing social structures		√√√	
D. Political			
1. War, instability, displacement	→←		√√√
2. Disempowerment, social exclusion			√√
3. "Government failures"		√√√	

not long-term enough—for example, that it does not identify the influence of historical factors, or "path dependence." The search for ultimate causes can continue almost indefinitely, but the approach here is pragmatic. While not denying the importance of historical factors, the focus is on long-term factors but those which, unlike history, are capable of change.

The Interaction of Causes and Effects

It is often hard to know what is cause and what effect, as indicated by the "→←" symbols in column 1 of the table.[1] The case of environmental degradation (item B2) provides a well-known example, where poor rural dwellers in their struggle for subsistence may overfarm or overgraze the land, thereby causing erosion and reducing its productivity, which, in turn, further aggravates their poverty.[2] The well-known association of poverty with high fertility is another example (discussed in chapter 10): chronic poverty (as opposed to transitory) induces large families in order to maintain an essential supply of labor

and old-age security for parents (and also because ignorance of, and/or lack of access to, contraception), but large numbers of children result in many mouths to feed and so aggravate a household's poverty. Such interactive processes create poverty traps, making it harder for the poor to improve their condition, and provide many examples of how the different dimensions of poverty can reinforce each other.

A few of the less obvious cases marked in column 1 may need explanation:

- The entry against gender biases (C4) arises from the observation in chapter 11 that much of what is sometimes described in those terms is actually a result of the coping strategies of the poor and of differences between the priorities of men and women within the household.

- The interaction intended under entry C3 (personal dependence, etc.) relates to the inability of traditional sharing mechanisms to cope adequately in the face of large-scale and increasing poverty. Where those afflicted are a manageable minority, they can be cared for; when relatively few would have to look after large numbers—as with famine, conflict, and the HIV/AIDS pandemic—the mechanisms tend to break down.

- The entry against market failures (A5) may seem surprising. Chapter 7 shows how market failures worsen poverty, but the additional hypothesis here is that when there is large-scale poverty, the domestic market is often too small, in terms of effective demand, to support a sufficient number of suppliers to achieve an efficient market outcome through competition.

- Perhaps the most problematic entry (note the question mark) is against A1, suggesting an interactive relationship between low economic growth/productivity and poverty. It is clear how causality can run from poor economic performance to poverty (see chapter 5), but how does it run in the opposite direction? Two examples may be given: (i) poverty implies small disposable incomes and low savings, resulting in low investment and, hence, low growth and productivity, and (ii) poor people cannot feed themselves well and, hence, suffer from ill health and low energy levels, again feeding through to low productivity. The reason for calling this type of two-way linkage problematic is that it implies the existence of a "low-level trap," a proposition that has been thrown into question by the progress of many Asian and other formerly very poor countries.[3]

Some Neglected Causes

Table 4.1 presents a substantial number of variables, all of which could, depending on the context, plausibly be described as causes of poverty in Africa. Most of these are dealt with in part II. But there are a few that are not. For the most part, they are underrepresented in this report because of a paucity of hard information and, hence, suggest themselves as particularly urgent future areas of research.

Arguably the most serious omission is the slow growth of employment (item A2 in the table). There is no question that "having a job," particularly a formal-sector job, is of huge importance to the economically active poor. This is obviously true of the urban poor but is also valid for rural poverty, for one of the best-established characteristics of the rural poor is their reliance on remittances from the towns. At the same time, much of what economic growth there has been in African countries has been capital intensive and has not therefore generated new

jobs fast enough to keep pace with labor force growth. There is an urgent need to know more about this topic and about how the workings of labor markets in Africa have impinged upon poverty in Africa.[4]

Environmental degradation (B2) is touched upon in chapter 8, where it is suggested that, in general, this set of factors is of secondary importance as a source of the continent's poverty, and some regions are relatively well endowed with environmental resources. But this view should be qualified by reference to poor soil quality in many areas and the incidence of soil erosion.

Lastly, economic instability (A4) receives only passing mention here, again because of a lack of hard research on its poverty effects. Chapter 3 points to the probability that there is much movement in and out of poverty, so that at any one time temporary poverty is likely to make up a large share of the total. Many of the temporarily poor will be pushed into penury, and may remain there, as a result of shocks of various kinds, notably economic movements. But here too there is little evidence—on the extent of mobility in and out of poverty, on the types of shocks that push people down, and, specifically, on the impact of economic fluctuations, at both macro and micro levels. Here, too, more research is a priority.

Proximate versus Primary Causes

In both columns 2 and 3 of table 4.1 the relative importance of each variable is indicated by the number of ticks entered against each, with three checkmarks ($\sqrt{}\sqrt{}\sqrt{}$) indicating the highest level of importance. Primacy is not synonymous with importance. "War, instability and displacement," for example, are identified as of the highest importance but are classified as proximate causes, on the grounds that they are a reflection, above all, of government failures of various kinds.

Underlying factors, labeled as "primary" causes, are identified in column 2. The hierarchy suggested here is intended to illustrate "the general case" on the continent but cannot apply equally to all countries. Rather than go through all the entries in columns 2 and 3, some main features are picked out here. First, a few points of illustration:

- Globalization (item A7) is categorized as a proximate causal factor. Why? The answer given in chapter 6 is that, although various influences from the global economy have done harm, the key factor has been the inflexibility of many African economies and their resulting inability to respond to the opportunities offered by the acceleration of world trade growth and the internationalization of capital markets. A more fundamental explanation, therefore, would refer to the factors creating that inflexibility.[5]

- The influence of location, for example, remoteness (B1), shown in chapter 3 to be important in Africa's rural poverty, is likewise classified as a proximate factor, on the grounds that it essentially reflects the poor state of the communications and, above all, transportation infrastructure, and is hence an outcome of political forces, although climate, low population densities, and poor natural resources add to the difficulties.

- Perhaps most controversially, poor human capital (C2) is classified as a proximate cause. As argued in chapter 9, a great deal of this disadvantage suffered by the poor is a result of avoidable deficiencies in the volume, quality, and incidence of social service (mainly education and health) provision by the state, so that it is more fruitful to look for the sources of those deficiencies.[6]

- Social exclusion, by which the poor can be denied access to the opportunities to move out of poverty, is an outcome of the interaction of political and social structures, and so appears as proximate cause of poverty.

The main outcome of the exercise in table 4.1 is to spotlight the importance of social and political factors. As repeated throughout this report, economic growth is crucial—but the poor growth record is a consequence of social and political factors, so that it is classified as a proximate cause of poverty.

To expand on this latter point, first take economic factors. There are, of course, manifold factors holding back the growth of Africa's economies. Some are sketched in chapter 5 and include a poor human capital base, weak physical and institutional infrastructures, and low investment rates (unfavorable perceived risk/return ratios). These factors can in large measure be attributed to the weaknesses of the state in many African countries and to political structures that exclude the poor, described in chapter 7. Hence the record of slow growth is a proximate—although very powerful—cause of widespread poverty.

Similarly, arguments apply to the case of inequality (A6). Chapter 5 shows inequalities to be large and probably increasing in Africa, a situation that provides a large contribution to the extent of poverty. But inequality is not intrinsic to Africa's resource endowments and economic structures. On the contrary, the continuing dominance of smallholder agriculture in many of the region's

economies offers a safeguard against large income differences. Rather, the emergence of large inequalities is a result of the nature of the political structures that have emerged since independence and the social forces underpinning these, so that it is sociopolitical factors that are the primary explanation.

A proximate factor that rates among the highest is war, political instability, and the resulting displacement of huge numbers of citizens (item D1). The terrible effect these scourges have had in intensifying the poverty problem in many countries is a theme of this report. Here again, the origins of the violence are varied and often have deep historical roots, but it is reasonable, as is done in chapter 7, to regard much of the post-independence growth of violence as an outcome of the "state failures" analyzed there.

In summary, the failings of political systems, and the social forces underlying these, are identified as the key primary causal factors underlying the poverty problem of many African countries. They stunt economic incentives and the processes of accumulation; constitute a major source of the inadequate human capital of the poor; remain unresponsive, for example, to the opportunities offered by globalization or (in many cases) to the ravages of the HIV/AIDS pandemic; in too many cases, they fail even in the basic law-and-order functions of the state, leading to both economic impairment and violent conflict. There is a substantial number of exceptions to this general view, of course, and the political weaknesses may, in turn, be seen as the product of the ill effects of colonialism and other historical factors. African governments have a thankless and extremely difficult task. But there is a huge gap between what the best and worst of them manage to achieve, and that is a gap that should be narrowed.

Some Policy Implications

The analysis just offered directs attention firmly toward domestic rather than external factors. This view is more fully argued in chapter 6, although it is recognized that there are various additional things that donor-creditor governments and international agencies could do in support of an antipoverty effort.

Directing attention to sociopolitical factors rather than to some of the, perhaps more amenable, economic and "situational" variables listed in table 4.1 is not encouraging. Social and political institutions can be notoriously slow to change and not very amenable to outside influence. However, the primacy of institutional issues does not mean that there is nothing that can be usefully done to improve the more proximate causes of poverty set out in table 4.1. For example, higher growth is needed and macroeconomic policy can make a difference here. Governments and donors will doubtless concentrate many of their efforts on these familiar and relatively tractable policy variables. However, the analysis here emphasizes that fundamental and lasting improvements in the poverty situation will require more deep-seated changes. Part III suggests a range of actions to tackle both proximate and some primary causes.

In some ways, however, the analysis gives grounds for optimism. For all the tenacity of institutions, there have been major political changes in many African countries during the last decade, and a good many governments are making serious efforts to improve the welfare of the poor (Greeley and Jenkins 1999, p. 34). Although much of the apparent democratization has been seriously flawed, it has left a better situation than previously obtained (chapter 7). By weakening the control of unrepresentative governments, democratization may yet prove a milestone in the greater empowerment of Africa's poor. Chapter 7 suggests a three-pronged approach for accelerating this process, and chapter 15 points out the scope for donors to engage more effectively with governments and with wider society in this area.

In the economic sphere, too, there are signs of improvement. Chapter 5 indicates that there is now greater macroeconomic stability—growth performance has improved somewhat, and there are reasons for believing this improvement may be sustained. Chapter 10 points out that there are signs of reducing fertility rates in much of Africa, with expected benefits for the poor, and chapter 9 refers to the fact that a few states (Senegal and Uganda are commonly mentioned) are leading the way in showing that effective action is possible in containing the spread of HIV/AIDS.

Lastly, the implications of the interaction between poverty and many of the proximate causal factors are important. One such implication is that initial progress may set a virtuous circle in motion. Once poverty begins to retreat, one of the sources of conflict is weakened, productivity begins to rise, the care of economic dependants becomes more feasible, and so on. In turn, these improvements further help the poor, and a self-sustaining process of improvement may be set in motion.

These interactions should be borne in mind in the account throughout the following analysis, which reviews the factors contributing to the severity of Africa's poverty problem, beginning in the next chapter with its economic performance.

Notes

1. This is not the same as saying that some of these factors are correlates rather than causes. Rather there is bidirectional causality, and it is not always easy, or even possible, to identify the "determining factor" in some settings.

2. Although, as recognized in chapter 8, there are cases where the poor can improve the environment.

3. The phenomenon of "jobless growth," that is, output growth outstripping employment growth, is simply the inverse of productivity growth, and points to the fact that productivity increases may not always be associated with poverty reduction.

4. See Teal (1999) and for a review of available evidence, though not with a specific poverty focus.

5. These have been argued elsewhere to be a result of political, social, and historical factors (see Killick 1995a, chapter 6).

6. There is some simplification here, however, because there is often a problem with poor people's demand for education.

CHAPTER 5

Economic Stagnation Has Caused Much Poverty

Economic growth has a major effect on trends in income poverty. Indeed, in economies that start poor, growth is indispensable if poverty is to be reduced at a satisfactory rate. However, the extent to which overall growth benefits the poor also depends on what happens to the distribution of income. This chapter starts, therefore, by examining the growth record of African economies, paying particular attention to the more encouraging record of recent years. It then surveys distributional trends in the region and the way these are likely to impact on poverty reduction, and decomposes the likely differential effects of growth on various poverty groups. Finally, since the bulk of poverty occurs in the rural economy, it examines the comparative performance of agriculture and the continuing weaknesses of this sector.

Growth and Distribution: The Overall Picture

Changes in income poverty can be decomposed into the effects of changes in gross domestic product (GDP) and changes in income distribution. Cross-country econometric studies (which have limited African coverage because of data problems) show that growth effects dominate in statistical explanations of changes in income poverty. A recent example, based on a sample containing 61 observations drawn from 26 developing countries (of which, however, only one, Nigeria, was African) finds a roughly one-to-one relationship between overall growth in per capita gross national product (GNP) and changes in the incomes of the poorest 20 percent and 40 percent of the population (figure 5.1).[1] In only six (mostly Latin American) out of 39 observations was per capita economic growth of more than 2 percent a year associated with falls in the incomes of the poorer segments of the population, although there were a number of additional cases where substan-

tial overall growth left the incomes of the poor largely untouched. In most economies that experienced periods of declining per capita GNP (Nigeria included), the incomes of the poor also fell.

These results are consistent with evidence from earlier studies. Fields (1989) found from a sample of 18 developing countries that in only one case was growth not associated with falls in income poverty. The World Bank (1995a, p. 45) similarly found growth to be the most significant influence on changes in income poverty. From a total of 33 developing countries (including a number of African countries), poverty declined in 19 of the 24 experiencing positive growth, and increased in all nine of those with declining GDPs. Other World Bank work produces comparable results, including a study of the experiences of 20 developing countries in 1984–93, which found that a 10 percent increase in mean incomes resulted in an approximately 20 percent reduction in income poverty (Bruno, Ravallion, and Squire 1996). Some studies, however, suggest that the incomes of the poor may rise less than those of the nonpoor (see, for example, Demery 1995), which is the case for all those observations lying below the line in figure 5.1.[2] On the other hand, the evidence suggests that the poorest are also included in improvements from growth, and some studies find proportionately greater reductions in poverty intensity indicators (Baulch and Grant 1999).

To some extent the trickle-down view of poverty reduction, commonly associated with the 1960s, has been rehabilitated. The employment-creating consequences of growth are seen as a particularly important mechanism through which it can reduce poverty, as a primary source of incomes for the newly employed, by stimulating the demand for informal-sector outputs and foodstuffs, and by permitting an increased flow of income remittances to poor rural households.

Figure 5.1 The income of the poor grows with overall growth

Income growth of bottom 20 percent (percent per year)

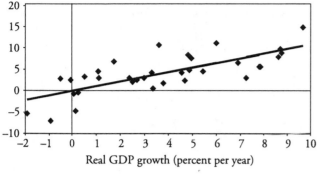

Real GDP growth (percent per year)

Source: Roemer and Gugerty (1997, table 4).

However, by comparison with the 1960s, there is now a better understanding of the importance of distribution in mediating between growth and poverty. Growth's impact on income poverty is found to be strongly sensitive to both the initial distribution and how that changes with growth. As regards the first of these, the elasticity of poverty with respect to growth has been found to decline with the extent of inequality: the greater the initial skew in income distribution, the smaller the power of growth to reduce poverty. Thus a recent study (Hanmer and Naschold 1999, table A2) of a sample of 105 developing countries, using the conventional Gini coefficient measure of inequality, obtained the following estimates of the growth-poverty elasticity:

	All countries	Africa
Low inequality (Gini < 0.43)	−0.93	−0.82
High inequality (Gini > 0.43)	−0.34	−0.55

For the high-inequality countries, results for Africa show consistency with those from other recent studies. For rural poverty, Ali and Thorbecke (1998) report an elasticity of −0.50, and for total poverty Baulch and Grant (1999) report one of −0.56. Thus, using the results of Hanmer and Naschold, in low-inequality countries a 10 percent GDP growth will be associated with an 8 percent fall in the headcount income poverty measure, whereas there will only be a 5.5 percent fall in high-inequality countries. A number of studies (see, for example, Demery and others 1995) find poverty elasticities to be lower in

Africa than elsewhere, pointing to structural problems that may impede the spread of the benefits of growth and the possible exclusion of some parts of the population from the growth process.[3]

Lastly, a growing body of evidence shows a negative association between initial inequality and growth. The reasons for this are not well established, but it seems likely that large income differences may be associated with inefficient use of resources arising from the untapped human potential of the poor and the tendency in such situations for wealthy elites to skew policies in their own favor to the detriment of overall productivity growth. Inequality thus penalizes the poor in three ways: (i) by leaving them with a smaller share of initial incomes, (ii) reducing the growth potential of the economy, and (iii) weakening the poverty-reducing power of such growth as does occur.

With respect to the pattern of growth, this is an area requiring further research. Recent work has argued that there is no systematic relationship between economic growth and inequality (see summary in Baulch and Grant 1999). However, what African data there are (discussed below) suggest cases exist in which inequality has worsened with growth. Experiences in African countries in the 1990s, sometimes combining the emergence of a wealthy urban elite with rural areas that seem largely untouched by growth, but this observation needs to be supported by harder evidence.

Africa's Growth Has Often Been Slow but May Be Improving

As is well known, economic growth has been slow in Africa, although this has not always been the case. In the 1960s and into the 1970s the pace of expansion, at over 5 percent annually, was comparable with that of other developing regions. It was not until around the mid-1970s that there was a general slowdown, leaving an increasingly wide gap between the records of Africa and other developing regions. The African experience is portrayed graphically in figure 5.2, which records per capita growth rates for both GDP and private consumption, showing declining average incomes and consumption during the 1980s and 1990s, although the deterioration is probably overstated by official statistics, as people increasingly retreated into (under-recorded) subsistence production. The deterioration in private consumption over this period is particularly noteworthy because material poverty can be expected to be especially sensitive to changes in this, as

Figure 5.2 Income and consumption show long-term decline

Average annual growth rates (percent)

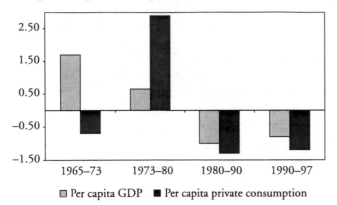

☐ Per capita GDP   ■ Per capita private consumption

Source: World Bank database; World Bank, *World Development Indicators 1999.*

to a lesser extent are other welfare indicators, such as health and nutritional status.

Such long-period averages can, of course, be misleading, both because they conceal variations within periods and because they smooth out differences in country experiences. The record of the 1990s is of particular interest because it throws a stronger light on the prospects for the immediate future, and it shows some revival of growth. This latter feature is portrayed in figure 5.3, showing GDP growth in excess of population growth in 1995–97. This recovery prompted optimistic statements suggesting that the region's economies had at last turned the corner and that, with continuing policy efforts, the recovery would be sustained.

Have Africa's economies really achieved a breakthrough or does the slowdown of 1998–99 suggest that the promise of 1995–96 was a false dawn? It is proper to be wary. In the mid-1990s the world economy was booming, creating an encouraging environment but one which subsequent events have shown should not be taken for granted for the longer term. In addition, 1994 was the year of the devaluation of the Communauté Financière Africaine (CFA) franc, after 46 years and serious recessions in many franc zone countries. Maybe the overall regional figures were unduly influenced by an essentially once-for-all response by the CFA countries, catching up on the income losses of earlier years. Perhaps the apparent return to declining per capita incomes in 1998–99 is simply a return to the long-run trend.

Against such an argument there are reasons for taking the more positive view that it is the recent downturn that

is the exception (see Fischer, Hernández-Catá, and Khan 1998). Although Africa was less affected than much of the rest of the world, it too was hit by the 1998 economic crises in East Asia and Russia and by the world economic slowdown that followed. Commodity prices, to which Africa's exports are particularly sensitive, fell sharply in 1998 and remained weak in 1999. And, although weather conditions were reasonably favorable in much of the region during 1994–96, contributing to above-trend agricultural growth, the weather was less favorable in 1997–98. In other words, it is at least possible that the slower expansion after 1997 was caused by external shocks whose effects were likely to be transient.

As a further positive consideration, the accelerated mid-decade growth was not confined to some small group of countries and not specifically to franc zone countries. Well over one-half of African economies grew at 4 percent or more. Multiplier (or contagion) effects may mean that growth in some countries helps lagging neighboring countries to step up their growth too. International efforts to further reduce external debt burdens may encourage investment and limit the diversion of government revenues away from economically productive uses. Even some of the more deep-seated development constraints show signs of improvement—for example, slowing population growth and improving educational indicators (discussed in more detail in later chapters). Moreover, there have been some important policy trends, notably toward more

Figure 5.3 The 1990s witnessed large growth fluctuations (annual real GDP growth)

Percent

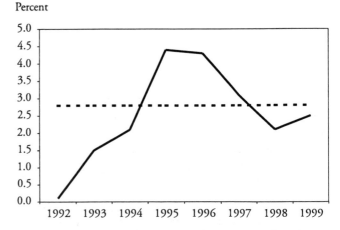

Note: The figure for 1998 is preliminary and for 1999 is a World Bank forecast. The horizontal line is drawn at 2.8 percent, to represent the average rate of population growth in this period.
Sources: International Monetary Fund and World Bank databases.

competitive exchange rates and reduced budget deficits, and there has been a long-overdue improvement in Africa's export performance.

But against these encouraging trends there are more negative considerations. First, while the growth recovery of 1993–97 was reasonably widespread, few African economies managed to sustain consistent above-average growth year by year, and two of the few that did so (Angola and Uganda) were in war-recovery situations. Many countries continue to be beset by conflict: the four countries with the poorest growth performance in the 1990s have all experienced war (figure 5.4). The region's economic giants, Nigeria and South Africa, were not in the vanguard of the recovery; both face formidable (but different) political and economic difficulties. While some reforms in many countries appear irreversible, there remain important areas in which it is possible to doubt the extent and depth of economic policy reforms. A serious factor for the sustainability of accelerated growth is the continued depressed levels of public and private investment, which remain at levels too low for sustained rapid growth. The continuing low levels of private investment suggest that there has as yet been little fundamental improvement in investors' perceptions of the balance between risk and reward.

No doubt perceptions are influenced by the intractable or slow-changing nature of some of the more fundamental

Figure 5.4 Growth experiences have varied widely (annual average GDP growth, 1990–97)

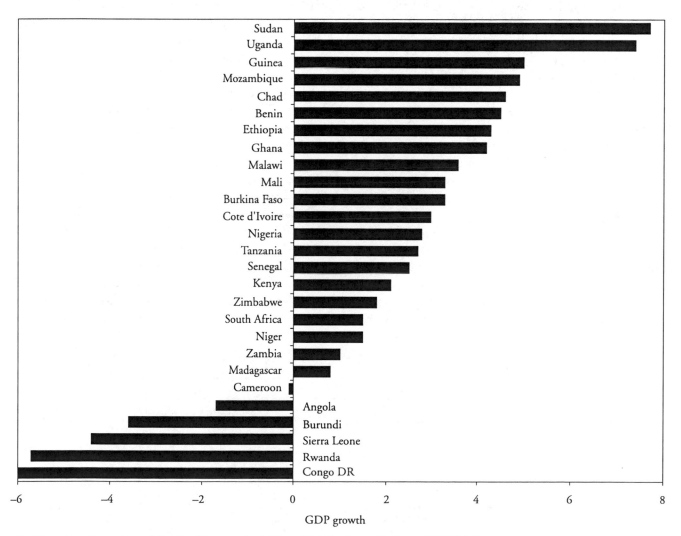

GDP growth

Note: Countries with populations below 5 million are omitted. *Source: World Development Indicators,* 1999, Table 4.1.

constraints, of which the poor stock of human capital, the associated weak ability to make productive use of modern technology, the parlous condition of the physical infrastructure, and the weakness of the institutions of the state suggest particular importance. The severity and intractability of these constraints help explain why Africa's economies have responded only weakly to the improved price incentives associated with structural adjustment programs, which, in turn, raises questions about the sustainability of the policy changes. There are questions, too, about the extent to which recent political changes are likely to strengthen the conditions for growth and provide assurance against policy and institutional reversals in the future. And far too many African countries still suffer from the turmoil of war and acute instability, with all their adverse consequences for investment and growth, as well as for human suffering.

Lastly, such considerations can be criticized as too general, not paying enough attention to differences in country experiences. The wide range of recent GDP growth experiences is illustrated in figure 5.4, from which it can be seen that in 1990–97 country growth rates ranged all the way from minus 6.0 percent in Democratic Republic of Congo (formerly Zaire) to more than 7 percent in Uganda, Botswana (not shown), and, according to the data, Sudan. In summary, of the 27 countries in figure 5.4, six experienced negative growth, 11 had growth rates in excess of 3.0 percent, with the remaining 10 in the 0.0 to 3.0 range, that is, below or about the same as the rate of population growth.

On balance, these considerations warn against any facile assumption that Africa can at last look forward to a prolonged period of catching up and growth-induced poverty reduction. Nonetheless, it is even more important not to overlook that there are points of light, with more grounds for optimism today than there have been for a long time.

The Poor May Not Be Able to Benefit from Growth

Whatever view one takes of prospects in Africa, there is the additional question of the power of growth to reduce poverty. Recall here the earlier conclusion from more global evidence, that large and growing inequalities considerably dampen that power. How unequal, then, is the distribution of income in Africa? Here the evidence is particularly incomplete and unreliable. It is not negligible, however, and the situation it portrays is summarized in table 5.1.

Inequalities are shown to be large in Africa—comparable with the extreme inequalities for which Latin America is notorious. The poorest one-fifth of the population receive only an estimated one-twentieth of total incomes, less than one-tenth of the share enjoyed by the richest one-fifth. The size of the Gini coefficient for the continent is shown as greater than that of Latin America and much larger than in the Asian subregions and industrial countries.[4] Moreover, there is evidence that inequality has been increasing during the last decade. Deininger and Squire (1996) show that the Gini coefficient for Africa rose from the 1980s to the 1990s, although the data are not good enough to be confident about this. Further analysis is required to know whether the income skew in Africa is a result of a small elite creaming off much of the national income, leaving most others more or less poor, or whether the essence of the problem lies more with extreme poverty at the lower end of the income spectrum.

As already suggested, with such large inequalities growth is less able to reduce income poverty than in a more egalitarian situation. One partially saving grace of African estimates is that they generally show the position of the poorest to be upgraded somewhat more as a result of general economic growth than those closer to the poverty line. However, it seems the nonpoor reap greater benefits from

Table 5.1 Inequality is severe in Africa

	Shares of total income		Ratio of richest to poorest	Gini coefficient[a]
	Poorest 20%	*Richest 20%*		
Sub-Saharan Africa	5	52	10.2	0.51
East Asia	7	44	6.5	0.38
South Asia	9	40	4.6	0.32
Latin America & Caribbean	4.5	53	11.7	0.49
Industrial countries	6	40	6.4	0.34

Note: Data relate to 1990s, with the figure for Africa adjusted to reflect expenditure basis of data.
a. A measure of departures from perfect equality, where perfect equality = 0.
Source: Deininger and Squire (1996).

economic expansion, as evidenced by countries that enjoyed recoveries in the 1980s. Kenya, Nigeria, and Tanzania were all countries that, in various periods during the 1980s and early 1990s, enjoyed periods of growth whose poverty-reducing effects were partially undone by rising inequalities (Demery and Squire 1996). In Kenya, for example, the estimates indicate that economic growth in 1981–91 would, other things being equal, have reduced the headcount index of poverty by over 6 percentage points. In the same period, however, inequalities worsened to an extent that, other things being equal, would have raised headcount poverty by nearly three-and-a-half points, so that combining the growth and inequality effects left a net improvement in the poverty count of under 3 percentage points. Evidence is also available from recent work analyzing asset holdings using demographic health survey data (Sahn, Stifel, and Younger 1999): although "asset poverty" has fallen in the 1990s in eight of the nine countries studied,[5] this effect comes largely from growth of asset holdings, with their distribution becoming more unequal over time in all but two cases (these data are presented in table A.6 of the appendix).

One problem, of course, is that rapid population growth absorbs much of any increase in total incomes and is especially concentrated in poorer households. Another is the failure of such economic growth as has occurred to generate new employment at a satisfactory pace. An important channel through which economic growth benefits the poor is the creation of new jobs, but the general belief is that growth in Africa has often taken excessively capital-intensive forms. Unfortunately, it is impossible to be more affirmative than this because employment data are particularly weak. In fact, the whole subject of the interactions between the operations of labor markets and poverty in Africa is, as suggested in chapter 4, a seriously neglected topic. If better information were available, it would almost certainly show formal-sector employment growing slower than the labor force as a widespread feature of African economies. There is also a need for a fuller understanding of the potentially large benefits of the informal sector as a source of employment, training, and enterprise, and of the institutional and policy environment required in order to tap this potential (Meagher 1995).

Growth Affects Poverty Groups Differently

The dangers of relying upon general economic growth to reduce income poverty are underlined by reference to the anatomy of poverty in Africa offered in chapter 3. The first observation here is that the extent to which growth raises the position of the economically dependent poor (the disabled, many children and old people, unsupported women) is entirely contingent upon the operation of traditional and other safety net provisions and, more widely, by changes in the distribution of income. In societies where income disparities are widening, governments are unable or unwilling to make adequate social provisions and the efficacy of traditional sharing mechanisms is diminishing, the position of the dependent poor is highly exposed.

As regards the economically active poor, an episode of economic growth will not, of course, raise sources of income equally, and some may be left out altogether. All will depend on the growth path and the extent to which it is pro-poor.[6] Box 5.1 on Uganda provides a positive example of what can be achieved when growth goes hand in hand with declining inequalities. The task is to identify the various sources of income of the economically active poor and to examine the extent to which these can be expected to be improved by GDP growth. While these groups cannot be quantified, table 5.2 identifies categories of the active poor who may benefit little from overall economic expansion. Growth will clearly be more pro-poor if it is more concentrated in areas (both geographical and productive) that have the largest contribution to poverty. However, regional growth patterns tend to discriminate against the poorest regions, and agricultural performance, particularly for subsistence crops, has been poor.

In the cases of the rural landless, reliant on selling their labor, and the urban unemployed, the crucial factor is the extent to which employment opportunities expand

Table 5.2 Groups of poor that may benefit little from growth

Economically active poor	
Rural	The landless
	Smallholders producing mainly subsistence crops
	Pastoralists
Urban	The unemployed
	Informal sector workers in defensive activities
Dependent poor	
Traditional poor	Elderly, widows, disabled
New dependent poor	AIDS orphans, refugees

Box 5.1 Combining growth with greater equality: a Ugandan success story

After years of internal strife and economic disintegration, Uganda's economy enjoyed a recovery during the 1990s to become one of the continent's adjustment success stories. As a result, per capita private consumption increased by one-fifth between 1991/92 and 1997/98. So what happened to poverty?

Here too there is a success story to tell. A household consumption survey and four follow-up monitoring surveys revealed a record of rising household welfare during this period of recovery. Using a nationally determined poverty line, the data revealed widespread initial poverty, with 56 percent of Ugandans falling below the poverty line as late as 1992. Just five years later this proportion was down to a still high 44 percent, and the record of improvement held both for both urban and rural areas. Growth proved a powerful means to reduced poverty because it was associated with some, albeit modest, improvements in the distribution of income. An important reason for that was that agriculture was fully included in the general economic recovery.

Examination below the surface reveals a more complicated picture, however. Inevitably, some benefited more than others and a few actually became poorer. Within agriculture, for example, it was the cash crop (mainly coffee) farmers, previously severely impoverished, who gained most. Their numbers below the poverty line were reduced sharply, while there was a more modest decline among food farmers, who started the period even more impoverished. The manufacturing and trade sectors experienced particularly large improvements, but mining saw much less improvement. Households whose heads were not working (mainly because of age) suffered actual increases in their already extreme levels of poverty. There were also substantial variations across different parts of the country and regional disparities widened somewhat. Broadly, the central and western regions enjoyed the greatest reductions in the headcount index, while the eastern region benefited least.

Overall, the Ugandan experience is an object lesson in what can be achieved when growth and reducing inequalities are combined. But there remain some questions. For instance, if households with elderly heads slipped further into penury, against the general trend, what happened to living standards *within* the households that gained? How did the women and children and other dependants fare? Survey results based on the household unit cannot answer this. Another question is about sustainability. To some extent Uganda's economic gains were based on a temporary boom in the country's main export, coffee. What will happen when that comes to an end? Similarly, the growth path of the 1990s is unlikely to be appropriate for the following decades. In that case will Uganda still be able to retain its pro-poor qualities?

Source: Appleton and others (1999).

---

as a result of growth. In the case of subsistence farmers who, more or less by definition, are only weakly integrated into the market economy because they have a limited surplus to sell, the crucial factor will be the extent to which changes may occur (for example, through improved farm-gate prices, extension services, the introduction of improved seed varieties, or the example of more progressive neighbors) that enable them to raise their yields. Pastoralist poor are even less likely to benefit from growth, as they are apt to resist the very economic modernization that may drive the rest of the economy forward.[7]

Lastly, workers and those self-employed in the urban informal sector may or may not benefit from growth elsewhere in the economy, depending on the nature of the enterprise they work in. For simplicity, the informal sector may be thought of as divided into modern and defensive categories. Those in modern enterprises will enjoy expanding demand for their outputs (positive income elasticities) as a result of growth and will be more or less connected to the more formal parts of the productive system.

But many informal workers will be in defensive enterprises, resulting from the coping strategies of the poor, as a way of scraping a living during hard times and declining employment. A wide range of such activities spring up, or become overpopulated, during economic recessions. Again, more or less by definition, they will tend to be hard hit by formal-sector expansion, because they will typically be producing goods or services with low or negative income elasticities of demand.

It also follows from the analysis in chapter 3 that the risk that the above categories of poor will be left behind by growth will be increased by the extent to which their situations are affected by certain of the correlates of poverty, particularly the following:

- Those who live in a remote region, relatively cut off from the mainstream of the economy by distance and poor infrastructure
- Members of female-headed households subject to gender biases in access to assets

- Those who are illiterate and unable to take advantage of improvements in technologies or increases in job opportunities requiring modern skills

Finally, chapter 3 showed that, at any one time, the temporarily poor are likely to be a substantial proportion of the total, thrust into their predicament by shocks of various kinds. While many of them are likely to be better placed to benefit from growth than those who suffer chronically, the nature of their poverty draws attention not so much to growth as the solution as to the avoidance, dampening, or counteracting of the shocks that push them below the poverty line—a policy issue taken up in part III.

Conclusion

Past growth, even in the 1990s and in the absence of widening income disparities, has not been fast enough to result in acceptable rates of poverty reduction. Moreover, there are formidable obstacles in the way of sustaining faster economic expansion, and the already large income inequalities may be widening. Finally, the agricultural sector (discussed in the next chapter) on which so many of the poor depend has performed weakly and remains backward.

Against these considerations, however, are the more encouraging factors of recent years helping to raise growth rates, and agriculture is by no means without examples of progress. There is a danger in overgeneralizing. If the situation appears dire in some countries, it is encouraging in others.

What definitely does emerge is that it will require major breaks with the past, with respect to the constraints on growth and the distribution of income, if satisfactory progress is to be made in the struggle against income poverty, and if the international targets to which governments have committed themselves are to stand any chance of being realized. It also emerges that, when considering the benefits of economic growth, it is dangerous in the extreme to think of the poor collectively. The situations of poor groups vary enormously, not least in terms of their abili-

ty to benefit from general economic growth. Antipoverty policies must be based on a recognition of this and include measures to safeguard those most at risk of being left behind.

It is evidently crucial to understand what have been the key constraints on growth, and how they may be addressed—issues that are the subject of the next chapter. It is equally evident that the notion of pro-poor growth must lie at the heart of any satisfactory antipoverty strategy, and that topic is taken up in chapter 12. What can be achieved when growth takes forms favorable to the poor is demonstrated in box 5.1 for Uganda, whose example might be taken as a model. Even there, however, the progress is not entirely without qualification, nor should its sustainability be taken for granted.

Notes

1. The coefficient from the simple regression is 0.92 with a t-statistic of 5.83; for the bottom 40 percent these figures are 1.01 and 8.95, respectively (see Roemer and Gugerty 1997).

2. Strictly speaking, the comparison should be with the 45-degree line, but the slope of the fitted line is close to unity.

3. On the other hand, Hanmer and Naschold (1999) find a higher elasticity for Africa among high-inequality countries. This is one area requiring further research.

4. The figure reported by Deininger and Squire is 0.47, but that is based largely on expenditure rather than income, which is not the case for other regions, so the figure here is that with the upward adjustment they propose (see also Ali 1999).

5. The eight are Ghana, Kenya, Madagascar, Mali, Senegal, Tanzania, Uganda, and Zambia, and the exception is Zimbabwe.

6. Like its predecessor, *broad-based growth*, the term *pro-poor growth* remains undefined. Three possibilities suggest themselves—the incremental income accruing to the poor (i) exceeds their population share, (ii) exceeds their existing income share, or (iii) exceeds some international norm (see White 1999b for more discussion).

7. As with any generalization, there are exceptions to this statement. Some pastoralists experienced a large windfall gain from the devaluation of the CFA franc.

CHAPTER 6

Why Has Growth Been So Poor?

Causes of Low Growth: The Usual Suspects

Since economic stagnation is so closely associated with the failure to reduce poverty in Africa, it is important to understand the causes of slow growth. Many possible factors present themselves, which fall into three broad categories:

- Adverse external environment: the colonial heritage, adverse movements in terms of trade and limited foreign capital inflows
- Poor policy environment: suppression of markets and macroeconomic instability and their consequences (low savings and investment)
- Societal, institutional, and geographical factors: from poor physical environment and adverse environmental trends to cultural attitudes and hot weather

This chapter attempts to sort out these various factors, starting with a discussion of regression results, which allows a focus on "bad policies." Attention is then focused on the agricultural sector, before coming to an assessment of the overall impact of economic reform programs. The role of external factors is then considered. Discussion of political issues is deferred until the next chapter.

Are Bad Policies to Blame?

Table 6.1 presents the results of seven studies that have estimated the determinants of growth in Africa.[1] There is a remarkable degree of consistency in these results. While differences in specification or data sets may mean that a given variable is significant in one test but not in another, there is much agreement on the direction of influence exerted by almost all variables. The uncontroversial results

are that (i) past (lagged) gross domestic product (GDP) growth is significantly negative, which supports the idea that Africa's past slow growth ought to permit faster growth in the future; (ii) higher investment promotes higher growth; (iii) lowering population growth will raise economic growth; and (iv) raising human capital will increase growth. In addition, there is more limited evidence to support the propositions that positive terms of trade movements and aid inflows are good for growth; that conflict is bad for growth; and, perhaps more controversially, that political freedom is associated with higher growth. Analysis in the 1998 *Poverty Status Report* also indicated that gender discrimination in education has a downward impact on growth.

Moving to policy variables, inflation is found to be bad for growth in one study but insignificant in others. However, running a large budget deficit is bad for growth. The close relationship between these two variables make it likely that at least one will be insignificant when both are included. The results confirm, therefore, the idea, for which there is much independent support, that macro stability is important for growth. It can be noted in passing that inflation is also likely to be directly harmful to the poor, particularly in the towns, who have few assets to diversify into inflation-proof portfolios.

Moreover, having an open economy may well be good for growth. The studies here use export growth or the trade ratio, but other analyses of the determinants of growth have used measures of openness that include a wider range of factors. Such indicators suggest that, even in the 1990s, Africa continues to be far less open than other developing regions: an index of openness (with 1 representing maximum openness) is estimated at just 0.04 for Africa and 0.37 for other developing countries (Collier and Gunning 1999b, p. 69). However, the significance of these

Table 6.1 Regression results for determinants of growth of GDP per capita in Sub-Saharan Africa

	World Bank	Mosley and others	White	Savvides	Ojo and Oshikoya	Blackden and Bhanu	Calamitsis and others
Lagged growth/GDP	–ve	–ve	–ve	–ve	–ve	–ve	…
Investment	…	…	…	+ve	+ve	+ve	+ve[a]
Population growth	…	…	…	–ve	–ve	–ve	–ve
Human capital[b]	…	…	+ve	–	+ve	+ve	+ve
Inflation	–	–	–	–	–ve	…	–[c]
Growth of exports/trade ratio	…	…	…	+ve	…	+ve	+ve
Growth in government consumption	…	…	…	–	…	…	…
Fiscal policy[d]	+ve	–	+ve	…	…	…	+ve
Financial development[e]	…	…	…	–	…	…	…
Real exchange rate	+ve	+ve	–	…	+ve	…	+ve
External debt	…	…	…	…	–ve	…	…
External transfers	–	–	+ve	…	…	…	…
Terms of trade	–	–	+ve	…	…	…	+ve
Political freedom	…	…	…	+ve	…	…	+ve
Conflict	…	…	…	…	…	…	–ve
Sustained adjuster dummy	…	…	…	…	…	…	+ve
Education gender equality	…	…	…	…	…	+ve	…

Note: +ve = significant positive effect; –ve = significant negative effect; – = insignificant; … = not included in regression. Dependent variable is growth turnaround for first three studies and growth for the other two.
a. Public and private investment included separately and both significant.
b. See papers for definitions of variables.
c. Regression also includes standard deviation of inflation, which is also insignificant.
d. Measure of fiscal balance and revenue collection, +ve indicates deficit is harmful for growth.
e. Ratio of quasi-liquid liabilities of the financial system to GDP.
Sources: Blackden and Bhanu (1999); Calamitsis, Anupam, and Ghura (1999); Mosley, Subasat, and Weeks (1995); Ojo and Oshikoya (1995); Savvides (1995); White (1997); World Bank (1994).

findings has been questioned owing to the conflicting results given by different measures of openness.

These results broadly support the idea that the pursuit of policies that closed off African economies to external competitiveness and fiscal laxity were detrimental to growth. Western culpability should be mentioned here too, since these policies (import substitution and expansion of the government sector) were supported by the international community throughout the 1960s and 1970s, and to some extent into the 1980s.[2]

These results do not, however, constitute support for an exclusively market-oriented development strategy, since none of the variables, with the possible exception of the measures of exchange rate misalignment, capture the extent of "market distortions."[3] As it relates to growth equations, the empirical and theoretical basis for liberalization is far weaker than that in support of macro stabilization and openness. It has also been contested by widely respected experts, including a former chief economist of the World Bank, emphasizing instead the importance of institutions. It is worth quoting these opinions at some length. Rodrik (1999, p. 4) has stated the following:

Countries that have done well in the post-war period are those that have been able to formulate a domestic investment strategy to kick-start growth and those that have had the appropriate institutions to handle adverse external shocks, not those that have relied on reduced barriers to trade and capital flow. The evidence from the last two decades is quite clear: the countries that have grown the most rapidly since the mid-1970s are those that have invested a high share of GDP and maintained macroeconomic stability.... Policy makers therefore have to focus on fundamentals of economic growth—investment, macroeconomic stability, human resources and good governance—and not let international economic integration dominate their thinking on development.

Similarly, Stiglitz (1998, pp. 5, 9, and 10) has argued that

many of the most successful countries (representing the largest part of growth within the low income countries) have not actually followed the "recommended" policies. . . . The Washington consensus failed [owing to] a failure to understand the subtleties of the market economy, to understand that private property and "getting the prices right" (that is, liberalization) are not sufficient to make a market work. An economy needs institutional structure. . . . Perhaps had [the East Asian] countries followed all the dictums of liberalization and privatization, they would have grown faster, but there is little evidence for that proposition.

These themes are taken up in chapter 7, where it is argued that market failures mean that liberalization alone is unlikely to succeed in the African context.

Agricultural Backwardness Is Particularly Serious, but the Causes Go Deep

Given the rural location of most poverty in Africa, the development of the rural economy is of key importance for raising the welfare of most of the poor: there is a negative correlation between the incidence of poverty and the level of value added per worker in agriculture. While fewer rural dwellers depend solely on agriculture, the health of the agricultural sector remains central to rural well-being. Besides providing the primary direct source of incomes in the rural economy, the multiplier effects of agricultural growth also have a potent effect on the expansion of the rest of the economy and on the development of off-farm sources of rural income. One estimate has it that a US$1 increase in agricultural output leads to a US$4 increase in induced demand for nonagricultural inputs (Adelman and Vogel 1992), creating the possibility of an agriculture-led growth path. Another estimate suggests that a US$1 rise in agricultural income generates additional rural nontradable production of US$1 to $2 (Delgado and others 1998)—a factor of the greatest importance because of the enormous importance to the rural poor of an ability to diversify income sources away from exclusive reliance on farm income.

The sad fact is, however, that African agriculture has proved too static to propel the broader growth of the economy, despite the enormous catching up potential of this sector. World Bank data indicate that, on average, there was no change in agricultural productivity per worker between the beginning of the 1980s and the later 1990s.[4] Similarly, the responsiveness of the agricultural sectors of African countries undergoing programs of structural adjust-

ment has been generally sluggish, although varying across countries. Thus in one recent study of a sample of 13 African countries, agricultural responsiveness was classified as weak, very weak, or zero in eight countries, and as strong or moderate to strong in the other five; moreover, average performance did not vary across the different economic regimes (White and Leavy 1999).

Agriculture is of central importance to the course of poverty in Africa for an additional reason—it is associated with strong seasonal variations in human welfare. The rural poor are particularly vulnerable to the effects of seasonality. Most of the very poor live in environments marked by a wet-dry seasonality, which affects all aspects of their lives, from income and consumption to health, nutritional status, and education. The wet season is the time of greatest difficulty. It is then that exposure to infection is often most pronounced and morbidity is at its highest. This is also the hungry season, with a combination of low food availability and a necessity for high-energy inputs into cultivation, for this is also the weeding season. This combination results in energy deficiency and weight loss, particularly affecting women and children.

Food prices rise in the wet season due to shortages, increasing debt. Families have fewer resources to meet the costs of treatment for illness and transport, and the labor lost because of this has high opportunity costs for the family. Acute or prolonged sickness risks making people permanently poorer through distress sales of assets, reducing family earning capacity and the possibility of rebuilding lost assets. Combined with all these factors, the health services at this time of year are likely to be at their least effective, due to high demand for treatment and shortages of supplies and personnel, which are apt to be disrupted by transport difficulties.

Agricultural improvement is key, therefore, and there is little doubt that there is much potential for improvement. Although international comparisons are open to objection because of the extent of variation within regions, differences between them in factor endowments, and the ecological specificity of recommended cultivation techniques, it is hard to quarrel with the general message emerging from tables 6.2a and 6.2b. In terms of the comparative levels attained in Africa for the four indicators presented, and the pace of change during the mid-1980s and 1990s, Africa is lagging far behind Latin America and South Asia. Comparable data for export crops tell a similar story (Killick 1995a, table 6.3). Africa's continuing heavy reliance on rain-fed agriculture—with all the associated vulnerability of poor people to adverse weather and the tyranny of

Table 6.2a Indicators of agricultural change, 1979–81 to 1995–97

	Sub-Saharan Africa		Latin America and Caribbean		South Asia	
	1979–81	*1995–97*	*1979–81*	*1995–97*	*1979–81*	*1995–97*
1. Irrigated land (percentage of cropland)	3.6	3.8	9.8	11.2	27.8	37.2
2. Fertilizer consumption (kg per arable ha.)	419	576	786	931	918	1370
3. Food production index (1989–91 = 100)	79.5	108.3	80.4	118.9	70.3	119.2
4. Cereal yield (kg per ha.)	1089	1050	1840	2576	1410	2197

Source: World Bank, *World Development Indicators 1999*, tables 3.2 and 3.3.

Table 6.2b Africa is lagging behind other regions

	Percent cropland irrigated	*Fertilizer consumption*	*Food production*	*Cereal yield*
1. Change, 1979–81 to 1995–97 (percentage)				
Africa	6	37	36	–4
Latin America	14	18	48	40
South Asia	34	49	70	56
2. Africa's level, 1995–97, as percentage of next lowest	34	62	91	48

Source: Author's computations from table 5.3a.

the hungry season—is especially disconcerting. Even within ecological zones, there is typically a large spread between the technologies and productivities of the best and the worst farmers. Such contrasts indicate a large scope for improvement.

At the same time, the constraints on the types of agricultural development that will most benefit the poor, notably greater production of cash crops, are formidable. Perhaps at the top of the list is the set of factors causing extremely high costs of transportation and distribution, which have the effect of dulling the price incentives for farmers to raise their yields and productivities, and to shift into potentially income-raising cash-crop production. For all of Africa's trade dependence, these high costs mean that much of its agriculture is relatively closed off from the benefits of international commerce (Delgado 1995, p. 5):

African economies are [only] "semi-open" because transport and other marketing costs to and from the ports for bulky items—including food staples and major exportables—end up doubling and tripling African port values . . . of exportables relative to their farm gate prices.

To a substantial extent, this phenomenon reflects the combined effects of often still low population densities and the limited past ability and willingness of governments to invest in rural infrastructure, as well as a past tendency to burden agriculture with inefficient, high-cost, state-owned marketing monopolies. The often underdeveloped and decaying state of rural roads[5] and other parts of the infrastructure system is a potent obstacle, dulling responses to price incentives, increasing market imperfections, and perpetuating agriculture's marginalization from the modern economy. So too is limited access to health services, which reduces productivity and detracts from the time available for women and children.

But market failures also contribute significantly. Although there has in recent years been a major state withdrawal from marketing, the response of the private sector to the opportunities thus opened up has fallen well short of the ideal. Besides the high transport and marketing costs resulting from underinvestment in infrastructure, weaknesses identified have included limited trade investment, thin markets, poor public market information, and high transactions costs (Gabre-Madhin and Johnson 1999, p. 52). The resulting weakening of farm-gate incentives in turn feeds into the continuing technological backwardness of much of smallholder agriculture, still substantially reliant on the methods of the past, aggravated by the low underlying levels of education, training, research, and extension support characterizing this part of the economy.

Although this is much harder to generalize about, the uncertainties and insecurity resulting from unreformed land tenure systems is often also an obstacle to investments in agricultural improvement, discouraging long-term investment and hampering the extension of credit to farmers anxious to make improvements. The gender biases already discussed add a further potent dimension. The inferior access of women to schooling and health, land, credit, and support services, as well as the excessive demands made on their time by the combination of farming work, childcare, and other household duties, quite apart from the inequities involved, hold back the progress of agriculture, where women's labor is particularly important. The extent and inefficiency of this was demonstrated in the 1998 *Poverty Status Report*, which estimated that the various disadvantages faced by women reduce economic growth in Africa by nearly a full percentage point (0.8 percent) each year, with the best explanation for this loss relating to agriculture.

Besides those already mentioned, various other factors lie behind Africa's poor agricultural record. First, many parts of the continent suffer from a weak ecological base, particularly poor soil quality but also a tendency toward drought. Second, Africa has experienced no equivalent to Asia's green revolution: there is great scope for technical advance, but it has not been realized. Finally, conflict has disrupted production in many countries.

In the past, policy biases have made the task harder. Macroeconomic incentives have been inadequate and governments have been unable to support the introduction of high-yielding technologies. In periods of economic austerity, extension services to farmers (or the means whereby extension workers can reach farmers) are often among the first items slashed. The rural infrastructure remains neglected and has in many cases deteriorated. Top-down and inefficient agricultural research and extension systems (often more oriented to the problems of the larger commercial farmers than to poor smallholders) have contributed, sometimes compounded by governmental unresponsiveness to smallholders' problems and always undermined by the weak farm-gate price incentives described earlier.

Some improvements have been effected in recent years, but much remains to be done, particularly in the development of research and extension services oriented to the needs of poor farmers. However, improved agricultural policies can be expected to make their best contribution to reducing the hardships of the poor only if the rest of the economy is also moving forward at a reasonable pace, and if the poor have both the incentives and the capabilities and assistance needed to be able to participate in the rural marketplace.

More fundamentally, there must be real doubts about the long-term sustainability of smallholder agriculture in the face of globalization and agricultural liberalization. This has huge implications for the rural poor. Africa's agricultural future is almost certainly bound up with accelerated commercialization and development of larger farms, with greater use of modern know-how and lower unit costs. The implication of this is to draw even greater attention, for the welfare of the rural poor, to the following:

- The importance of developing the industrial, service, and other aspects of the urban economy, to create alternative employment and enterprise opportunities for migrants from the villages.
- The development of a wider range of nonfarming opportunities within the rural economy, heightened by the already large importance of off-farm income sources for the rural poor.
- Efficient labor markets that will encourage labor-intensive development paths and facilitate the absorption, at reasonable levels of productivity and earnings, of rural labor within both the rural and urban economies. This latter point underscores the importance of the assertion of the importance of gaining a fuller understanding of the operation of labor markets in Africa and their impact on the poor.

Economic Reform Programs and Poverty Reduction

There has been much controversy about the impact of economic reform programs (often labeled "adjustment") on vulnerable groups.[6] There are two questions to pursue: (i) how reforms have affected poverty-reducing growth and (ii) the extent to which there have been measures to protect the poor during the adjustment process.

Has reform promoted pro-poor growth?

Not surprisingly, the influence of programs on economic performance is a function of the extent to which they have actually been implemented. When implementation is good, there is strong evidence of an associated improvement in economic performance, and with that improvement comes an enhanced potential to reduce poverty. Implementation is often weak, however. One symptom of this is that reform programs have high mortality or interruption rates. A high proportion of IMF programs break down before the end of their intended life and, on average, past World Bank programs have taken twice as long to complete as intended, with both shortcomings largely due to nonimplementation of policy conditions.

A further symptom of poor implementation is that programs have only modest impact on key policy variables, even less on institutions. There is little evidence that IMF programs exert restraint on domestic credit, although they do strongly influence exchange rates, and there is also quite a strong association with reform of other price variables, such as interest rates. But reforms have much greater difficulty in influencing institutional change, for example, in financial sector reforms and privatization programs. The World Bank's 1994 *Adjustment in Africa* report judged that only six out of 29 adjusting countries had achieved decisive improvements in macroeconomic policies. In a follow-up study (Bouton, Jones, and Kiguel 1994), 15 out of 25 adjusting African countries were still judged to have poor or very poor macroeconomic policy stances in 1991–92 even though between them these countries had received 110 World Bank adjustment credits and 95 IMF programs since 1980. The quality of policy was judged to have deteriorated during 1992 in eight of the 25, even though seven of the eight had Bank structural adjustment programs during that year and five of them also had IMF programs.

If the growth effects of programs have been mixed, what about their distributional consequences? They have often been criticized for imposing excessive burdens on vulnerable groups. However, the evidence suggests that the distributional effects of reforms have been quite complex. Evidence on Côte d'Ivoire, Ghana, Tanzania, Kenya, and Nigeria suggests that reforms have either been associated with, or have been unable to prevent, growing inequalities. For Côte d'Ivoire, Ghana, and Tanzania, there is also evidence that the differential effects of adjustment measures have been sufficiently powerful to induce a measurable narrowing in the size of urban-rural inequalities, but mainly by squeezing urban incomes. In fact, that a disproportionate part of the burden of adjustment is borne by the urban labor force is one of the few firmly established generalizations in this area.

Women are often regarded as being put particularly at risk by adjustment policies. They are apt to be constrained by household duties and discrimination in credit, product, and labor markets from taking advantage of the new opportunities that reforms may create. Some traditional divisions of labor in the rural economy, in which the men are responsible for cash crops while the women grow the food, would weigh against women when reforms shift prices in favor of cash crops, for which there is evidence from Malawi. However, a contrary speculation suggests that, since the incidence of poverty among households headed by women is greatest in rural areas whereas poverty in the towns is related more to the low incomes of male household heads, reforms that shift relative incomes in favor of the rural economy may improve the relative position of female-headed households. Unfortunately, there is little more than anecdotal evidence against which to test these speculations, and what does exist produces mixed results.

Indeed, this is the overall picture, too: apart from the earlier generalization about the impact on the urban population, there is a distinct lack of evidence that programs change income inequalities or poverty to any large extent. Perhaps this is not so surprising, since reform programs are not much addressed to the causes of poverty as set out in this report. Apart from their impact on government services, reforms are not intended to address the social structures and demographic factors contributing to the poverty problem, nor the civil and political strife that aggravate it. Economic reforms can do little for the empowerment of the poor. They are rarely addressed to the initial inequalities that aggravate the poverty problem. Reforms are addressed to some of the sources of low productivities that underlie the poverty problem, and to correcting the past capital intensity of growth by raising the cost of capital relative to labor, but the responses of African economies to measures intended to shift prices in favor of job creation have been disappointing. Overall, adjustment measures are somewhat peripheral to the causes of poverty and, therefore, unlikely to make a large impact in either direction. What is clear, however, is that more energetic execution of agreed programs could be expected to improve economies' growth performance and, hence, the scope for poverty reduction. Halfhearted reform has been a major weakness, for which both national governments and international agencies share responsibility.

The poor have not been adequately protected

There are two chief aspects here: (i) the ways in which the composition of government spending has been changed by the introduction of reforms, particularly spending on the social services, and (ii) the effectiveness of safety net provisions designed to alleviate programs' possible poverty-worsening effects.

Reforms appear not to have made a decisive difference to social spending. To summarize drastically, research on the effects of adjustment on state spending points to the following conclusions:

- The interest cost of servicing public debt, domestic and external, has been rising in many countries, placing a squeeze on nondebt spending.
- When faced with the necessity to cut nondebt spending, governments generally try to protect social spending, with the heaviest cuts falling on capital budgets and economic services, so that social spending actually tends to claim a rising share of total nondebt spending.
- This *relative* protection has not prevented large *absolute* declines in social service provision in some African countries. This has often been worsened by a deteriorating quality of services (schools without books, clinics without medicines). However, IMF data show increasing real per capita social spending in its African program countries in 1986–97, although that still left nonprogram countries with higher average social spending levels. It should also be pointed out that substantial declines in social spending took place in many countries prior to the adoption of adjustment programs.
- Comparisons of expenditure patterns in adjusting and nonadjusting countries reveal little systematic difference, suggesting that programs per se are not particularly a source of regressive budgetary cuts. This is reinforced by findings of a positive link between social spending and program implementation: it may be that the worst outcomes are in countries that adopt reform programs but only halfheartedly.
- In many cases, reforms have not been able to improve the quality of government spending. Micro-level changes in social spending patterns often reinforce the tendency for the richer portions of developing country populations to capture a disproportionate share of social services, with shifts away from the primary education and preventative medicine services that bring greatest benefits to the poor (see chapter 9).

The indications are that safety nets have had a mixed but improving record. Provisions have been increasingly employed to protect groups especially vulnerable to adjustment measures, notably public sector employees who lose their jobs as a result of civil service reforms and pri-

vatizations. These schemes have included targeted subsidies and transfers of various kinds; employment-creation and retraining schemes; and special infrastructural development schemes in poor areas. Early evidence suggested they had made little impression, being too small, reaching only a fraction of the targeted poor and with regional, gender, and class biases. But lessons have been learned and later results (although mostly relating to non-African countries) are more encouraging. Targeting and project designs have improved, and schemes have been made more accessible to the poor. However, their international sponsors are at pains to stress the limitations of what can be achieved by safety net measures in the absence of wider antipoverty strategies. Box 6.1 on Tanzania illustrates the dangers to the poor of reform measures that are not set in the context of an overall antipoverty strategy. Moreover, there is a possibility that distress and dislocation caused by adjustment measures may have contributed to the weakening of traditional sharing mechanisms described elsewhere in this volume.

In summary, the evidence surveyed does not support the strongest allegations of those who criticize reform programs for causing poverty. When properly implemented, they have tended to bring improved economic performance and, with it, increased *potential* for reducing poverty, but incomplete implementation has been a major weakness. Programs have had adverse effects on the urban poor, have been unable to prevent widening inequalities, and have often not effectively protected those placed at risk. At the same time there is little strong evidence of systematically adverse poverty effects; perhaps most reform measures have left the more basic causes of poverty largely unaffected.

While the Bretton Woods institutions have been slow to act to at least reduce the dangers that reform measures may harm vulnerable people, there have more recently been important and welcome moves in this direction, for example, in connection with the Enhanced Highly Indebted Poor Country (HIPC) debt relief scheme. Such moves should be supported for, while concern for the welfare of the poor is not a good reason for rejecting adjustment, more could be done to reduce programs' ill effects on vulnerable people.

Global Factors Have Not Been a Major Reason for Slow Growth

There is a clear sense in which the outside world, in the form of colonialism, has had a determining influence on

Box 6.1 Economic reform in Tanzania has neglected the poor

Over the last decade there have been substantial liberalization and other policy reforms in Tanzania. How have these affected the poor? In several instances, there has been a mismatch between the policies implemented (or to be implemented) and the needs of the poorest. Evidently, it is not the first goal of SAPs to tackle the problem of poverty but to confront the more general economic problems of a country. However, in Tanzania, the mechanisms by which this effect could potentially happen are faulty, since policymakers sometimes depart from wrong assumptions concerning the situation and attitudes of the poor. As Castro-Leal and others (1999) rightly point out, "improving targeting to the poor involves not simply rearranging the public subsidies but also addressing the constraints that prevent the poor from accessing these services."

Our findings show that, in terms of agricultural policy, movements towards the favoring of export crops and liberalization of input and product markets may be decisive for the country but will either neglect the poor or negatively affect them. In terms of education, the message is not so clear-cut. The situation is deficient but deficient for everyone. Educational infrastructures in rural areas are slowly collapsing and both poor and wealthy families are affected, although this is a larger problem for the less well-off. The health sector is also in a critical state in rural areas.

Thus it is clear that strategies aimed at alleviating poverty must be directly focused on the poor. Indirect approaches that rely on trickle-down and the functioning of the microeconomy may not benefit the poor. Poverty alleviation plans must be part and parcel of overall social-economic plans.

Source: Cortijo and Lebrun (1999, p. 57).

Africa's economic condition. While it is increasingly implausible to attribute the continent's economic ills to colonialism, the neglects of that period—in the development of the physical and human capital stocks, technological capabilities, and institutions—made it predictable that the new states of Africa would have great difficulties in sustaining reasonable rates of economic progress, just as it is not surprising that the colonial experience, and the way this interacted with traditional social structures, resulted in postindependence states that would often prove incapable of responding adequately to emerging economic deficiencies.

But what of the contemporary influence of the world economy? The long-standing debate about the balance between external and domestic influences on Africa's economic problems has been given new life by concerns that the quickening pace of globalization may be increasing inequalities and disadvantages among the poor in developing countries. In taking up this set of issues, trade questions are first considered and then the influence of the financial connections between Africa and the rest of the world.

World trading conditions: some difficulties but big opportunities

One major way in which the outside world affects Africa is through movements in the prices of the primary product exports on which the continent remains heavily dependent. Through these are transmitted fluctuations in world

activity and shifts in demand, and they have a potent influence on Africa's commodity terms of trade. There is now widely agreed to be a long-term deteriorating trend in real commodity prices. There are fluctuations around the trend and periods of recovery, but the most recent years have shown a fluctuation in the adverse direction, in response to the slump in world growth following the 1998 economic crises in Russia and East Asia. In 1998 alone (in nominal dollar terms), nonfuel commodity prices fell by nearly 15 percent and oil prices by 32 percent, with prospects for further substantial falls during 1999.[7] Figure 6.1 shows very clearly the great variability in Africa's terms of trade, and the decline since the boom in the mid-1970s.

Both the trend and the fluctuations naturally affect Africa's terms of trade and these, in turn, affect domestic investment and economic performance, including ability to respond to the poverty problem, particularly in the short term. However, the scale of the terms of trade deterioration is easy to exaggerate. According to African Development Bank data, Africa's terms of trade actually improved at an average rate of 1 percent a year in the 1980s and, although they worsened in the 1990s (1991–98), this was only at 2 percent per year.[8] It is similarly easy to unduly emphasize the negative influence of external shocks like the East Asian crisis. By virtue of their poor long-term export performance and exceptionally high protectionism, most African economies are less fully integrated into the world trading economy than would be predicted by their small size, as already reported. This situation is strongly adverse to Africa, but it does provide a degree of insulation

Figure 6.1 Macroeconomic indicators

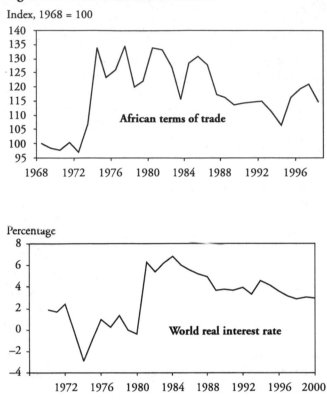

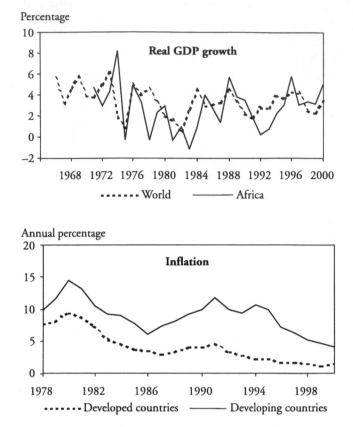

Source: IMF, *International Finance Statistics; Global Economic Outlook.*

from global economic shocks. It seems that the 1998–99 world economic downturn may have knocked 1–1.5 percentage points off Africa's growth in both years—serious enough against a fragile background but less than traumatic and with a recovery forecast for 2000.[9]

Concern is also sometimes expressed about the negative effects of the long-term slowdown in world economic growth that appears to be under way. The data do indeed suggest the existence of such a trend but against this has to be set a more potent compensating factor: the growth of trade relative to world output. Consider the statistics in table 6.3. These confirm a slower world GDP growth rate in the 1990s but show a faster trade growth, with trade in the 1990s growing three times as fast as output, underlining the accelerating trend toward globalization.

A situation in which world trade is growing at more than 6 percent a year ought to be enormously favorable to small, trade-reliant economies, as it has been for many countries outside Africa. This is the big truth about the influence of the world trading environment. The big question is why Africa's economies have generally been unable

to take advantage of the opportunities created by this development, a failure illustrated by figures showing Africa's share of total world exports to have more than halved over the last two decades, from 3.9 percent in 1980 to 1.5 percent in 1997.[10]

Why has Africa become such a tiny actor in world trade? It cannot be explained in terms of the trade barriers of the rest of the world because exporters from other developing regions have faced, and often overcome, far more discriminatory treatment, whereas Africa has been rather favorably treated. This conundrum is closely related to another big question. Africa's exports and terms of trade

Table 6.3 World trade has been booming (annual real growth, percent)

	1981–90	1990–99
World GDP growth	2.8	2.1
World trade growth	4.5	6.2
Multiple of trade to GDP growth (ratio)	1.6	3.0

Source: Computed from United Nations, *World Economic and Social Survey 1999*, table I.1.

are vulnerable to adverse price movements because the continent has made much less progress in diversifying out of reliance on primary product exports than any other developing region, as illustrated by the statistics of the share of primary products in total exports (table 6.4). The share of primary products in total exports was more than 90 percent in both South America and Africa in 1970; in the 1990s it was close to 60 percent in South America but still nearly 80 percent in Africa. This dependence is only partly explained by Africa's rich endowment in natural resources—it is also an outcome of poor policies and infrastructure that mitigate successful investment in manufacturing, and it has also been shown to be the result of the continent's weak skills base on account of low levels of education (Wood and Mayer 1999).

The question of the causes of Africa's weak response is returned to below, but the expansion of world trade also poses another issue, concerning its impact on the distribution of income. Such rapid growth implies major structural changes, as economies adapt to this shift in global demand. In all structural change there are winners and losers and an ever present danger that prominent among the losers will be the already vulnerable (see box 6.2). Is this happening in Africa? There are reasons for fearing that it might. Changes in the pattern of world demand hardly favor the foodstuffs grown by most African farmers, to say nothing of its myriad informal-sector workers. Trade is a potent vehicle for technological change, but most technology originates in capital-rich, labor-scarce industrial countries and is thus apt to be biased away from the job creation that is so central to any attack on poverty in Africa. And, to the extent that jobs are created, they may call for modern skills the poor lack.

There is, unfortunately, scant hard evidence to bring to bear here, partly because of the research complexities involved. The balance of the (mainly non-African) literature predicts that the relative growth of international trade is growth- and employment-enhancing, and therefore pro-poor, so long as appropriate supporting policies are in place. The literature also predicts that trade will raise

Table 6.4 Africa's exports have not diversified (percentage share of primary products in total exports)

	1970	*1984*	*1993*
Sub-Saharan Africa	95	93	78
South America	93	76	62
East and South Asia	51	37	16

Source: United Nations Conference on Trade and Development (UNCTAD) Commodity Yearbook 1995.

Box 6.2 Trade reform and poverty in Zambia and Zimbabwe

The experience of Zambia and Zimbabwe illustrates some of the ways in which the poor may gain from trade liberalization, but also that such gains may fail to be realized. The majority of Zambian farmers are maize producers who have been most affected by internal trade liberalization, with the removal of panterritorial and panseasonal pricing along with subsidies on inputs. These changes have hit many farmers, some of whom have retreated into subsistence, at a time when their cash needs are greater than before (as user charges have been introduced for social services and inputs must now be purchased). Many traders engage in barter rather than pay cash.

The Zimbabwean experience has been more positive, with a greater degree of diversification. This success brings different problems of increased vulnerability to the volatility of international markets.

In both countries liberalization has brought more goods to the shops in rural areas. But, particularly in Zambia, many of the poor can afford few of these items. Evidence from both countries suggests that both men and women engage in cash crop production but that men control the income earned from these sources, which will affect the pattern of household expenditures.

Source: Stevens (1999).

---

real wages, not only among traded-goods producers but also in nontraded good industries that service them (McKay and others 1999). However, these predicted benefits are long term and net. There are losers as well as gainers, and there are apt to be particularly substantial losses during the process of adaptation and change. Evidence on the impact of structural adjustment programs on smallholders' incomes varies from case to case and leads to no strong conclusion. Influences operating through the trade channel may be contributing to the widening inequalities in Africa hinted at earlier, although it is likely that the main explanations lie elsewhere. The influence of trade growth on Africa's poverty problem would, perhaps, be a more acute issue if the continent participated more fully in the global trade explosion.

Capital flows and aid could help more but are not central to the poverty problem

There is a clear but essentially trivial sense in which trends on Africa's private capital account are hampering growth and the potential for poverty reduction. This refers to the only slight extent to which foreign direct investment (FDI) and other private flows have gone to Africa in recent decades, by contrast with other developing regions. In fact, the United Nations actually estimates that, on a net basis, the FDI balance was negative in every year from 1987 to 1997, that is, there was net disinvestment. IMF and World Bank figures are less adverse but also show Africa's receipts to have been small relative to other developing and transitional economies.[11] This absence of flows is described as trivial not because it is unimportant but because the key question is why private capital still stays away. The reasons why the risk-reward balance is still seen as unfavorable again focus attention on economic and political conditions within Africa.

One other factor that should be recorded here is the movement of world real interest rates, for although African countries receive only limited variable-interest credit, this factor has apparently exerted a significant influence on growth in the past.[12] The trend in that variable is also traced in figure 6.2, from which can be seen a large rise from the mid-1970s to the mid-1980s, with a downward drift thereafter. The rise may well have been influential in the economic deterioration from 1975 to 1985, but the poor economic results of most years since have been despite an easing in real rates.

What now of the position with regard to public flows, of which development assistance is the most important element? There are questions here about the scale of aid receipts and the uses to which it is put. On scale, there has been alarm about the declining real value of total development assistance, with some talk of the existence of an aid crisis. The figures do indeed show a serious recent

decline, as shown in figure 6.2. However, much of this reduction was concentrated in a few countries (Kenya, Somalia, Sudan, and the Democratic Republic of Congo), and aid nonetheless remained above the early 1980s level in real terms (but has declined in per capita terms). It is still the case that Africa is strongly favored in the distribution of aid and receives far more, relative to other economic variables, than the other major developing regions (table 6.5).

But has the aid been of the right type? In particular, has it sufficiently addressed the reduction of poverty? At the broadest level the facts must suggest that aid has failed to live up to its promise: as many infants die in their first year as 30 years ago despite billions of dollars of aid, indicating some culpability among aid donors for the limited progress. This culpability has been both economic and political—economic because well into the 1980s donors supported the sorts of government interventions they now blame for Africa's poor growth,[13] and political because aid was often given to support regimes who were clearly bad for the well-being of most the country's population (see chapter 7). Issues of the impact of aid are further detailed in chapter 15. The main conclusions regarding poverty are listed below (some of which are also illustrated in box 6.3):

- Despite donors' rhetoric, only a modest proportion—perhaps 15–25 percent—of total aid has been directly poverty oriented, although that proportion is rising.
- Many donors have yet to bring poverty reduction criteria into the mainstream of agency work by, for example, staff incentives and training, provision of guidance, and establishment of poverty-related monitoring systems.
- Agencies have been poor at trying to understand country poverty situations, and few have engaged recipient governments in policy dialogue on this subject.
- There is little information about the effect of donors' interventions, but the indications are that most projects

Figure 6.2 The real value of aid to Africa is declining (net disbursements in constant prices)

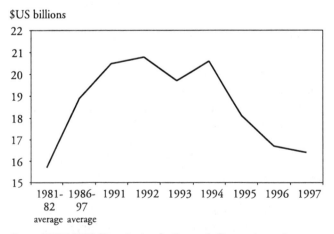

$US billions

Source: OECD-DAC (Organization for Economic Cooperation and Development (Development Assistance Committee), *Development Co-operation*, 1998, and earlier issues.

Table 6.5 Africa's 1997 aid dependency ratios remained high (percentages, except aid per capita)

	Africa	Latin America and Caribbean	South Asia
Aid per capita ($)	26	13	3
Aid/GNP	5.0	0.3	0.8
Aid/investment	27.7	...	3.6
Aid/imports	12.7	1.4	4.3

... Not available.
Source: World Bank, *World Development Indicators 1999*, table 6.10.

Box 6.3 Mixed poverty-reduction results from aid to Zimbabwe

A study of European aid to Zimbabwe concluded that "with the partial exception of Sweden, the donors we have studied could not be said to have given the PR [poverty-reduction] objective much consistent priority. Most had tried to improve the well-being of poor groups with specific interventions but the PR content of their programmes was quite limited, none had come near to applying best-practice PR standards and some were quite explicit in stating that PR had not in practice been given priority." Of total aid to Zimbabwe by five European donors in the mid-1990s, only about one-tenth was directly targeted at poor groups, with another third having significant indirect PR benefits. Three-fifths of total aid fell into neither of these categories.

There were some mitigating factors, however. A sample of projects nominated by donor agencies as having antipoverty objectives was found, by the criteria of livelihoods, knowl-edge, resources, and rights, to have made positive contributions to the welfare of poor people, particularly by enhancing their access to knowledge. There are, moreover, legitimate objectives for aid programs in addition to PR, particularly in a country not among the more seriously poverty stricken in Africa and where the national government itself apparently gives rather low priority to PR.

Nonetheless, the donors could have done more. The study urged them to engage with the government in a policy dialogue on this subject. It urged donors to improve their own knowledge and conceptualization of the poverty situation in the country, to buy into locally generated schemes, particularly those based on beneficiary ownership and participation, to improve coordination among themselves, to move towards better targeting of poor beneficiary groups, and to strengthen their own monitoring and evaluation procedures.

Source: Killick, Carlsson, and Kierkegaard (1998).

---

with antipoverty objectives produce beneficial results, particularly those specifically targeted at poor groups. Few of these projects would be financially sustainable if donors withdrew, however.

Overall, it is difficult, in comparative terms, to argue that the rise of poverty in Africa has been due to the deficiencies of external assistance. Although the recent volume trend is adverse, and donors could have done much better in using aid to reduce poverty, Africa has been comparatively well treated for a long time, to such an extent that excessive aid dependency is now recognized as a problem.

Debt overhang aggravates the poverty problem, but the benefits of debt relief have been exaggerated. Much of past aid, particularly from multilateral agencies, created debt. To this should be added a large volume of export credits and a more modest volume of private, mainly bank, credit. As of the end of 1998, the total size of Africa's outstanding external debt was about US$220 billion, equal to about one-half of GNP, a higher ratio than for other developing regions. Debt service payments for Africa as a whole averaged about 13 percent of export earnings, but this ratio was artificially low because about one-half of debts were not being serviced. Even so, some debtor countries had ratios of well over 20 percent. A succession of debt-relief schemes for heavily indebted, low-income countries had been introduced and found inadequate in the face of debtors' continuing inability to repay. The most recent of these, the 1996 HIPC initiative, itself had to be substantially enhanced in 1999.

There is a clear connection between the burdens of the more severely indebted African countries and their poverty situations. The prior claims that debt servicing makes on domestic saving and on foreign exchange availability impedes both the utilization of existing resources and the rate at which productive capacity can be increased through investment. Moreover, there is evidence that the existence of such a large debt discourages private investment by depressing complementary public sector investments, increasing investor uncertainties and reducing expected rates of return. All these factors impede economic growth and, hence, the potential for reducing poverty. Also, since most of the debt in question is public or publicly guaranteed, debt servicing can make a large claim on governments' scarce budgetary resources and—depending on their spending priorities—can compete directly with pro-poor spending on education, health, and rural infrastructure.

At the same time, there is often an exaggerated view of the strength of the debt-poverty connection. Widespread poverty predated the emergence of the debt problem and would remain if all debt were written off. Its fundamental causes lie elsewhere, as described in this volume. Similarly, concentration on the terms of debt relief may divert attention from the underlying source of the debt problem, which is the low efficiency of investment. Only exceptionally have African countries borrowed on harsh terms. On average, terms are below commercial rates and have been for many years. Thus in 1997 the average rate of interest on new credit for all African countries taken together was 3.9

percent, with an average maturity of 22 years and a grant element of 40 percent (with even softer terms for low-income Africa). Even as early as 1984 the equivalent statistics were 5.4 percent, 23 years, and 34 percent. In addition, much capital (including, nowadays, most bilateral aid) is provided as grants. In 1997 capital received as transfers amounted to $10.3 billion, against new long-term borrowing (including IMF) of exactly the same value, so the true grant element of total capital receipts is much larger than just reported.[14] The question that has been neglected in recent debates is how it can be that economies receiving capital on such favorable terms can encounter acute debt difficulties. The answer must lie with low returns to the capital invested (including its capacity to generate additional foreign exchange earnings and fiscal revenues), which takes us back to the manifold causes of Africa's weak past economic growth. So long as these underlying causes are not addressed, large-scale poverty will persist, whatever debt relief is provided.

To this cautionary note should be added another: there is no necessary assurance that resources released by debt relief schemes will actually be devoted to raising the welfare of the poor. As argued elsewhere in this volume, not all African governments have an established record of giving priority to pro-poor measures. It is true that spending on education and health, relative to GDP, is high in Africa (chapter 9), but it is also the case that much of this takes the form of most benefit to non-poor users, and there are considerable political and other obstacles to more effective targeting of services on poor groups. Uganda is among the countries that have established a mechanism for channeling revenues saved by debt relief into pro-poor services, but so far not many others have followed suit. In any case, fungibility limits the value of such devices unless there is genuine political commitment to poverty reduction and the released resources can be fed into comprehensive antipoverty strategies and policies. Finally, there is a danger that increasing the generosity of debt relief could divert aid resources from countries that have much poverty but have avoided large-scale debt difficulties. African countries falling into this category include Burkina Faso, Malawi, and Senegal.

The primacy of domestic inflexibility

Has globalization increased poverty? Not as such. Rather, Africa's main problems have been (i) a weak export record, both with respect to growth and diversification, reducing the continent to insignificance as a trading force; (ii) pri-

vate investors' continuing perceptions of an unfavorable risk-reward balance; (iii) low returns to past investments, giving rise to major debt problems, the alleviation of which would, by itself, make a limited difference in the extent of poverty; and (iv) that these problems have been experienced despite favorable treatment of Africa in the global distribution of aid. Although there are specific ways in which globalization makes poverty reduction harder, the argument here has drawn attention to the primacy of the domestic economic and political environment, conditioning Africa's responses to globalization.

Why, then, has there been so much concern about the impact of globalization on Africa's poor? Much of the answer has to do with the inflexible nature of Africa's economies, making it more difficult and costly for them to adapt to changing global conditions and to take advantage of newly developing trading opportunities. Besides its poor export record, symptoms of inflexibility include a widening technological gap, rather low supply responses to changing price relativities, a generally inferior record of results from policy reform programs, and political structures that too often remain either unstable or unresponsive to demonstrated policy deficiencies. The extent of this inflexibility is illustrated in table 6.6, which shows the shares of various sectors in GDP. The most striking fact from this table is how little the structure of African economies has changed: agriculture's share has remained at around 25 percent, whereas in South Asia it has fallen from 41 to 30 percent.

Underlying these deficiencies are often weak information flows and incentive systems, resulting from faulty policy interventions and an underdeveloped infrastructure but also from market failures of various kinds (chapter 7). Relatively weak technological capabilities are particularly serious, flowing from the continent's narrow base of skills and knowledge, and the deficiencies of its institutions, raising transactions costs. Africa, in short, is ill-placed to realize the promise which globalization holds out. The costs of adaptation tend to dominate perceived benefits, particularly in the shorter term, and various categories of the poor are placed at risk. For example, coming to terms with the inefficiency (in international terms) of the bulk of a manufacturing sector which owes its existence to high protective barriers poses acutely difficult problems of management and restructuring which may threaten the livelihoods of many workers on whose remittances many poor households depend. And yet, if poverty is to be conquered and Africa's future growth is to be sustained at a reasonable pace, adaptation is essential.

Table 6.6 The structure of African production has not changed over time (sectoral shares of GDP, period averages)

	Agriculture			Manufacturing			Other industry			Services		
	1970–79	*1980–89*	*1990–96*	*1970–79*	*1980–89*	*1990–96*	*1970–79*	*1980–89*	*1990–96*	*1970–79*	*1980–89*	*1990–96*
East Asia and Pacific	31.4	26.9	21.4	26.1	29.8	31.2	11.4	11.0	10.7	31.1	32.3	36.8
Europe and Central Asia	...	15.2	13.7	...	...	...	...	...	...	...	36.3	45.6
Latin American and Caribbean	12.2	10.0	10.1	26.0	26.8	21.7	11.1	12.3	11.9	50.7	50.9	56.2
Middle East and North Africa	10.5	14.6	16.9	8.4	10.0	12.5	45.6	29.2	22.3	35.5	46.1	46.8
South Asia	41.3	33.8	29.6	16.0	17.0	17.6	7.0	9.4	9.9	35.7	39.8	42.9
Sub-Saharan Africa	25.3	24.1	24.0	13.7	14.5	14.7	15.8	17.6	17.0	45.1	43.9	44.4

... Not available.
Source: World Bank, *World Development Indicators.*

Conclusion

Africa's low growth may be explained by a range of factors. A poor policy environment has certainly been a major part of the explanation, by which is meant a failure to maintain macro stability and undue neglect of external competitiveness. Although the inefficiencies of state intervention also undermined growth, there is less evidence in support of an exclusively market-oriented development. Rather the problems of low growth are ones to do with the traditional determinants of growth, such as investment and human capital. It is the failure to improve these fundamentals, combined with weak implementation of agreed reforms, that underlies the modest success that reform programs have had in turning around African economies. In addition, such programs have contained little of direct relevance to poverty reduction and have not contained adequate protection for the poor where there have been adverse effects.

There are various ways in which the global economic environment has aggravated Africa's economic problems and lessened the ability of the region's governments to cope with the problem of mass poverty: unstable trading conditions and secularly deteriorating export prices; a possible tendency for the relative growth of trade to leave many of the poor behind; a continuing perception by investors that many African states remain unacceptably high-risk locations for FDI; a decline in real aid flows in recent years, coupled with limited donor effectiveness in using their resources to reach the poor; creditor reluctance to offer debt relief in line with the debtor countries' abilities to pay, leading to a continuing debt overhang problem; and reform programs that are still insensitive to the needs of the poor and in some cases unnecessarily worsen their condition.

However, there have been some strongly positive forces at work, too, notably an extraordinarily rapid expansion in world trade and, notwithstanding recent reductions, amounts of development assistance that remain very large by comparison both with other low-income regions and with economic aggregates in Africa. The most important issues are why Africa has been unable to take advantage of the trade expansion, so that today it is a negligible force in world trade, why it continues to be seen as an unfavorable environment for FDI, why its debt servicing capacities remain so weak despite large inflows of public capital on favorable terms, and why its implementation of, and responses to, policy reforms have been generally weak.

In short, domestic structural, and policy inflexibility are the key factors. If these could be satisfactorily addressed, the global economy could be seen more as enhancing Africa's ability to tackle its poverty than as an aggravating force. This is why the bulk of this report is about conditions and policies within African countries, rather than about the wider environment in which they operate.

Notes

1. Many more studies include African countries in addition to those from other regions. The advantage of using larger samples is that the growth differential attributable to included variables may be calculated, as done in Easterly and Levine (1997). However, such studies typically impose constraints on model coefficients, so that the estimates may not be valid for African countries. Hence results presented here are for studies using African countries only.

2. For example, donors continued to use import support to "underwrite" failing parastatals and so impeded restructuring.

3. The "sustained adjuster" dummy used by Calamitsis, Anupam, and Ghura (1999) is based on staying on track with the International

Monetary Fund (IMF), which cannot be taken as a good measure of overall policy stance.

4. Gabre-Madhin and Johnson (1999, table 1) give data for 20 African countries from which it can be calculated that agricultural value added per worker, in constant 1987 dollars, averaged US$479 in 1979–81 and US$468 in 1994–96 (unweighted means). The usual caveats are, of course, necessary concerning the reliability of the primary data on which these figures are based.

5. As an indicator of this, Gabre-Madhin and Johnson (1999, table 1) provide data showing that, on average, well under one-fifth of Africa's roads are paved.

6. The following paragraphs are based largely on Killick (forthcoming). See also White (1997); ODI (Overseas Development Institute) (1999); Sahn, Dorosh, and Younger (1996); and Bredenkamp and Schadler (1999).

7. *Source:* IMF, *World Economic Outlook,* May 1999, table 1.1.

8. African Development Bank, *African Development Report 1999,* table 2.5. These averages include North African countries (including Egypt). Examination of data for these countries suggests that excluding them would result in an outcome for Sub-Saharan Africa marginally less positive for 1980s but about the same for the 1990s.

9. These comments are based on data and discussions in World Bank, *World Development Indicators 1999* and the IMF's *World Economic Outlook,* May 1999.

10. Author's calculations from data in *World Development Indicators 1999,* table 4.17.

11. The U.N. source, which is the only one we found that gave a time series confined to Sub-Saharan Africa, is the *World Economic and Social Survey 1998,* table A.25. For IMF estimates, which, however, include North Africa, see *World Economic Outlook, December 1998,* table 4.9. This indicates an average net inflow of FDI of US$3.8 billion each year. in 1990–98, against a total for all developing countries of US$70.9 billion a year.

12. Rather surprisingly, Ghura's (1995) exploration of the determinants of economic growth in Africa found a rise in world real interest rates to have been a significant and substantially negative influence on African growth in 1970–90.

13. An early collection by Coulson (1979) documents several of these failed projects in Tanzania. The World Bank's own review of its assistance to Tanzania found that, from 23 projects 14 had a negative rate of return, and all but one a return substantially below the estimate made at appraisal (World Bank 1990).

14. The statistics for borrowing terms are averages for new borrowings by Sub-Saharan African countries, from World Bank, *World Debt Tables, 1989–90,* p. 84 (for 1984 data), and *Global Development Finance, 1999,* p. 200 (for 1997).

CHAPTER 7

Both Governments and Markets Have Failed the Poor

Political Systems Have Contributed to Economic Stagnation

A major cause of Africa's poor growth record has been "government failure." Following the spirit of optimism at independence, by the 1970s the competence of many governments was being eroded by both major and petty corruption, democracy abandoned in favor of the one-party state with power changing hands by the bullet rather than the ballot, and accountability undermined by reliance on external support, including aid, or resource-based taxation.[1] One authority describes these changes as follows:

> Within an astonishingly short period . . . the imposition of control from the top, rather than the mobilization of support from below, became the predominant relationship between African rulers and those who had now become their subjects. . . . There is no doubt of the virtual universality [of this phenomenon]. . . . In no state on the African mainland, from independence through to 1990, did any opposition party gain power as the result of winning a general election against an incumbent government.

In the second phase, even the governing parties atrophied as their mobilizing functions were removed, their electoral organization became redundant, and their leaders were appointed to governmental positions which depended on the favor of the head of state rather than the support of their constituents. . . . Within a few years of independence [African] states were turned into organizations of a broadly similar kind, which may be characterized as "monopoly states." (Clapham 1996, pp. 56–57)

The 1990s have seen some changes, and there have always been exceptions to the above picture. But in general African states since independence moved away from accountability and towards what have been variously called regimes of personal rule, and the patrimonial, predatory, or even parasitic state. In the words of one author, "the dominant form of political economy became a crony statism consisting of three interrelated characteristics: (i) clientelist networks used to build support through the extraction and distribution of rents; (ii) expansion of state size, including the creation of an extensive parastatal sector; and (iii) purchase of primarily urban support via state welfare services and subsidies" (Callaghy 1991, p. 258) (see box 7.1 for what is perhaps the extreme example of Democratic Republic of Congo).

These developments have held back poverty reduction in several ways. First, and the concern in this section, is that states have failed to deliver growth: growth has not been part of their agenda, and at best they have failed to provide the stable framework it requires, but at worst their actions have undermined growth or state structures have dissolved as conflict has erupted. Second, the state has not addressed the needs of the poor, which has been manifested in various ways, such as poor and skewed service delivery. The next section takes up the issue of the neglect of poverty.

African states failed to deliver growth for at least four reasons: (i) absence of a stable legal and institutional framework for economic activity, (ii) implementation of controlled economy policies that were amenable to rent seeking and detrimental to growth, (iii) the rise of corruption, and (iv) state collapse.

Box 7.1 The predatory state in Democratic Republic of Congo

MacGaffey (1988, pp. 172, 175) has provided a vivid account of the consequences of the political system that developed in Zaire (now Democratic Republic of Congo) as it developed during the Mobutu period, and the consequential decay of the state:

> In Democratic Republic of Congo those with political position have used the power of their office to seize control of the economy . . . to acquire manufacturing, wholesale and retail businesses and plantations. However, they have neither managed their

enterprises in a rational capitalist fashion nor invested their profits in expansion of their businesses and improved production. . . .

The ruling class is not a true economic bourgeoisie; it is one that loots the economy and collapses effective administration. It is thus unable to exercise the control over production necessary to maintain its dominance and must resort to consolidating its position by participating in the more lucrative activities of the second [parallel] economy.

Source: MacGaffey 1988.

A minimum function of the state is the provision of a legal and institutional framework to facilitate the economic life of its citizens. Essentially, this is a matter of ensuring that the rule of law prevails both to provide peace and security, and so that property rights are respected, contracts enforceable in a predictable and cost-effective way, transactions costs minimized, and competitive markets facilitated. Often even these basic responsibilities have not been fulfilled. An African writer has put this as follows: "Government as it is known in the West does not exist in much of Africa. . . . One expects at a minimum a government to be responsive to the basic needs of the people. Or at least, to perform some services for its people. But even this most basic requirement for government is lacking in Africa" (Ayittey 1998, p. 150). Equality before the law has been flouted in favor of political elites and their friends and supporters; property rights have been pushed aside when they clashed with the interests of these groups; markets have been overridden or manipulated in order to yield monopoly profits for favored minorities; police and judicial systems have been corrupted or subverted.

Although the state failed to provide the conditions for growth, the state itself (if not individual governments, as takeover by extra-parliamentary means has been rife) was remarkably resilient for over two decades. Clapham (1991) offers two reasons why the state survived. First, there has been a large degree of external support—foreign aid as well as direct military intervention to prop up tottering regimes. Second, the support from politically important groups who did benefit: "It is possible for a country's economy to fall into ruin, for development to be insignificant, while at the same time the members of a large number of (informal) networks continue substantially to enrich

themselves. It may even be true that economic failure is in this respect at least more profitable for many than development" (Chabal and Daloz 1999, p. 133). Or, as it was put more prosaically in a Ghanaian newspaper, "poverty is rife in Africa because African military despots have raped our economies" (quoted in Ayittey 1998, p. 155).

The opportunities offered by administrative controls have been a principal means of extracting wealth from the economy: "The rise of the 'policed economy' came about in Africa when the post-colonial state . . . began to seek the interest of the ruler and the ruling elite" (Deng 1998, p. 37).[2] The interests of the powerful were served by both the official activities of the state and through unofficial channels: the main interaction of the politically excluded with the state was to pay taxes and bribes rather than to receive any benefits from state-financed activities. Infrastructure was not maintained and preference given to trunk roads rather than feeder roads: maintenance and feeder roads are much less likely to yield rents than new construction contracts. By the 1980s, however, few governments were paying for any physical investment from their own revenues, which were funded from donor assistance. The declining fiscal situation, resulting from a weakening tax base, lax collection, and growing subsidies to failing enterprises cut into capital budgets. The soft budget constraint, corruption, and inefficiency turned once profitable public enterprises into loss makers whose principal purpose was often to provide a basis for patronage. Social service provision was also deteriorating, and the wage bill consumed an increasing share of expenditure (even though real public service wages have been severely reduced in most countries). Eventually these circumstances strengthened the domestic constituency for the reforms that, during the last decade, have started to alter the situation described above, but not until per capita incomes had fallen well below their levels at independence in many countries, with obvious adverse implications for poverty.

The same set of political forces combined to frustrate the development of private enterprise. Rather than providing a stable environment for private activity, the systems of government that developed in many African countries restricted and preyed upon the private sector, being called in a study of Ghana "the Vampire state" (Frimpong-Ansah 1991). These tendencies were partly due to an ideology of African socialism suspicious of markets, entrepreneurs, and the profit motive, by which the state should control at least the commanding heights of the economy (although in many countries nationalization extended far further, into retail trade and small services, such as car repair workshops). In agriculture, state-run farms were often created but failed to feed the growing towns and cities as intended. Private agriculture was not left untouched, as state-marketing boards, export taxes, and overvalued exchange rates all acted to transfer surpluses from the rural community to the government or urban areas.

Rulers and supporters have benefited from the spread of corruption: "bureaucratic values were readily subverted by patronage and financial corruption that, though in large measure simply a means through which the powerful reaped the rewards of office, also helped the rulers to meet the expectations of their more favored constituents" (Clapham 1991, p. 98). There was little notion of officials being there to serve the people. Rather, bureaucratic obstacles were created with little concern for the inconvenience caused and with bribery often the only way to get over them. At both formal and informal levels, these attributes debilitated private initiative. The rewards from corruption have been very high: Mobutu's billions are well known, but there are many other cases. Charles Taylor is estimated to have made US$75 million a year since beginning the war in Liberia in 1990, and Niger's President Ousmane, by his own declaration, tripled his personal fortune within one year of taking office (Ayittey 1998, pp. 156–57, 181). The culture of corruption runs through government, with ministers regularly receiving large payouts to foreign accounts (as one example of many Ayittey provides, the US$50,000 paid to a Swiss bank account for Sierra Leone's minister of transport in the early 1990s (Ayittey 1998, pp. 152–53).

Corruption is bad for both growth and poverty reduction in several ways.[3] First, it is the equivalent of a regressive tax, directly or indirectly drawing resources from the poor to the rich. In many countries in Africa, government-supported farmers' credit programs were often ruined by corrupt managers and bureaucrats. Second, high-level corruption erodes the goodwill of the population, the business community, and the donors, encouraging "exit." It makes the population less amenable to mobilization. Likewise, if businesses lose confidence in the government's ability to curb corruption, they might seek to "cut their losses" by paying less tax, since corruption is simply a deferred tax, or even to relocate to other countries. Since corruption affects producer incentives and costs, it also inevitably leads to factor substitution, not necessarily in favor of labor-intensive production. Corruption also erodes donor goodwill, threatening resource inflows that are still important for development. Donors have learned from experience that development and the fight against poverty are difficult to achieve in corrupt environments. Finally, corruption diverts the attention of state employees and the activities of the state away from the tasks that need to be undertaken to achieve growth, especially if it is to be of a pro-poor variety.

The systematic abuse of state power for personal enrichment is argued by some observers to be so widespread as to constitute a "criminalization of the state" in Africa, with official involvement in drug trafficking, dumping of hazardous waste, trading in arms, and international fraud (Bayart, Ellis, and Hibou 1999). Fairhead (2000) argues that the systematic abuse of natural resources to appropriate profits from rapid depletion is at the roots of much conflict across the continent,[4] and is clearly bad for the poor as the environment is destroyed by the rich and an unaccountable elite wastes the nation's wealth. The role of multinational corporations in these activities highlight the fact that Western culpability is not an issue of the past. As one example, former Rwandan president, Habryimana, has been implicated in rackets involving aid money, drugs, illegal forex dealing, and body parts of gorillas (Ayittey 1998, p. 177).

Combined with the absence of effective choice at the ballot box, such conditions have led to alienation, disaffection, and violent resistance. In the worst cases, these have led to large-scale civil disturbance and war. In fact, war has been a common feature of recent African history, affecting at least 28 countries during the 1980s and 1990s. Somalia and Liberia have essentially been stateless in recent years. It is indeed difficult to find civil wars where a peace settlement may be said to have solved the political problems. Conflict has thus become embedded in economic and political structures. Poverty is linked to conflict at several levels (Luckham, Ahmed, and Muggah 1999). There are the direct effects of loss of life, which has reached up to 5 percent of the population per year in Burundi in 1993–95, with several other cases of around 1 percent. Child soldiers should be singled out as among the most tragic victims. Others are victims of torture and rape, or witnesses to such acts, who suffer psychological trauma. Many more are displaced, often spending years as refugees. Social indicators rapidly deteriorate as services collapse and people's livelihood and social capital are destroyed. Indirect effects operate at several levels, with worsening growth performance undermining governments' revenue bases and distorting their spending patterns. The destruction of physical infrastructure is obvious, but institutions are also destroyed, and similarly need to be rebuilt for sustainable growth to occur (Haughton 1998). It can take years, even decades, for investor confidence to be restored following bouts of political instability.

Although this report emphasizes the dangers of overgeneralization, there appears to be a remarkable degree of consensus over the picture of the African state presented here and its widespread nature. The puzzle is rather why it persisted in the way it did. The evidence presented here supports the model of the African state in terms of personal rule, or patrimonialism, where the position of the ruler and his government is maintained by patron-client relationships, based for the most part on familial and ethnic loyalties. Followers are rewarded with preferential access to loans, import licenses, contracts, and jobs and in the distribution of government spending. Institutional rules and constitutional checks and balances are swept aside by the competition for patronage and the struggle to maintain power. As a result rulers became presidents for life, the dubious virtues of one-party rule became the official ideology, open political competition was banned or carefully delimited, and the distinction between the public and private domains became blurred.

- One of the strengths of this model is that it explicates some of the economic distortions described earlier, notably the following:
- Emphasis on the appropriation and distribution of resources by the state, rather than on growth and wealth creation
- Growth of the state relative to the private sector, in order to maximize the opportunities for patronage and reward

- Forms of intervention that provide the agents of the state with direct and discretionary control, as against operating impersonally through market mechanisms
- Growth of crony capitalism to the frustration of local entrepreneurial talent
- Persistence of antidevelopmental policies long after their ill effects have become apparent, because their primary function was to provide a system of rewards and maintain the ruler in power, rather than promote development per se.

Why such systems have flourished particularly well in African soil goes beyond this report. Likely explanations are rooted in the colonial experience: "The African state system as we know it today is the direct and obvious descendant of European colonialism" (Clapham 1991, p. 95). These origins interacted with precolonial social and demographic conditions, bringing into being at independence nation-states whose fragility reinforced the tendency to use patronage and centralized authoritarianism in an attempt to hold the state together. As with economic decline, the culpability of foreign powers cannot be ignored, with their willingness to underwrite corrupt and unaccountable regimes. The case of Mobutu (see box 7.1), supported by both the United States and France, is one extreme case, but there are other extremes (such as Obote's second period of rule in Uganda), and a general disregard for democracy and human rights in dealings with Africa.[5]

Political Systems Have Also Tended to Keep Poverty off the Agenda

Distributional concerns are central to a patrimonial model of politics, to the extent of being at the expense of economic growth and long-term development. But these concerns are only incidentally about the poor. Resources of the state are used to reward those who support those in power. The base for this is often ethnic and regional, sometimes religious, sometimes military. The poor within such groups may benefit from the resulting largesse; those outside will not. Indeed, many of those seen as in opposition, or just politically unimportant, will rather be forced into poverty through neglect, discrimination, and the ill effects of the economic stagnation resulting from this form of rule.

This prediction is consistent with evidence concerning the policy priorities of African governments. Quite recently, the World Bank (1996, p. 16) reported that African governments give low priority to poverty reduction as an objective. Poverty was rarely identified as a policy problem in governments' Letters of Development Policy and only about one-quarter of them had explicitly identified poverty reduction as a policy objective in their programs with the Bank. Addison (1993, p. 1) similarly suggests that "many African countries present a difficult political environment for any donor agency that is intent on reducing poverty," although the problem is by no means confined to Africa. Addison states the following:

> [M]any of the policies that benefit the poor work against the interests of higher-income groups who are politically influential ("vocal") in their demands. These are often the very people who constitute the political power base of the region's governments. Thus governments often direct public expenditures to the benefit of high-income groups, both as government employees and as users of services, rather than to services that are important to poor people such as preventative health care and primary education. Paying farmers a low share of the world price of their commodities taxes the rural poor but creates public revenues with which to buy political support among the vocal. Import controls, by limiting competition, create profits for favored manufacturers and economic rents for those who trade in scarce goods but tax the rest of society, especially those on low incomes who have the least access to scarce goods. (Addison 1993, p. 2)

Today the poverty reduction goal would probably receive more frequent mention by governments and a number of them have moved to draw up national antipoverty strategies (which are further discussed in chapter 13). But there is a danger that some of these are merely in response to the rise in interest among donors, rather than reflecting a deep-rooted commitment. One manifestation of the relative indifference of political systems in Africa is that public service provision has been notable for its lack of relevance to the poor (see chapter 9). This situation is in contrast to developing countries in both Asia and Latin America, where explicit attention has been paid to the plight of the poor under both democratic and nondemocratic governments, and where the poor have been a political force in their own right.

Africa's poor are well aware that political systems work against them. The summary by Larivière and others (1999, p. 20) of the results of a Participatory Poverty Assessment reports the poor as perceiving their governments as having neglected the economic and social infrastructure, especially in rural areas, resulting in limited access to markets, health, and education; as having placed obstacles in the way of individual initiatives; and as biasing the delivery of public services away from the poor, particularly in favor of those who can afford to pay bribes. The lack of accountability in political structures in Africa is part of the explanation of this neglect of the poverty issue. But the reasons also lie in the absence of a constituency for pro-poor measures. The experience of both industrial and developing countries in implementing antipoverty programs—from the Poor Laws in sixteenth-century Elizabethan England to the Employment Guarantee Schemes in India—is that there needs to be a middle class lobby for such policies (Toye 1999). For much of the elite, these concerns may be motivated by self-interest, seeing the poor as a threat of unrest, crime, and disease. But social reformers inspired by altruism have also often played an important part.

The situation has frequently been worsened by the slow rate of economic growth. It is easier for people to accept schemes to help the less fortunate in conditions in which they themselves are well provided for. A daily struggle to survive in the face of declining incomes stunts altruism and has led to replies by governments to questions about their lack of an antipoverty strategy to the effect that such strategies are redundant because "we are all poor." Indeed, one of the greatest challenges facing African policymakers is precisely the scale of the poverty problem. While not all are poor, very large numbers are indeed engaged in a daily struggle for existence.

Another factor contributing to past political neglect is the heterogeneity of the poor. Hence their interests vary and sometimes conflict. The poor are far from being a single class and are not confined to any particular ethnic group. They therefore rarely exist as an organized political entity. Antipoverty measures thus tend to relate to particular poverty groups, according to the basis of their livelihoods. In particular, there is a constant danger that the interests of the poorest—the least powerful, least integrated into the modern economy, and least articulate—will lack an effective voice and be left aside. The absence of effective political mobilization is an important feature. In the Latin American context it has been noted that "the macropolitics of poor people's pressure were critical in increasing their potential to benefit from growth," but that in Africa there has been no such realignment of civil society (Lipton and van der Gaag 1993, p. 25). There is, of course, a host of African nongovernmental organizations (NGOs) working at grass roots levels to alleviate the plight of poor people, but most of them have limited objectives and are closely watched by their governments.

The situation described in the last paragraph restricts what even well-motivated governments can do because, politics being the art of the possible, they have to operate within constraints set by more or less organized interest groups. Notwithstanding the large scale of the poverty problem, governments may weaken their own power base by introducing antipoverty measures, especially if these involve any form of redistribution from the less poor. South Africa stands as an exception that nonetheless illustrates the general rule. Because of its own unique recent political history and the democratic nature of its current political system, the poor there have a unity based on race, are well organized, and are strongly represented in the ruling party. It is no coincidence, then, that the South African government has one of the strongest antipoverty stances of any on the continent.

Some Markets Fail the Poor

Confronted with the failings described above, the temptation is to wash our hands of the possibilities of effective state intervention and leave the matter to the market. But such a reaction would ignore the characteristic of the market system that, unless there are safeguards, it sets up dynamic forces whereby "money makes money" while many others fall behind into a poverty trap. When it operates within an appropriate institutional and policy framework, capitalism is entirely compatible with low and declining poverty rates, but there is little within the market system itself to produce such an outcome. Thus the well-known cases of "equitable growth" in some East Asian countries rested on massive public investment in health and education, as well as on redistributive measures such as land reform. This is the view expressed in chapter 6, and this section elaborates on this view by discussing which markets may be missing or failing in Africa and how such a situation harms the poor.

These market failures may be of two types. One is where there are externalities (say, health and education) or public goods (providers cannot capture the returns to their investment, which applies to much public infrastructure). In such cases a free market will underprovide, creating a case for either state provision or state support (subsidies)

to private providers. Underprovision can also occur if there are information asymmetries—the most common example being that of rural credit, where potential borrowers, particularly those without existing businesses, cannot signal their creditworthiness. The second form of market failure occurs from noncompetitive practices, such as monopolies (single seller) or monopsonies (single buyer, for instance, agricultural marketing boards). Monopolies may be created by the state, even if they are in private hands, or they may be created by the market. In both cases regulation is required to ensure competitive behavior and so protect consumers. Table 7.1 summarizes some of the market failures that impinge on the poor, which are now discussed in more detail.

As just mentioned, a common justification for state intervention in the past has been either the presence of positive externalities (where the social gain from an activity exceeds the private gain, leading to underinvestment from a social point of view if the market is relied upon) and public goods (where private investment will not occur because the investor cannot adequately capture the benefits to make a profit). Infrastructure is the most frequently cited example of a public good. Although some infrastructural development, such as railways in the United States, have been undertaken by private capital, market pricing of transport facilities remains the exception rather than the norm, and the still relatively low densities of population in much of Africa further reduce the potential for private sector provision here. The role of rural infrastructure in poverty reduction in Africa has already been stressed—further development of infrastructure will help remote communities, which include many of the poorest; facilitate market access for those without it; and put essential services within reach. Infrastructure is one of the most important public goods for poverty reduction.

There are positive externalities to investments in health, education, water, and sanitation. These externalities arise in part through productivity effects, but the health benefits of investment in all these areas are perhaps even more important given the prevalence of communicable diseases. In Africa, over 70 percent of the burden of disease is accounted for by communicable disease, compared to only 50 percent in most other developing countries and as little as 25 percent in China, so that there are very large public benefits from improved health services, of a kind which could not be captured through private provision alone. Given the present inequalities in access (chapter 9), expansion of services will benefit the poor. Some

Table 7.1 Market failures and distortions as barriers to poverty reduction

General area	Specific area	Market failure/ distortion	Link to poverty reduction	Groups of the poor	Policy intervention	Experience (government failure)
Factor markets						
Physical capital	Infrastructure	Public goods	Growth/supply response; pattern of growth; access to social services; reduced work burden	Rural, remote	Public provision	Maintenance
	Investable resources	Asymmetric information; barriers to entry	Strengthen and diversify livelihoods	Those with potential and access to productive opportunities, i.e., not the poorest	Legal reform; institutional subsidy	Targeting, sustainability
Labor	Human capital: health, education, and family planning	Positive externalities	Growth/enhanced productivity; social indicators worse for poor	All, but bias to rural poor	Public provision or subsidy	Targeting, quality
	Labor market rigidities	Legal barriers to migration	Improved earning opportunities	Migrants	Remove national and international barriers	
Land	Absence of land markets	Traditional tenure systems	Liberalizing land markets has ambiguous effect on poverty reduction	All		
Product markets						
Agricultural produce	Marketing	Uncertainty, monopsony	Supply response	Smallholders & dependants	Infrastructure development, competition policy	State marketing bodies often inefficient or exploitative
Informal sectors	Retail/ microenterprise	Legal restrictions	Income generation/provision goods and services	All, but bias to urban	Remove restrictions	Government intolerance

interventions, such as malaria eradication and reproductive health services, clearly have poverty-reduction benefits at both macro and micro levels.

Other markets are affected by information asymmetries and uncertainty. These concepts have traditionally been applied to explain underinvestment and, in particular, high interest rates in rural areas. But they also affect technology—both research and extension—and some marketing channels. The existence of information asymmetries, resulting from the high costs of obtaining information about small-scale depositors and borrowers, especially in rural settings, has been frequently cited to explain the paucity of financial services in rural areas. In particular, a poor person with a creditworthy idea is unlikely to gain access to loan funds. In consequence, an array of public sector, or not-for-profit, "microcredit"

initiatives have been launched in recent years as an antipoverty provision.

Market conditions in Africa also often fail the poor by confronting them with monopoly and monopsony forces against which they have no effective defenses. Agricultural marketing is perhaps the most important case in point. In the past the state itself was the cause of the problem, through the creation of state-owned monopoly marketing boards. There has fortunately in recent years been extensive privatization or liberalization in this area, but the results have by no means been without problems. A well-documented case has been Zambia in which government had to step in to purchase the bumper budget following liberalization of agricultural marketing. Because of low levels of competition among private traders, farmers are all too often confronted with a single buyer for their produce who offers only a low farm-gate price. Participatory analysis reveals the continuing dissatisfaction of many producers, and evidence from Zambia and Zimbabwe shows that traders are often only willing to engage in barter (consumer goods and secondhand clothes) rather than pay cash (Stevens 1999). A substantial part of the apparently weak responsiveness of the agricultural sector to improved relative prices is due to this factor. Weak competition within the banking industry is another example that also contributes to the weak provision of financial services for small-scale savers and borrowers.

What Does the Future Hold?

The prognosis from this chapter may appear poor: both state and market have a history of having failed the African poor. The previous section argued that redressing market failure requires state action, but there seem little grounds for believing in either the capacity or commitment of the African state. But there need not be pessimism. Many changes have taken place in the African political scene in the 1990s. This section identifies three major areas of change and assesses how they affect the prospects for poverty reduction. The three are the following:

- Empowerment and democracy
- Extending beyond central government (decentralization and civil society)
- Coalition-building

Empowerment and democracy

There has been a major shift in Africa in the 1990s from nondemocratic to democratic regimes. Since lack of political voice is one dimension of poverty, this step is in itself poverty reducing. However, the importance of these changes should not be overemphasized since (i) when it comes to the other dimensions of poverty, such as income poverty, it is far from readily apparent that there is a clear link between democracy and poverty reduction; and (ii) there are limitations to the extent of democratization.

Several analyses have shown that, while regimes that have been the least successful at reducing poverty are nondemocratic, democracies are not inherently better at poverty reduction than nondemocracies (see summary in Moore and Putzel 1999, which is the main source for the following arguments). Although democracy in principle "gives the poor a voice," many of the poor remain excluded and, particularly poor women, do not participate in the political process, or if they do they may vote according to

allegiances other than being a member of some group of the poor. Even if a class awareness is present, the poor person may calculate they are better served by selling their vote than casting it for a party claiming it will change their situation. On the positive side, the link between democratization and poverty reduction breaks down, as the government can take decisive steps of its own to reduce poverty, although the record on this front has not been good in Africa.

A sharp distinction should be drawn between formal and "real" democratization. There has been a good deal of progress at the formal level, with reformed constitutions and electoral rules to accommodate multiparty elections in many African states in recent years. During the 1990s, 42 out of 50 African countries held multiparty elections, to which should be added four functioning democracies that already existed at the start of the decade. But in only 10 of these 42 states did the elections result in a change of government, and at the subsequent election government changed in a mere two countries (Madagascar and Benin), in both cases in favor of former military rulers (*Economist* 1999, p. 69). In a high proportion of these countries, already ruling and apparently unpopular parties were able to manipulate formal electoral processes with some ease, using the resources of state and the advantages of incumbency to ensure their own reelection. And in a large proportion of cases electoral politics has found expression as ethnic and regional politics, which is unlikely to result in a satisfactory antipoverty strategy. Finally, there is no apparent increase in women's political participation. Genuine empowerment of the poor appears some way off.

On the other hand, the move towards electoral politics is not meaningless. The entrance of opposition parties, liberalization of the press, and the emergence of civil society into the debate has helped to keep pressure on incumbent governments, with the plight of the poor and the rural sector receiving increased focus. The days of "silent eating," that is, corruption without public outcry, are past. Sen (1990) has pointed to the strong link between political freedoms and the end of famine: "The diverse political freedoms that are available in a democratic state, including regular elections, free newspapers and freedom of speech, must be seen as the real force behind the elimination of famines" (cited in de Waal 1997, p. 4). De Waal extends this notion of an "anti-famine contract" to Africa, arguing that even where it exists—in Botswana and Kenya— it is shaky and that in general African governments have not been required to submit themselves to such contracts to maintain power.[6] If it is not yet difficult enough, it is at least harder than it formerly was for incumbent regimes to control political processes. Formal democratization, in other words, may lead on to the genuine variety in due course, bringing with it a greater empowerment of the poor.

There are implications here for donor governments that have been prominent in advocating democratization. They need to build a recognition of the distinction between formal and real change into their own policies and aid allocation processes, to encourage the genuine reformers, to penalize the more cynical manipulators, and to work with wider society to support the forces for genuine reform wherever they arise. The desirability of doing this is enhanced by the socially embedded nature of much poverty and the need, therefore, to work with those who can form and change opinions and values.

Extending beyond central government: decentralization and civil society

Working through central government is not the only possibility. Depending on the local political system and the realities of power within it, donors can work through local government agencies, which are closer to the problems, with particular scope within federal systems. In fact, donors currently evince a perhaps excessive faith in decentralization, for at the local level, too, there is a danger of elite capture. The less poor are more articulate, confident, and have the time available for participation (the time factor particularly weighs against poor women). There may be even fewer checks and balances at the local level than there are nationally to restrain the elite from promoting their own interests, partly because capacity of local government may be weak, as was found in examination of local government in both Ghana and Nigeria (see Crook and Sverrisson 1999). While there have been genuine achievements at the local level, the pattern of spending from recently expanded district-level budgets does not appear particularly pro-poor. A cross-country study of decentralization found that the African cases in general had a poor record (other than improved spatial equity) with respect to both participation by the poor and impact (see table 7.2).

Table 7.2 Impact of decentralization

	Participation of the poor			Socioeconomic impact			
	Participation	Representation	Responsiveness	Growth	Equity	Human development	Spatial equity
Africa							
Côte d'Ivoire	Low	Low	Very low	...	...	Improved	Improved
Ghana	Improved	Fair	Low	Low but little evidence	Low but little evidence	Low but little evidence	Fair
Kenya	Very low	Very low	Very low	Low	Low	Low	Fair
Nigeria	Low	Low	Very low	Low	Very low	Very low	Low
Other regions							
W. Bengal, India	Improved	Improved	Improved	Improved	Improved	Improved	...
Karnataka, India	Fair	Improved	Low	Low	Low	Fair	Fair
Colombia	Ambiguous	Ambiguous	Improved	...	...	Improved	Improved
Philippines	Improved	Improved	Ambiguous	...	...	...	...
Brazil	Low but limited evidence	Low but limited evidence	Low but limited evidence	...	Mixed	Mixed	Low
Chile	...	...	...	Improved	Improved	Ambiguous to low	Ambiguous to low
Mexico	...	...	...	...	Low	Low	Low
Bangladesh	Fair	Very low	Low	Very low	Very low	Very low	Fair

... No evidence available.

Source: Crook and Sverrisson (1999).

The other shift away from central government that has been strongly supported by the donor community has been an emphasis on civil society. Civil society is a very broad concept, reflecting a great diversity of social organizations. Only a small subset of these are concerned with poverty reduction (and some may impede it), and it is these NGOs that have been the focus of donor attention. NGOs and their supporters claim they are better at working with the poor because they are closer to the problems, more likely to adopt participatory approaches to the design and execution of their programs, and often have stronger antipoverty motivation than official agencies. Systematic evidence in support of these propositions is scanty. However, NGOs offer a way of operating in countries with an unsupportive political climate. This modality has limitations, however. Many NGOs have an essentially ameliorative and often quite narrow remit, not geared to tackling the causes of the poverty they address, although others are active campaigners against the status quo. Some are opportunistic, existing largely because of the availability of donor and private monies. It is also difficult to channel large sums of assistance through NGOs without changing their nature or diminishing their grassroots credibility and other advantages. It would be a mistake, therefore, to think that NGOs can offer a satisfactory substitute for sympathetic governments.

Despite these qualifications, however, working through local government and broader civil society both have the potential to make real contributions to the antipoverty drive, particularly in situations where the central government is unsympathetic.

Building coalitions

It is a large weakness of the recent resurgence of interest in measures to reduce poverty that it has been largely donor driven. Little progress can be expected unless it becomes possible to build domestic political coalitions in favor of pro-poor action. At the heart of this proposition is the premise that achieving successful poverty reduction is not a matter of identifying an optimal set of policies but rather one of achieving that set of measures that is the most feasible within a given political setting. In short, it is necessary to work within existing political constraints while also seeking to loosen these. This will often involve working with local elites to convince them that antipoverty measures, such as improved educational provisions, are also in their own long-term interest. Historical experiences from beyond Africa indicate that this is indeed

possible, for key groups within political elites may well see that mass poverty is an obstacle to the economic modernization on which their own prosperity depends, and that it may also threaten their interests as a source of crime, disease, and disaffection.[7]

Nevertheless, it is commonality of interests that has to be stressed, which implies avoiding measures that appear to pitch the interests of the poor and less poor against each other. A case in point relates to the politics of targeting. Targeting is a key element in a poverty reduction strategy, especially in a context in which resources are scarce and substantial numbers of the poor will be bypassed by growth. But targeting may be either broad or narrow. The former concentrates on activities, such as primary health and education or rural development, most likely to benefit the poor. Narrow targeting aims to deliver benefits to defined poverty groups, and is either "indicator targeting," identifying group members by certain characteristics such as rural landless women, or self-targeting, providing food for work or selling inferior goods that would be of no interest to the better off.

Broad targeting has been criticized for its high leakage, large revenue costs, and inefficiency, with a large share of benefits going to the nonpoor. Indeed, as discussed in chapter 8, in Africa health and education spending has been skewed in favor of the nonpoor, as has what little investment there has been in rural development. Namibia and South Africa are the two countries to have state pensions; while these have positive benefits for the poor, they are also received by better-off pensioners who do not depend on them so much. Broad targeting thus fails in the important task of minimizing claims on scarce fiscal resources and is a blunt instrument for providing what the poor need.

These drawbacks have led to some replacement of broadly targeted schemes with narrower ones (this trend has been more apparent in regions other than Africa, although there are exceptions like the *Gabinete de Apoio à População Vulnerável* (GAPVU) scheme in urban Mozambique). But there are both technical and political constraints on narrow targeting, which suggest that more universal benefits may be better after all.

The political dilemma is a real one. Broad targeting creates a substantial constituency with a vested interest in maintaining a provision that is also likely to bring substantial benefits to the poor. Narrow targeting tends to do the opposite because it acts through exclusion. The more precisely defined the target group—the larger the numbers excluded—the less likely it is that the provision in question will command wide political support and the more likely it is that it will be opposed by those excluded. In the extreme case, political support may be so eroded that eventually a lower level of provision will go to the poor than in the pretargeting situation. That was the experience in a number of countries, including Colombia and Sri Lanka. The dilemma is well illustrated where poverty is concentrated in some specific region or in a particular ethnic group. Targeting in these cases involves excluding other regions or other groups, not a proposition likely to commend itself to those excluded. Thus Glewwe and van der Gaag (1990) show that the theoretically poverty-minimizing policy in urban Côte d'Ivoire was to concentrate transfers on the East Forest region. However, the implication was that no households outside that region—some also living in poverty—would receive any transfer and would have no self-interest in supporting such provision. It was therefore politically unfeasible.

On the practical side, targeting can be administratively costly, with per recipient costs rising the narrower the targeting. The management of GAPVU reduced administrative costs to just 7 percent, but this was at the expense of proper monitoring of eligibility, with the result that at least one-half of the benefits were lost to ineligible beneficiaries or corruption. Following changes, a greater proportion of benefits reaches the intended poor beneficiaries now that more, rather than less, is spent on administration. But the narrower the targeting the greater the likelihood that significant numbers of the poor will not benefit. There is also a danger of creating incentives against work: those near the poverty line to begin with are particularly likely to fall into a poverty trap in which there is no incentive to raise themselves above it.

These issues mean that targeting schemes must be tailored to the local political and social context. Self-targeting may command support by, for example, offering low wages for hard work. But if the work is too onerous it may exclude some, such as the elderly, the moderately disabled, and some women, who may be among the poorest. There may also be arguments for awarding wages or food sufficient to feed the whole family rather than the individual worker (as has been done on the Employment Guarantee Scheme in Ethiopia). But doing so is likely to lead to an oversupply of labor, so that jobs have to be rationed, most probably to those with easiest access rather than those from more remote, and so poorer, communities. Besides applying either stigma or discomfort, obtaining assistance acts both as a targeting mechanism and may increase political support for the scheme. Targeting women may simply increase their workload, adding to their burden the additional task of providing food that was previously undertaken by men.

To conclude, this discussion of targeting illustrates both the complexity and delicacy of the policy decisions confronting governments wishing to embark on an antipoverty strategy and the central importance of keeping closely in mind the need to maintain breadth in public support for the measures undertaken. While it is for statesmen to exercise leadership in poverty reduction, they need to maintain a coalition of support sufficient to sustain the strategy and prevent its reversal.

Notes

1. A single sentence cannot capture the diversity of experience, although there appear to be common elements for many countries. As selected counterexamples, the Kenyan civil service performed competently into the 1980s, Botswana never discarded democracy, and corruption was held in check in Malawi under Banda.

2. It is difficult, however, to maintain the argument that controls were introduced because of the rents they would provide. As Mkandawire (1998) points out, and as was discussed in the last chapter, such policies were favored by the development community at the time and received the support of international donors. However, the availability of rents certainly built constituencies that resisted reform.

3. See also the analysis, and empirical verification, provided by Gupta, Davoodi, and Alonso-Terme (1998).

4. Statistical analysis by Collier and Hoeffler (1999) confirms a significant link between natural resource endowment and the probability of civil conflict.

5. The most notable exception to this rule was South Africa, although other particular leaders lost foreign support as a result of their excesses (Amin, for instance). Under President Carter the United States attempted to incorporate human rights into its foreign relations, but this only affected Ethiopia under Mengistu.

6. De Waal's book is also about sharing culpability with other actors so that African governments are not seen as solely to blame. High on his list of those responsible are humanitarian agencies that "do not subject themselves to any antifamine political contracts; directors, professors, and consultants do not lose their jobs if there are famines" (de Waal 1997, p. 24).

7. On this theme see the special issues of *IDS Bulletin*, 30(2), April 1999 on 'Nationalising the anti-poverty agenda?' See also Ascher (1984).

CHAPTER 8

The Poor Have Inadequate Capital

A Weak Asset Base Undermines Sustainable Livelihoods in Rural Areas

This chapter mainly focuses on the rural poor for several reasons. First, they comprise 90 percent or more of the poor in most countries. This is partly because the rural population share is large in most countries. But the contribution to poverty of rural areas exceeds this population share: rural people are disproportionately poor. The poor have lower incomes and lack access to facilities. Lack of access to facilities explains the result that, even once the impact of income is taken into account, then the larger the share of rural residents in the total population the lower the level of welfare, as measured by the Human Development Index (HDI); this relationship is shown in figure 8.1.[1, 2] This inverse relation between

Figure 8.1 A larger rural population is linked with lower social indicators: the partial regression of HDI on rural population share

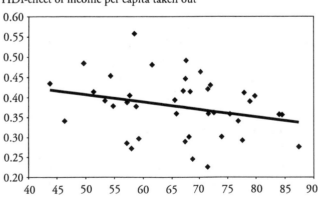

HDI-effect of income per capita taken out

Note: Rural population (percent)—effect of income per capita taken out.
Source: Calculated from World Bank *World Development Indicators* and UNDP *Human Development Report.*

national well-being and rural population share is a second reason for paying particular attention to rural poverty. A third reason is the contribution of the agricultural sector to growth and poverty alleviation, in both rural areas and at the level of the economy as a whole. Research from Zimbabwe shows that this sector has a larger multiplier than other sectors; the ripple effects generating additional economic activity are greater for agriculture than they are for manufacturing or services.

We adopt a sustainable livelihoods approach to rural poverty, which directs our attention to the issue of assets. A sustainable livelihood is one that does not run down the asset base on which it depends, undermining future welfare. In addition, the livelihood strategy should be such to withstand shocks occurring in the environment in which it operates. Vulnerability to shocks also depends crucially on assets, as these can be turned into income in times of need.

The poor are more vulnerable since they do not have the ability to build up reserves for hard times, and hold fewer assets to draw upon. In Ethiopia just over one-half of households in the upper tercile had food stores six months after harvest, whereas only 2 percent of those in the lower tercile did so. Without food stores, hardship turns a vicious circle into destitution. Beyond a certain point there is no turning back. Analysis of famine in Ethiopia and Sudan shows that households first sell off livestock. Next they sell housing materials (for instance, metal roofs and wooden posts) and household items such as beds. Finally, they sell their clothes and cooking utensils.[3] Once destitute many die. If they survive they have little chance to be able to return to their prefamine level of well-being.

In the analysis that follows assets are divided into three main categories: physical, human, and social. In all cases our analysis concerns both the level of capital, which is generally inadequate in African countries, and access of the poor to these assets. But there is diversity across the continent as to the relative importance of the constraints imposed by the lack of these various assets. Table 8.1 divides Africa into six agroecological zones. These categories, of course, apply most readily to natural capital, that is, land and the environment.

Africa Lacks Physical Capital of All Kinds, Stocks of Many Are Being Denuded, and the Access of the Poor Is Increasingly Restricted

Five areas of physical capital are considered: infrastructure, credit, land, environmental capital, and livestock.

Infrastructure

As argued in chapter 5, infrastructure in Africa is low by international standards and has in many respects deteriorated over the last two decades, a trend resulting from declining and squandered state resources and exacerbated by conflict. The length of paved roads per person grew by about 50 percent from 1965 to the end of the 1970s but declined in the 1980s, picking up only slightly in recent years to return to the level of the early 1980s (ADB 1999 p. 113). Similarly, per capita electricity production doubled in the two decades from 1965, but has since remained relatively stagnant. With respect to roads and irrigation Africa does not just lag behind other developing regions but is in a worse state than was India four

Table 8.1 Land resource base of Sub-Saharan Africa

Region	Climate	Growing period (days)	Soils	Vegetation	Major agricultural activities	Climate and soil constraints	Countries
Sudano-Sahelian Africa	Precipitation exceeds potential evapo-transpiration from 2 to 7 months annually. Annual rainfall : 100–400 mm.	1–74	Most common soils are red to grey ferruginous leached soils with low natural fertility.	Predominantly desert (32%) and arid areas (36%)	Extensive grazing of sheep, goats & camels. Cereals occupy 70% of cultivated land. Millet and sorghum account for 80% of cereal production. Dry season valley bottom farming.	Has shorter crop seasons than other semiarid tropics with similar rainfall.	Mauritania, Senegal, Gambia, Mali, Niger, Burkina Faso, Chad, Cape Verde
Humid and subhumid West Africa	Dominated by moist subhumid (47%) and humid (35%). Annual rainfall: 1,200–1,500 mm.	75–119	Acid soils in the humid areas, less leached and higher nutrient content in the drier savannah areas.	Forest in the humid and savannah woodland in the sub-humid forest areas. Forest-savannah mosaic.	Suites for a wide range of annual and perennial crops and some small ruminants	The alternation of wet and dry seasons leads to formation of lateritic crusts not conducive to farming activities.	Guinea–Bissau, Guinea, Sierra Leone, Liberia, Côte d'Ivoire, Ghana, Togo, Benin, Nigeria
Humid Central Africa	Virtually humid throughout the year. Annual rainfall: over 1,500 mm.	180–260	Acid soils cannot be cultivated continuously under low-input farming.	Forest	Suited for perennial crops and root crops such as cassava.	Fertility declines rapidly when vegetation is removed.	Cameroon, Central Africa Rep., Gabon, Congo Rep., Congo
Subhumid and mountainous East Africa	About 88% of East Africa has a single rainfall season. Temperatures decrease with altitude. Rainfall is generally not more than 1,200 mm.	120–179	Dark clay soils	Grass steppes	Wide range of uses. Temperate and tropical crop production and grazing in the semiarid parts of the region.	Relative land scarcity due to differences in the rainfall and high population density Rwanda, Ethiopia,	Madagascar, Reunion, Malawi, Seychelles, Tanzania, Comoros, Burundi, Somalia, Sudan, Uganda, Kenya, Eritrea
Subhumid and semi-arid southern Africa	Up to 6 months humid rainfall. Arid to semi-arid conditions in 48% of the area.	1–74	Reddish chestnut, reddish-brown, and brown soils.	Montane forest and grassland.	Cereal cultivation and grazing in the drier parts.	Rainfall is inadequate and unreliable.	Angola, Zimbabwe, Namibia, Zambia, Botswana, Mozambique, Lesotho, Swaziland

Source: Benneh (1996).

decades ago: in the 1980s less than 3 percent of tropical cropland was irrigated in Africa compared to around 30 percent in India in 1950, and roads per kilometer squared in Africa were one-fifth those in India in the earlier period (Hayami 1997, pp. 94–95).

By definition, the remote have less access to facilities. There is a strong correlation between mean incomes and access to facilities, such as the closest road. In Ghana, for example, the poorer regions have greater proportions of their population without access to a drivable road or public transport, have fewer schools, and spend more time in tasks such as fetching water (table 8.2). These data also reinforce the importance of intranational variations in well-being. Some groups of the poor may have limited access for special reasons: the elderly, infirm, and disabled by virtue of limited mobility. Children, even those responsible for the well-being of siblings in child-headed families, will not have the legal standing or authority to exercise control over capital.

However, much infrastructure spending is biased toward the needs of the nonpoor. Most countries have a high-quality road, frequently of several lanes, to the (modern) international airport. But large tracts of most countries are not served by all weather roads, or roads at all. Small infrastructure investments, such as bridges, can bring great benefits in terms of greater access and reduced workloads. These benefits accrue in particular to women who carry the greater load—one source states that in Ghana (table 8.3) and Tanzania women spend nearly three times as much time on transport and transport four times as much as men in volume (World Bank 1999), and another shows that their transport burden can be up to five times as high. Women's heavier transport burden, which includes items such as water and fuelwood but also reflects their role in agricultural marketing, is one aspect of their relative time poverty. Women usually work two to three hours a day longer than men.

Credit

Investment rates in African countries are low by international standards, as is the share of private investment.

Table 8.2 People in poorer regions have less access to transport and education: the case of Ghana (early 1990s)

| | | Percent of communities with: | | | | | |
	Mean expenditure	Access to drivable road	Access to public transport	Primary school	Primary enrollments at least 50 percent (male)	(female)	Time spent fetching water (minutes per day)
Greater Accra	234	100	57	100	57	58	15
Ashanti	191	100	89	100	93	93	28
Central	181	100	76	94	67	67	21
Eastern	164	59	48	59	94	90	30
Volta	160	78	39	78	73	70	40
Western	146	100	85	96	100	100	24
Upper East	145	78	0	78	55	23	71
Brong Ahafo	136	78	28	78	87	81	38
Northern	133	63	19	63	44	19	37
Upper West	104	60	40	60	30	30	37

Sources: Ghana Statistical Service, *Ghana Living Standards Survey: Report on the Third Round; Rural Communities in Ghana.*

Table 8.3 Women have a heavier transport burden than men (ton-km. per person per year)

	Kasama (Zambia)	Lusaka – rural (Zambia)	Mbale (Uganda)	Kaya (Burkina)	Dedougu (Burkina)
Females	35.7	30.3	39.0	10.3	15.5
Males	7.1	9.8	8.6	3.6	4.4

Source: ADB (1999, p. 108).

The commercial banking system barely touches rural areas, least of all the smallholder sector of most relevance to the poor. Rural credit has thus been provided through traditional associations and micro finance schemes. However, both of these have mainly benefited the relatively less poor in rural areas. Savings scheme often exclude the poorest, or producers associations collect funds from all members but only loan to the more prosperous, so that the poor subsidize the nonpoor. Women are further disadvantaged through social and legal restrictions on their access to credit. The process by which women are excluded is documented for the case of Zambia, where, although nominally as eligible as men, women are at a disadvantage because the procedures for securing project assistance (both a loan and other services) are alien to women, normally being carried out at meetings restricted to men. Moreover, although it is not written as a rule, it is assumed by both project staff and villagers that a loan to a woman would have to be guaranteed by her husband (Crehan 1997, p. 169). Women's labor is therefore less productive, since it is employed with fewer complementary inputs (table 8.4). Donor-financed micro finance initiatives are seen as a major instrument for poverty reduction, and are the main tool of the Consultative Group for the Abolition of Poverty (CGAP). But research shows there to be a clear trade-off between returns and targeting, a trade-off that has usually been made at the expense of the poorest (Hulme and Mosley 1997).

Land

Historically, Africa has had an abundance of land, with scope for new settlement through migration. This is no longer the case in several areas, and there is now a land constraint in eastern and southern Africa and part of the humid zones of western Africa. Other than in humid and subhumid West Africa, soil is of limited fertility, resulting in cropland accounting for 5–6 percent of total land, less than one-half the average for all low-income countries. Much of Africa has been characterized by dual land

Table 8.4 Male-headed households have more resources than female-headed ones: ownership of equipment in Senegal (percent)

	Tractor	Plough	Cart
Male-headed household	2.0	36.1	23.2
Female-headed household	0.6	9.5	5.1

Source: World Bank (1995b).

tenure systems since colonial times,[4] that is, land that was settled or was clearly in use for agricultural purposes remained under traditional land tenure systems, whereas all other land became the property of the state, being sold to settlers in eastern and southern Africa, and for plantations in West Africa. This system, which has been continued in the postcolonial period, alienated people adopting migratory livelihood strategies, such as pastoralists, from much of the land on which they relied. Access to land is unequal, with women frequently having no access (in the North West Province of Cameroon, for example, less than 5 percent of registered titles were issued to women (World Bank 1999, p. 35). Under many kinship systems, the property of a dead man passes to his brothers. If young, the widow is also passed to a brother as a new wife, or older women become the responsibility of their children. Hence the phenomenon of "land grabbing," whereby a husband's relatives seize his property from the widow on his death. In rural areas traditional land allocation system through a chief would make some provision for the woman, but this protection is not available in urban areas. Furthermore, the impact of AIDS and conflict on the middle-aged population leave many elderly women with no one to support them.

The scattered available evidence suggests that land holdings are becoming more unequal and that landlessness is increasing. Bonte (1999) documents growing inequalities in land holdings in the Sahel as certain ethnic groups acquire large amounts of land, mainly for commercial farming purposes. For example, in Mali first colonial pacification and then the installation of a series of wells since independence have allowed Dogon farmers to extend control over larger stretches of the country at the expense of Fulani herders, many of whom are reduced to becoming employees to look after the newly acquired herds of wealthy Dogons. Various countries have introduced land legislation that has aimed to reduce the role of chiefs in land allocation. Basotho chiefs resisted the 1979 Land Act in Lesotho on the grounds that the new measure to allow inheritance would eliminate the redistributive mechanism in traditional allocations (Franklin 1995). Franklin documents growing land acquisition for commercial farming in Lesotho by the wealthy, who acquire land through numerous individual land deals. Agreements are made with small farmers either for immediate use, sharecropping, or to inherit the land; there may be no legal agreement between the parties, but the chief approves the deal, for which payment may be building a house or providing food and clothing.

Despite these growing inequalities, in Africa, as elsewhere, there is a case for equitable land holdings on grounds of both efficiency and equity (or growth and poverty reduction). There is a well-established inverse relationship between yield and size of holding: in settlement schemes in Kenya the smallest holdings produced gross output per hectare worth more than six times that of larger holdings; similar patterns observed for large farms in Trans Nzoia (Kenya) (Hunt 1984, pp. 254–55). These higher outputs are, of course, based on higher labor inputs, which are up to 10 times higher per hectare—small-scale agriculture is the archetypal labor-intensive growth. Yet current policy changes toward liberalization of land markets are more likely to further concentrate land holdings.

The agenda of privatizing land is being pursued (and promoted by the donor community) with little thought for its consequences for poverty. What evidence we have shows that regressive land reform is being carried out in the 1990s.[5] For example, in Zambia land that was previously held by the state has been made available to urban settlers, but the procedures discriminate against the poor even for small plots, requiring, for example, bank statements as evidence of sufficient funds to develop the site. Meanwhile squatters are given registration certificates that in fact provide virtually no legal protection against eviction. Analysis of the situation in the copperbelt region of the country shows well-connected individuals to be acquiring land in forest areas on which they build homes (Hansungule, Feeney, and Palmer 1998).

Environment

The picture with respect to the environment is rather more complicated. The conventional view supposes a poverty-population-environment nexus in which increasing population creates environmental pressures that are exacerbated by the measures the rural poor are forced to take to survive. Environmental degradation undermines livelihoods, generating a vicious circle in which poverty and declining environmental quality feed off one another. But two important caveats must be made to this conventional view.

First, in terms of international comparisons, Africa's environmental situation is relatively good with respect to both the level of indicators, which is to be expected, but also the rate of change (table 8.5);[6] though this table does not include an indicator of soil quality, which is poor in many parts of the continent's agroecological zones and a critical constraint on agricultural growth. It is not surprising that water pollution in Africa is less than one-tenth that in high-income countries, and the level of CO_2 emissions per person under one-fifteenth. If the poor are bad for the environment, the rich are worse. The rates for Africa are also lower than those for other developing regions. What is perhaps more surprising is that the rate of increase in CO_2 emissions is lowest for Africa, though this can be explained by poor growth performance, and that the rate of deforestation is around the average for low-income countries. This caveat should not, however, be taken as cause

Table 8.5 Africa still has relatively good natural resources: international comparison of environmental indicators

	Levels indicators					Change indicators	
	Forest area as a percent of total land area (percent)	Forest area per capita (km²/000 people)	Water pollutants per capita (kg/day/ person x10⁶)	Motor vehicles per capita (vehicles/000 people)	CO_2 emissions per capita (metric tons/ person)	Rate of deforestation (1990–95, percentage)	Percent change in CO_2 emissions 1980–95
East Asia and Pacific	23.7	2.2	2.2	15	2.4	0.8	126
Europe and Central Asia	36.0	18.0	3.0	142	7.8	−0.1	320
Latin America and Caribbean	45.2	18.7	3.9	92	2.5	0.6	43
Middle East and North Africa	0.8	0.3	1.6	53	3.6	0.9	97
South Asia	15.6	0.6	1.3	6	0.8	0.2	161
Sub-Saharan Africa	16.8	6.7	0.8	20	0.8	0.7	36
Memo items:							
Low income	15.8	1.9	1.6	8	1.4	0.6	121
High income	21.0	7.1	9.8	559	12.1	−0.2	27

Source: World Bank, *World Development Indicators 1998*; data for 1995 except where indicated.

for complacency. Further development may well be expected to put further pressure on environmental capital.

But the second caveat follows from several studies showing that environmental quality has improved rather than worsened over time, and that the poor are frequently good guardians of the environment. The best known example is of the Machakos District in Kenya. There was widespread concern about soil erosion among colonial officials in the 1930s; but by the 1990s, after a sixfold increase in population, agricultural yields had increased fivefold and the density of trees had increased (Tiffen, Mortimore, and Gichuki 1994). Similarly, Fairhead and Leach (1996) demonstrate that "forest islands" in the savanna of Guinea are not, as was long believed, remnants of a more extensive forest degraded by population pressure, but were created by the very people held responsible for that degradation. This argument is not to say that poor people will always enhance, rather than degrade, the environment, but that they may do so when conditions permit, so that the problem shifts to that of identifying these conditions. Conditions for enhancing the productivity of land have been identified as security of tenure, low agricultural taxation, good infrastructure, and access to markets and credit. However, rather than enhance these conditions, government and donor interventions often operate in the other direction.

Livestock

Livestock accounts for 25 percent of agricultural GDP in Africa, up to 30 percent if by-products such as manure are included. Livestock is thus of critical importance to the rural economy and, hence, the well-being of the poor, but it has been subject to neglect, misguided interventions, and outright attack.

Government and donor interventions to increase the welfare of pastoralists have failed to meet their objectives of "improved" stock practices and raising living standards: "the last thirty years have seen the unremitting failure of livestock development projects across Africa. Millions of dollars have been spent with few obvious returns and not a little damage" (Scoones 1995, p. 3). These interventions have been misconceived because they have seen the problem as one of overgrazing leading to environmental degradation. The solution imposed has thus been to limit access to what is seen as the carrying capacity of the land for sustainable grazing. The misconception here is to see the environment as being in an equilibrium that can be main-

tained by careful management. In fact, most of Africa's livestock is in arid and semiarid areas with highly variable rainfall. Drought is the main determinant of both livestock numbers and vegetation status. Blueprint approaches are doomed to failure in such a disequilibrium environment. Indeed, by restricting movement they undermine the core of the survival strategy to follow in a such an uncertain setting, which is to move to where vegetation is available (called "tracking"). Tracking strategies have also been frustrated by interventions with less benign intentions. Both colonial and postcolonial states have alienated land they see as "unused," using it for resettlement schemes, state farms, and nature reserves. Conflict can also disrupt tracking by blocking migration routes.

Accumulation of Human and Social Capital Is Slow and Frequently Biased against Rural Areas

The main components of human capital—health and education—are discussed in the next chapter. There it is shown that service provision is uneven, being woefully inadequate in many areas, and that quality of services tends to be low. Biases act against the poor benefiting from services. Urban areas are better served than rural ones, with nonpecuniary access costs being correspondingly higher for rural residents. The poor are more responsive to prices, so that user charges may bias services still further unless effective exemption schemes are put in place. Enrollment rates are lower for girls than for boys, and women are less likely to avail themselves of health services. There are some important exceptions—the Expanded Program of Immunization (EPI)—has raised immunization rates in many countries since the 1980s. In recent years several countries have successfully raised primary education. But these achievements are indeed exceptions to the general underinvestment in human capital.

Extension services

Knowledge and the dissemination of knowledge are important components of human capital. But research and dissemination remain weak; there has been no green revolution in Africa (Mosley 1999; see also chapter 6), and extension services do not reach the poor. Many colonial systems were oriented to serve settler farmers rather than indigenous ones, and some of these practices have been slow to change, and that change has focused on a minority of better-off "progressive" farmers. Such an orientation meant that women, who are responsible for the bulk of agricultural output, were missed. A study of reports from the colonial Department of Agriculture in Kenya found just 15 references to the gender of the farmer from 1914–52, and it was only in that last year that women were first referred to in an annual report, which commented that "the women do all the planting and until a greater interest is taken in the work by men, we shall be greatly retarded in our efforts. It is most difficult to change the ways of overworked women." (MacKenzie 1998, p. 99). After independence, many extension services have continued along the same lines. In Senegal fewer than 5 percent of students enrolled at agricultural colleges were women, and only 3 percent of extension workers were female (World Bank 1995b). Although it is not necessarily the case that women extension workers are needed to reach women, the practice has been to have separate services for women, with nonagricultural staff focusing on domestic tasks. It is not the case that entrenched social relations will necessarily frustrate attempts to introduce gender sensitivity to extension services: experiences from Siavonga District in Zambia demonstrate that, with changes in the process and content of extension to a more participatory approach, women's involvement could be greatly increased, and that men were at least as forthcoming as women in views as to how to overcome gender barriers (Frischmuth 1997).

Social capital

By contrast it may be thought that social capital in Africa is high and can act to support the poor. It is certainly the case that the extended family, with its associated networks of support, persists. On hearing of the more limited role of kinship in Britain, a Kaonde (Zambia) woman exclaimed, "You Europeans, you're just like fish!" (Crehan 1997, p. 87). But such a view has to be subject to several corrections. The first is to state that the poor have little political capital. As elaborated in the previous chapter, African political processes have had adverse implications for poverty reduction for several reasons. Institutional capital is also low. Rural institutions, such as cooperatives and marketing channels, are often weak or nonexistent. Where they do exist, they often exclude the poor (see, for example, Howard and Millard 1997).

A more nuanced picture emerges with respect to traditional social capital built on community relations. Such capital is undoubtedly high, though of course runs along traditional lines of association, which are usually

ethnic, although urban-based groupings may be organized on a nonethnic basis (Tripp 1998). This point can be summed up by saying that economic relations are mediated by social space. Transactions are based on trust and reciprocity. While this situation can protect the vulnerable and support the poor, it can also disadvantage them under two sets of circumstances. First, individuals unable to reciprocate in any way may "drop out of the system" and so not be supported in times of need. Second, when whole communities are in crisis, no one can reciprocate and systems of social support can collapse; in other words, in times of general hardship social capital rapidly depreciates.

PPAs often report (but do not elaborate upon) the view that "the poor only have themselves to blame" for their situation. Some examples from anthropological work reveals that this indeed *can be* an important cause of poverty. Not, of course, that the poor are to blame but that the social exclusion embodied in the attitudes expressed creates a poverty trap. An example comes from Howard and Millard's longitudinal study of the Chagga from Mount Kilimanjaro (Tanzania). Community members and local government officials dismiss the poor as "these people" (*hawa watu*), responsible for their own plight—they drink too much, are ignorant, do not plan ahead, and so forth. These attitudes mean that a poor individual cannot get a loan; the attempt of one of the authors to help the creation of a woodworking cooperative was frustrated by lack of support from both church and government, and the children of the poor are allowed to die the slow death of malnutrition living next to, or even in the same compound as, wealthier relatives.

Box 8.1 illustrates how illness, in this case leprosy, results in social exclusion, that is, a loss of rights, and that widowhood has the same effect. Children born disabled are not likely to be allowed to survive. Increased numbers of disabled from conflict will put a strain on both traditional and official support systems.

It is of course not possible to generalize from the above examples, and counter examples can be found of the support afforded to the needy in a wide range of African societies, and of customs that ensure that the elderly, infirm, and orphaned do not become destitute. The widespread reliance on "help from others" in times of hardship reported in PPAs testifies the extent of these traditions and how they have adapted to changing circumstances. But these traditions can be severely tested at times of general hardship.

If whole communities are affected by poverty, then social capital depreciates as the usual support systems break

---

Box 8.1 The disadvantaged are often excluded from normal social relations: Saran's story

At 15 Saran, now in her 70s, married Janko, a powerful man, who was head of the hunters' association from a distant village. The marriage was arranged as a substitute after Janko's older brother refused Saran's leprous sister, Hawa.

When Saran developed leprous sores a year later, Janko threw her out of his house. She went to live in isolation in a shelter outside the village where Janko visited her periodically to beat her and steal her crops. Eventually she returned to her own family, but her isolation from community life continued.

Colonial officials came to inspect villagers for illness, and Saran accepted the offer of treatment in Bamako, despite local fears that the white men simply rounded them up to kill them. She joined her sister already at the institute, and her condi-

tion gradually improved as more effective treatment with antibiotics was introduced after some time.

She married another leper, Bakari Kamara, and together they farmed unused land by the river. Saran had two children and became involved with a women's association whose members were of many different ethnicities.

After Saran's husband died, Hawa's daughter and son-in-law took away her compound, later selling it and moving away. However, she managed to live on a small strip of land selling vegetables in the local market and gained a reputation as a healer. Despite all her hardships, she now had a wide circle of friends and lived in a community where she felt accepted and valued.

Source: Eric Silla (1998).

---

down. Replying to questions about a period of famine in Ethiopia, households "argued that things were so bad that they could not help anyone but themselves. In the Ethiopian lowlands, where the famine was most intense, many people did feel a moral obligation to bury a dead neighbor, but that was the limit of mutual expectations. It was hard for respondents to talk about such matters. Sadness, guilt and fear all mingled in hushed conversation about the still recent deaths of neighbors, friends and relatives. . . . There was kindness in the darkness; but most individuals averted their eyes from the despair of others" (von Braun, Teklu, and Webb 1999, p. 110). Turnbull's (1973) study of the Ik from the borders of Sudan, Uganda, and Kenya, a tribe deprived of their traditional livelihood when their main hunting ground was turned into a national park, illustrates how virtually all social life collapsed. People would no longer share food, or even steal it from other family members. The Ik represent a clear case in which the social fabric has disintegrated. Finally, prolonged or severe economic crisis can have the same effect on social networks as more extreme shocks. In the Chawama community of Lusaka (Zambia), poor women reported they no longer borrowed from the neighbors, as they could no longer repay, and reciprocal links with rural areas had become strained (Moser 1996). Economic crisis can also strain the social fabric as deprivation provokes rises in crime, violence, alcoholism, and drug abuse, undermining relationships of trust. To generalize, social safety nets may help the vulnerable who are subject to an idiosyncratic shock but will not survive a more widely felt crisis.

Overall, the question of whether the social fabric is disintegrating is more difficult to answer. It is argued that social forces such as urbanization are causing this social fabric to disintegrate, so that society becomes more polarized as the better off no longer share their fortunes with their less fortunate brethren. Three important caveats must be placed on this picture. First, it is all too easy to paint too cheery a picture of a distant "merry Africa," as we have seen there have been limits to traditional safety nets (Booth and others 1999). Second, the pace of change is not as rapid as might be expected. While there is extensive migration, this has been an established feature of African life for at least the last few decades and provides the cash income that flows through the kin network, paying school fees and the like. Finally, social organizations develop, so that traditional structures change their nature or are replaced by alternatives, such as the church, which assume the role of social safety net.

New forms of social capital are built around nontraditional groupings. A study in Tanzania identified the church, political party, burial society, women's group, and farmers' group as organizations contributing to social capital, and only one of these groups (burial societies) may be regarded as traditional. Another study documents the rise of women's groups in urban areas in the 1980s, organized around their role as market traders, and crossing ethnic boundaries (see Tripp 1998). Household incomes were shown to be positively related to the level of social capital in a village, supporting the idea that such groups are indeed "capital" and have a social element (as it is village rather than just household capital which matters).

Equally important as village-level groups that may support those who fall upon misfortune is the emergence of civil society organizations at the national level that will place poverty on the national political agenda. Democratization in the 1990s has opened the way for this path. Experience from other countries shows that political mobilization of the poor cannot be relied upon alone: it does not always happen and they may lack voice if it does. A poverty-conscious middle class has a role to play in highlighting issues, including exposing corrupt and exploitative practices, and supporting redistributive policies.

Conclusion

African capital of all kinds is not high and the poor have unequal access to what of it there is. Some groups of the poor are affected worse than others. Those in remote communities are, by definition, cut off from infrastructure, and ill-placed to access credit. The landless are defined by their lack of access to land. Women are frequently disadvantaged in access to land and credit, undermining their productivity. Those not in a position to reciprocate—orphans, the disabled, and childless elderly—may be ill-served by social networks. Different dimensions to poverty serve to reinforce these barriers. Those with low human and political capital will have less access to credit. Social capital helps the powerful use institutions to their benefit, thus excluding the less well off. Those with few assets cannot invest in the education of their children or pay to preserve their health, laying one basis for unequal access to social services. Access issues and what is needed to improve social indicators is the subject of the next chapter.

Notes

1. Figure 8.1 shows the partial scatter plot. Of the Y axis are the residuals from regressing the HDI on log(GNP) and the X axis the residuals from the regression of rural population share (RURAL) on log(GNP). The partial regression passes through the origin, as residual means are necessarily zero. But in the figure the series means have been added to the respective residuals. The corresponding multiple regression results are (t-statistic in brackets):

2. An alternative approach to illustrating the same point comes from Moore and others (1999) who regress the residual of the regression of HDI on (logged) income per capita on a range of variables, finding population density to be significantly positive.

3. The failure of Early Warning Systems is not a failure to predict famine—this they can do—but the failure to respond before people have become destitute (see box 13.1 in chapter 13).

4. A systematic review of land tenure systems in each country is given by Bruce (1998).

5. Mozambique at least appears to be an exception in which the new land law was passed through a highly consultative process, with resulting legislation that should protect the rights of the poor, although it is too early to say if this is so in practice (see Greeley and Jenkins 1999).

6. The number of threatened species (mammals, birds, and higher plants) is higher in both absolute and relative terms (relative meaning as a percentage of total species in that country) in the United States than in any African country.

CHAPTER 9

Sustaining Improvements in Social Indicators Requires Growing Income and Better State Service Provision

The Direct and Indirect Benefits of Improving Social Outcomes

As recognized by their prominence among the International Development Targets (see chapter 13), health and education have vital roles to play in both direct and indirect poverty reduction. First and foremost, avoiding ill health, disability, and ignorance are in themselves empowering and raise the quality of life. But improving social outcomes also contributes to higher incomes at both the household and macroeconomic levels. Econometric analysis, presented in chapter 6, supports the view that human capital accumulation matters for growth. There are clear reasons why this is so. For poor families education can provide the stepping stone out of poverty, providing access to formal-sector employment, and enhance productivity in informal and agricultural activities, whereas sickness can remove the main income source and condemn a family to a vicious circle of deepening deprivation. An otherwise healthy person can be permanently disabled in the absence of timely health interventions. At the aggregate level, no industrialized or newly industrialized country has developed with literacy rates as low as they are in Africa today. In short, enhancing the capabilities of the poor will lift them out of poverty and reduce overall poverty.

Higher social indicators can be achieved by increasing private incomes and by provision of health, education, water, and infrastructure services. Growth is of central importance, as it both allows welfare-raising expenditures and provides the tax base for public service provision. But Africa has proved relatively poor at turning income growth into improved welfare indicators. Figure 9.1 shows the relationship between life expectancy and income per capita.[1] Three important messages emerge from this graph. First, life expectancy is highly correlated with income per capita—higher income results in improved social welfare. Second, although there is a high correlation between the two variables, it is far from perfect: there is considerable variation around the line, indicating that some countries are better able to convert income into higher social indicators. Although income matters in raising social indicators, other things are also important. Third, African countries are almost all "underperformers," having lower levels of life expectancy than expected given their income levels.[2, 3] Hence Niger and Nepal have the same income per capita, but life expectancy in Nepal is 10 years greater than that in Niger (57 versus 47). The following pairs of countries also all have the same income levels but widely differing life expectancies: Nigeria and Vietnam (54 and 68), Zambia and Nicaragua (43 and 68), and Zimbabwe and Honduras (52 and 69). Clearly, in many African countries the "other factors" that promote better social outcomes are not in place. Chapter 7 argued that the political situation is critical among such factors. This chapter focuses more closely on the provision of social services and water supply (other infrastructure was discussed in chapter 8).

The African poor are thus triply disadvantaged. First by the widening international gap as African social indicators lag behind those in the rest of the world, which is partly explained by the continent's history of poor growth.[4] Second, by the underperformance of African economies in turning what growth there is into welfare improvements. And, finally, by national disparities in health and education between the poor and the nonpoor. Where sickness prevails, or children go uneducated, it is the poor who bear a disproportionate part of the burden. What are the sources of these gaps and can they be closed?

Statistical analysis shows that investments in service provision account for some of the variation in social indicators, which is not explained by income (Hanmer and White 1999). While it is clear that improvements in health, education, and water supply all have an enormous potential contribution to make in reducing poverty, both directly by improving the well-being of the poor and indirectly by supporting growth,[5] this potential is far from realized in Africa for two reasons. First public provision appears plagued by low levels of efficiency, with quite high spending levels not being translated into appropriate outcomes. Second, social spending remains misdirected, with state subsidies disproportionately benefiting the nonpoor. A range of factors interact to restrict the access of the poor, yet universal primary education and greatly improved health status are achievable goals. To attain these targets, social service reform must overcome the constraints the poor face in accessing services, rather than reinforce them.

The theme of this report that the different dimensions of poverty interact with one another deserves special emphasis here. The positive linkages between health and education have long been recognized—for example how

maternal education can reduce infant illness and death.[6] The links from these to productivity, and thus income poverty, were mentioned above. Education clearly enhances the possibility for effective political participation. Recent macro evidence suggests that lack of education is a critical factor in explaining Africa's underperformance, illustrated in figure 9.1. Ranis and Stewart (1999) classify good performers as those countries whose ranking on the Human Development Index greatly exceeds that on income per capita. Two factors are consistently present in good performers: high levels of primary enrollment and a high ratio of female-to-male primary enrollment. A final key linkage comes from clean water, where the African poor are again disadvantaged. A recent review of studies of water use from a number of African countries (Rosen and Vincent 1999) reviews the various ways in which water supply can enhance productivity. One route is in reducing the time spent carrying water, which averages more than two hours a day, this being a burden that falls almost entirely on women and children. The need to carry reduces usage: the average was found to be about 10 litres/person/day,

Figure 9.1 Social indicators improve with income but Africa underperforms (scatter plot of life expectancy against income per capita)

Life expectancy

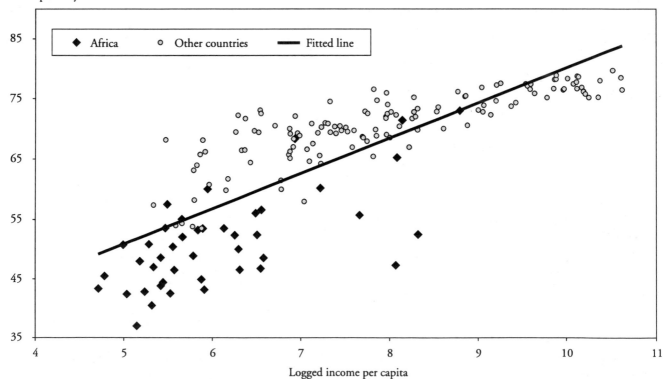

Logged income per capita

Source: World Bank, *World Development Indicators 1999.*

which is far less than that required for proper hygiene. Thus, unsurprisingly, there is a high level of water-related diseases, which account for over 10 percent of all mortality and morbidity. Rural water supply is shown to be a cost-effective way of preventing diarrhea and other diseases.

This interaction also has a downside. Improving education, or any other single intervention, is not a magic bullet. Increasing the number of school leavers when there are not productive opportunities for them will only swell the ranks of the unemployed. These arguments point to the need for "balanced development."

Africa Lags Behind on Social Indicators—and the Gap Is Widening

Improved health comes in substantial part through improved diet and shelter. Better-off families are more able to educate their children. Growing private incomes are thus central to improved social outcomes. But the existence of productivity gains, and other positive externalities, from investments in health and education, form the basis for an argument for state subsidy. There are two important caveats to this argument. First, the private sector may be willing and able to provide some services. In an African setting the appropriate role for the modern private sector is likely to be the "top end" of health and education services, which the poor cannot afford, leaving more state resources available for the poor.[7] The argument against such a policy is that it will create a twin-track system, running into the problem that "services intended solely for the poor are poor services." The balance between public and private provision is a political decision that countries must decide for themselves. The second caveat is that expanding social service provision is not in itself sufficient, since healthy school leavers need productive opportunities to apply their skills, emphasizing once again the importance of growth. But there is ample evidence that raising the quantity and quality of health and education will play a pivotal role in Africa's attempts to reduce poverty.

Colonial governments did little or nothing to promote education among the African population, which was left in the hands of missionaries. At independence very few universities had been established, and most countries had but a handful of graduates and secondary school leavers that numbered in the hundreds. New governments embarked on rapid expansion of the education system. In Zambia the number of children attending primary school more than doubled in the 10 years after independence (from 378,600 to 858,200), and there was a five-

fold increase in secondary students. Zimbabwe achieved an even more rapid expansion with the end of white rule in 1979 and independence the following year, more than doubling from well under one million to over two million from 1979 to 1983; the enrollment rate rose from 60 to 100 in just two years. In Africa as a whole the enrollment rate nearly doubled in the first 15 years following independence (table 9.1).

A somewhat similar situation prevailed in health care, with the health infrastructure, at least that outside urban areas, being the provenance of missionaries. The postindependence expansion was at least as rapid as that in education. In Zambia the number of hospitals rose from 48 in 1964 to 76 only 10 years later, and the number of health centers and clinics nearly doubled over the same period (from 306 to 595).

The drive to higher service provision faltered in the 1970s. Economic decline hit many countries so that real spending fell. Both quality and quantity suffered, with some countries, such as Ghana, experiencing declines in primary enrollment rates of 10 percent or more. Today Africa not only has the lowest enrollment rates, but the gap has widened over time as African enrollments have fallen in 1980s (table 9.1). In no country outside Africa are gross enrollments below 70 percent, but it is below this level for 19 out of 46 African countries. In Somalia the figure is less than 10 percent, and only 29 percent in Niger. Accurate measures of quality are not available, but parents regularly complain of lower standards, such as this Nigerian parent: "In our days, I started writing letters to my parents from the time I was in Primary 3. Nowadays, many Primary 6 pupils cannot even spell their own names properly" (Francis and others 1998).

Illiteracy in Africa remains at close to one-half of the population. It has fallen more rapidly than that in South Asia (though definitions of literacy vary), but South Asia's stronger performance on enrollments suggest that this situation may soon be reversed.

Despite continuing improvements in health, as captured by the infant mortality rate, the gap is also widening. In 1970 the infant mortality rate in Africa was comparable to that in South Asia, the Middle East, and North Africa, but by the late nineties, the rate in Africa was over one-third more than that in South Asia and nearly double that in the Middle East.[8] Rate reduction in Africa has decelerated as economic decline, conflict, and HIV/AIDS have all taken their toll, and the downward trend has even been reversed in some countries (Mozambique, Uganda, Zambia, and possibly Zimbabwe).[9] Conflict

Table 9.1 Africa lags behind in health and education—and education performance deteriorated in the 1980s

	1965	1980	1985	1990	1995
Gross primary enrollment rate (percent)					
Sub-Saharan Africa	41	78	77	73	74
South Asia	67	76	85	90	94
Latin America and Caribbean	98	106	105	106	112
East Asia and Pacific	87	111	118	118	114
	1970	1980	1985	1990	1997
Illiteracy (percent)					
Sub-Saharan Africa	71	61	56	50	42
Middle East and North Africa	69	57	53	45	38
South Asia	68	61	58	54	49
Latin America and Caribbean	26	20	18	15	13
East Asia and Pacific	45	31	25	20	16
Infant mortality rate (per 1,000 live births)					
Sub-Saharan Africa	137	115	107	99	92
Middle East and North Africa	137	99	75	62	54
South Asia	139	122	106	90	75
Latin America and Caribbean	85	62	51	43	37
East Asia and Pacific	80	56	48	45	40

Note: Primary gross enrollment rate is the number enrolled as a percent of relevant age cohort.
Sources: World Bank, World Development Indicators 1998 and 1999, United Nations Educational, Scientific, and Cultural Organization (UNESCO) Yearbook, 1998.

has both direct and indirect effects: indirectly it diverts resources away from social spending and undermines growth, and directly it destroys facilities (in Mozambique Renamo targeted health posts and schools) and displaced people: in refugee camps infant mortality rates of over 300 have been recorded. Around one-third of children whose mothers are HIV-positive will get the virus, and 80 percent or more of these will die in the first five years of their life.

Despite these figures, universal primary education is achievable in Africa. There are four compelling arguments why this is so. First, the record is not uniformly poor: 11 out of 46 African countries have enrollment rates in excess of 100 percent, and another three above 90 percent (though the data only run to the mid-1990s). Second, countries such as Malawi and Uganda have made substantial progress in increasing enrollment in the 1990s.[10] Third, the issue is at least as much one of increasing efficiency as of increasing resources. Public spending on education as a percent of GDP is higher in Africa than in any other developing region, and considerably higher than East Asia (5.6 percent versus 3.0 percent in 1995) where performance is best. East Asian countries with comparable levels of income per capita to Africa have achieved universal primary education (notably China and Vietnam). This achievement is partly a product of demographics: lower population

growth reduces the proportion of school age children, thereby requiring lower educational expenditure in relation to GDP. But there are other reasons: in China teachers' salaries are equal to mean income per capita, whereas the African norm is four to six times and is considerably higher in some countries (reaching 12 in Senegal).[11] High teachers' salaries mean that they typically consume 90 percent or more of the education budget. Consequently, spending on teaching materials is 1 or 2 percent of education spending, compared to 5 to 6 percent elsewhere. Finally, the start of the demographic transition in Africa (see next chapter) will make this target easier to achieve.

Unlike the case for education, spending in Africa on health is a lower percentage of GDP than elsewhere, with differences in both public and private spending (table 9.2). Nonetheless, substantial improvements in health status are achievable in Africa for two reasons. First, there is great scope for quality and efficiency improvements. Second, the pattern of disease in Africa differs greatly from that elsewhere, with over 70 percent of disability adjusted life years (DALYs)[12] lost being from communicable diseases, compared to around 50 percent in most other developing regions (25 percent in China and 10 percent in industrial countries). HIV/AIDS, tuberculosis, and malaria are among the main communicable diseases, with an

Table 9.2 Spending on health is lower in Africa than elsewhere (spending as a percentage of GDP, period averages for 1990s)

	Private	Public	Total	Public share
Africa	1.7	2.0	3.7	56.4
Other developing countries	2.4	2.7	5.1	53.0
Developed countries	1.9	5.9	7.8	76.0

Source: World Bank, *World Development Indicators 1999.*

estimated 270–480 million cases of malaria annually, equal to 90 percent of all cases worldwide.

Africa's environment means that water scarcity is a problem in many parts of the continent. The Sahelian region is at risk, as are many countries in eastern and southern Africa, which have experienced severe droughts during the 1980s and 1990s (Sharma and others 1996). Partly related to these factors, the average level of access to save water, at just 50 percent (and under 40 percent in rural areas) compares unfavorably with the 80 percent achieved in other developing regions. The figure varies widely across

Africa: from less than one-tenth in Eritrea to nearly 80 percent in Zimbabwe (see tables 1.4 and A.4 in chapter 1 and the appendix, respectively).

The Poor Are More Sick and Less Educated than the Nonpoor—and Resources Remain Skewed

The poor are more sick, less educated, and have worse access to basic infrastructure than the nonpoor. Mortality rates are typically twice as high for poor men as they are for nonpoor and three times as high for poor women as nonpoor ones; rates for poor children are three to five times those for the children of the nonpoor, and again the ratio is higher for girls than boys (table 9.3). Tuberculosis is twice as high among the poor. Finally, figure 9.2 shows that malnutrition is higher among the poor than nonpoor; there is not always so much variation between the bottom three quintiles, but the percentage of children who are malnourished in the top quintile is usually around half that for the bottom quintile. The same pattern can be found with respect to education. Figure 9.3 shows a pattern that is typical across the continent: enrollment rates are lower for lower income groups than higher ones.[13] Secondary enrollment among the poor is negligible, often around 1 or 2 percent or even less (and rises sharply

Table 9.3 Mortality and disease are higher among the poor

	Adult (15–59)		Children (0–5)		
	Male	Female	Male	Female	TB
Botswana	2.3	4.0	4.9	4.8	1.2
Côte d'Ivoire	1.5	1.5	2.4	3.3	1.6
Ethiopia	2.2	3.6	3.0	4.0	2.9
Guinea	2.1	3.5	3.7	5.6	1.9
Guinea–Bissau	1.7	2.1	2.2	3.0	2.6
Kenya	2.1	3.8	3.7	3.8	2.6
Lesotho	2.6	5.4	3.9	5.2	1.7
Madagascar	2.0	3.4	3.8	4.1	2.6
Mauritania	1.9	3.4	3.0	3.7	1.3
Niger	1.9	3.5	3.4	4.8	2.4
Nigeria	1.8	2.8	3.1	3.7	2.2
Rwanda	1.2	1.0	2.7	4.2	2.3
Senegal	2.2	3.8	4.0	4.9	2.5
South Africa	1.7	3.6	4.7	5.3	1.0
Tanzania	2.1	3.3	5.6	5.0	1.4
Uganda	1.4	1.4	2.1	2.5	1.3
Zambia	2.5	3.6	3.5	3.9	3.8
Zimbabwe	2.1	2.3	4.1	5.0	1.2

Note: The table shows the ratio of mortality and the prevalence of tuberculosis for the poor and the nonpoor.
Source: WHO (World Health Organization) 1999.

Figure 9.2 The children of the poor are more malnourished than those of the non-poor

Percentage malnourished

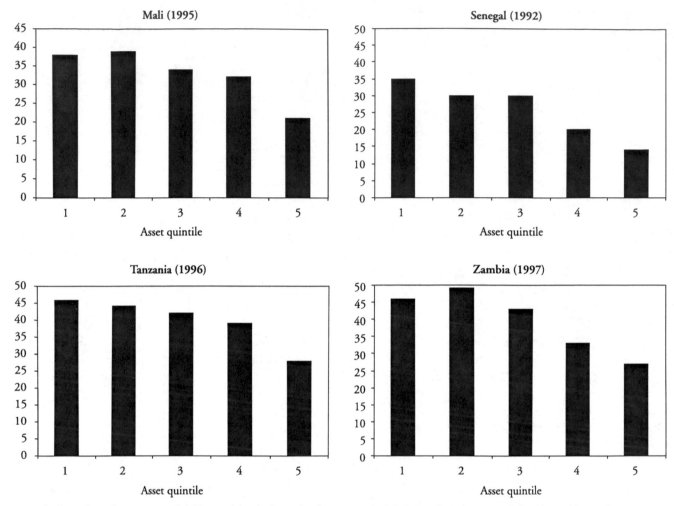

Note: The figure shows the percentage of children with height for age less than two standard deviations from the mean, tabulated by wealth quintiles. Wealth is calculated from an asset index (radio or bicycle, for instance).
Source: Sahn, Stifel and Younger (1999).

thereafter through the income quintiles). The children of the poor are thus likely to make up the poor of the next generation.

Similarly the gender gap closes as the enrollment rate rises: the gap is more than 20 percent in low enrollment countries like Chad, Guinea, and Ethiopia but small or nonexistent in high enrollment ones like Kenya, Botswana, and South Africa (see table A.13, appendix).

These factors interact with one another to undermine the well-being of the poor. Education helps the spread of health messages, and malnourished children are at best listless, but it is also likely that their intellectual development is impaired. The primary cause of many diseases is water related (typhoid, cholera, dysentery, gastroenteritis, and hepatitis are all waterborne, and scistosomiasis and guinea-worm are water based) through lack of safe water for drinking, for hygiene purposes, and for sanitation (Sharma and others 1996). These problems are being exacerbated as pollution of water sources increases from urban waste water and industrial effluent.

People are of course aware of these problems, water access being identified as a major priority, especially by women, in Participatory Poverty Assessments; in the words of a South African woman, "The shortage of water is a serious problem in this area which needs immediate attention. . . . I know about eight people who have died of

Figure 9.3 Enrollment rates are higher for the non-poor than the poor, urban residents than those in rural areas, and men than women (in percent)

Male   Female

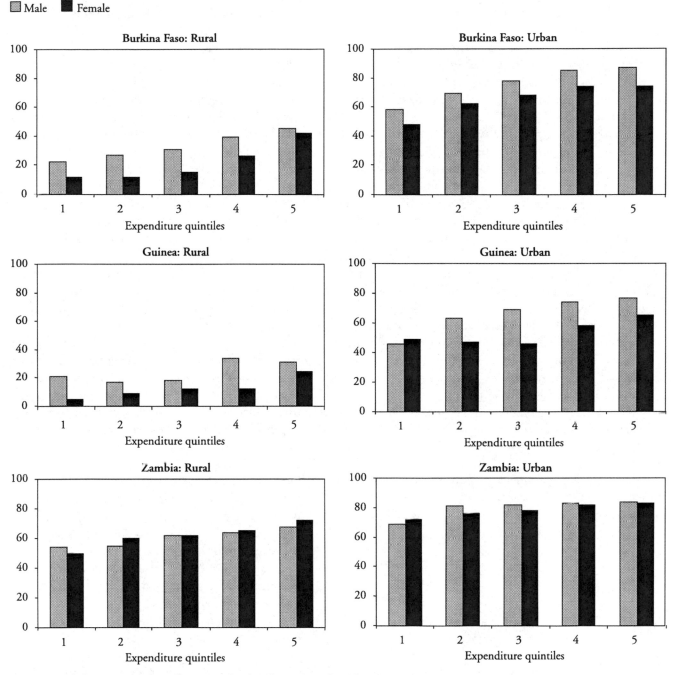

Note: The graph shows net primary enrollment rates for selected countries in the mid-1990s.
Source: Appiah (1999, table 4).

contagious diseases from water here" (Levin, Solomon, and Weiner 1997, p. 105).

Biases in enrollments and use of facilities mean that state spending on social services disproportionately ben-efits the nonpoor. The primary sector typically receives half the education budget, although since it has by far the largest number of pupils, spending per head is, of course, much lower than at other levels. On average, public spending on a university student is 20 times that spent on a primary pupil, although this figure exceeds 100 in Malawi (table 9.4). Combining spending per pupil with information on enrollments by income quintile provides a picture of how much each quintile benefits from spending.[14] Data from a number of African countries show that the bottom 20 percent receive between 5 and 17 percent of public spending on education, whereas the top 20 percent get between 21 and 44 percent (Castro-Leal and others 1999).

Similarly, the nonpoor use all levels of health services more than do the poor, with the disparities being greatest for higher service levels. In Tanzania the bottom quintile uses primary facilities only slightly less than the top quintile but are more than one-third less likely to use hospital facilities. As a result, the per capita subsidy to individuals in the top quintile is two to three times that received by those in the bottom quintile (Castro-Leal and others 1999). However it is not necessarily the case that higher budgetary shares for social services result in improvements in the quality of service delivery in rural areas. In Uganda this disjuncture has been blamed on the methods of disbursing funds from the center to the districts, and the knowledge gap on implementation that currently exists between the ministries and the local level (Ablo and Reinikka 1998).

One key constraint on the access of the poor to health, education, and clean water is thus the simple lack of

Table 9.4 University students get nearly 20 times as much public money as primary pupils

	Primary	*Secondary*	*Tertiary*
Burundi	1.0	4.9	66.3
Chad	1.0	2.7	19.0
Guinea	1.0	3.7	47.9
Kenya	1.0	2.7	30.5
Lesotho	1.0	4.0	31.7
Malawi	1.0	15.1	102.0
Mali	1.0	2.0	29.8
Mauritania	1.0	4.6	12.4
Togo	1.0	3.5	43.8
Zimbabwe	1.0	2.1	12.4
Sub-Saharan Africa	1.0	3.3	18.9
East Asia and Pacific	1.0	8.3	3.6
Portugal	1.0	1.2	1.5

Note: The table shows public spending per student as a ratio of the figure for primary.
Source: Appiah (1999), table 10.

facilities. But there are others. Participatory analysis with poor communities identifies the following key constraints:

- *Financial*—Both the direct pecuniary costs and the indirect opportunity costs are high for the poor, who are not able to be make large one-off payments for school fees or to readily change assets to cash to meet medical emergencies. There is a seasonal or cyclical element to the ability to pay that is particularly severe for the poor. The opportunity cost may also be seasonal so that children are kept away at busy periods. The costs and benefits of education, combined with cultural perspectives, can favor boys. A study in Kenya found that 58 percent of parents would rather have a girl drop out of school compared to only 27 percent for boys (with the remaining 15 percent having no preference). The nonpoor are better able to afford water supply systems to ensure continuous access to water, although, paradoxically, the poor in urban areas may then pay *more* for their water by being reliant on street vendors; in rural areas poor women spend a large part of the day collecting water.

- *Physical*—Lack of physical access to health services is repeatedly identified as a problem by rural communities who stress the need for all-weather roads and some form of public transport. The problem is seen to be exacerbated by poor geographical coverage of services, especially regarding access to emergency health care, and opening hours that make it impossible for people to attend. In urban areas access is constrained by increased lack of security, a problem that particularly affects women, and is most commonly mentioned in relation to women collecting water early in the morning or late at night. The breakdown of law and order is also seen to adversely affect education.

- *Gender biases*—Gender biases reduce women's access to education, health, and water. Girls' education is frequently less valued than that of boys given the view that "a son belongs to his parents whereas a daughter belongs to her potential husband," and some rural communities may be skeptical of the value of education more generally. Girls may be kept away from school, or at least be late, because of domestic chores such as looking after siblings, but may also be kept away if there are not properly segregated facilities such as toilets, or if it is thought unsafe walking to (or at) school. Surveys in several countries show that women are less likely to seek medical attention at times of sickness. Although women are responsible for water collection, which may consume several hours each day, the decisionmaking power to ease this burden, through constructing a well, or installing a rain catchment, lies with men. Drangert (1993) documents several cases of proposals to improve access to water in villages in Sukumaland (Tanzania) that failed through men's unwillingness to engage the problem.

- *Cultural*—In addition to gender biases, other cultural factors may limit utilization of state services. Anthropological work suggests that belief in witchcraft as a cause of illness remains strong, so that reliance on traditional health is probably greater than that revealed by surveys (both qualitative and quantitative), with home remedies and traditional healers being used first, with recourse to modern medicine only if these alternatives fail. If modern medicine becomes more costly, they will rely on traditional approaches more as an alternative.

- *Political*—There is a strong awareness among the poor that services intended for them are consumed by others. Political factors may adversely affect inter- and intrasectoral spending allocation, geographical coverage of facilities, and those who benefit at the local level. The apparent poor targeting of exemption schemes may be partly attributable to such factors. The poor may be excluded by administrative requirements, such as the need to show birth certificates, which are diffi cult and costly for them to meet. A Zimbabwean commented, "Only the people in our area who are powerful and well off get the assistance meant for us" (Brocklesby and Holland 1998, p. 16).

- *Quality*—Services are not always utilized because of poor quality, or, if utilized, there is dissatisfaction with quality: the Core Welfare Indicators Questionnaire (CWIQ) in Ghana found 80 percent of rural residents to be dissatisfied with educational quality (as were 50 percent of urban residents). This comment applies to both health and education in terms of facilities (lack of drugs or textbooks) and to staff (rude health workers and drunk teachers). Education may also be seen as irrelevant, with a preference for an emphasis first on basic skills, notably literacy, and then on vocational training. Health programs may also be seen as lacking, with some studies revealing a perceived need for more family planning services. Quality problems are partly a function of low morale among health workers, who do not have the means to perform their

tasks, and often earn insufficient salaries to survive, so that drug supplies find their way into the private market, and teachers set their pupils to work growing vegetables for sale.

What is the scope for further reform to overcome these obstacles?

Further Reforms Can Close the International and National Gaps

One message of this report is to reaffirm the importance of economic growth for social development and poverty reduction. Nearly all social indicators are correlated with income. Growing private incomes will support health and educational development and provide the revenue base for sustainable public services. But it is not enough to rely on growth alone: there are good economic and social arguments for investing in human capital while urgently addressing efficiency issues. Social service reform must be undertaken in such way as to redress, rather than reinforce, the barriers to access the poor face, in part by better targeting of resources for the poor.

User charges have been a central component of social service reform programs in many countries. By the mid-1990s all but one country (Botswana) was charging for health services. Proponents of fees argued that charges would improve both efficiency (through improved resource allocation by private providers and discouragement of the use of high cost services) and equity (by exempting the poor), as the revenues collected allowed for better quality service with greater accessibility to the poor. However these views underestimated the extent to which fees would exclude the poor, who have a higher price elasticity of demand for health than the nonpoor, and overestimated likely revenues; in the case of health, charges have amounted to about 5 percent of recurrent costs. These arguments have also not fully taken into account the externalities that mean that the poor should receive health and education if they cannot afford to pay. Collection costs can also be high. In the case of water and sanitation, it has been claimed that the costs of metering and billing can exceed the revenue thus raised. There is ample evidence that primary school fees have discouraged participation, particularly of girls, and that exemption schemes are poorly targeted. Even with fees, the costs of education—books, uniforms, "voluntary contributions," and the opportunity cost—can be a considerable burden to the poor. The introduction of primary charges in Malawi in the early 1980s led to a temporary drop in enrollments, followed by much slower growth than had been achieved before fees were introduced. When fees were abolished in 1994, enrollments increased by about two-thirds, from 1.9 to 3.2 million. A similar increase was achieved in Uganda when primary education was made free for four children from each family. Attempts to target exemptions have had nowhere near the same effect: an exemption scheme in Zimbabwe only reached 12 percent of the target population. In Lesotho people could be exempted if they were certified as paupers, having no income or assets, by the village chief or district officer. While 200 people were thus eligible, another 30,000 people enjoyed free health services, such as doctors, nurses, and village health workers.

During the 1990s there has been a move away from the simple application of user charges toward a more nuanced approach. Many countries do not charge for primary education, and this stance commands international support. There is however a view that there should be "community level financing," although the practice and implications of this problematic concept remain to be worked out, especially where the wealthy are reliant upon private facilities. In the case of health and water supply, charges seem more firmly established, but means of exemption and cost sharing are being explored. Health insurance schemes have been established in several countries. But there remains a case for free access for certain areas (poor districts), facilities (rural health clinics), or treatment (preventive interventions such as immunization). Water supply presents a different set of issues, since experience has shown that services are not maintained without an element of either cost recovery by the provider or community involvement in management, or both.

It should of course be recognized that there are different groups of the poor. The dependent poor are more likely to need free access, whereas some of the economically active poor may be able to pay for some services but not make lump sum payments. Hence, installment payments or insurance schemes are the appropriate means of paying.

Financial reform that charges those who can afford to pay—for example, replacing the grants for board and lodging to university students with loans—to help subsidize those who cannot is one area in which reforms can be made. But there is also scope for improvements in efficiency and quality, including a role for the private sector in providing services not used by the poor. In the education sector many countries have yet to undertake exten-

sive administrative reform and decentralization or measures to raise quality to reduce dropouts and repeats. Efficiency can be raised with no loss of quality, as the experience of some countries, for example, Senegal, shows. Measures undertaken include double-shifting (also called hot-desking), using more teaching assistants, and turning educational administrators into teachers.

In health a stricter use of the referral system can increase efficiency, but application of targeting also affects the nature of services provided. The current trend is to identify the most cost-effective way of reducing the burden of disease as measured by DALYs. But a number of caveats should be placed on this approach for a poverty-oriented health program. First, there are social constraints on such an approach: it is not cost-effective to provide care for the terminally ill, but it is socially unacceptable not to do so. Second, the relative opportunity cost of sickness is greater to the poor—they can ill-afford the lost income from those who are sick or from those who care for them, and a marginal family may be pushed into permanent poverty by a period of illness. Third, there are complementarities between different interventions so that they are more attractive taken as a package than when considered individually.

Conclusion: The Need for Balanced Development

This report has emphasized the importance of growth for poverty reduction. But it has been stated here that enhancing the capabilities of the poor is necessary for growth. So which should come first?

There has been a "sequencing debate" as to the ordering of investing in human capital and investing in growth (see the review in White 1999b). Countries that have emphasized growth alone have failed to sustain improvements in either growth or human development. By contrast, pushing on human development may eventually yield a growth dividend. But the best returns appear to come from a balanced development strategy, which is indeed suggested by the interrelatedness of the various dimensions of poverty. Such a finding is hardly surprising. Social service provision needs a tax base to support it or it cannot be financed. But growth needs healthy, educated workers. Although the view that adjustment policies squeezed social sectors cannot be sustained as an argument applying across Africa (see chapter 6), they can be criticized for insufficient effort in building human capital. This situation has been changing in the 1990s. But this chapter has documented the persistence of wide disparities in access that need to be addressed if the potential of the poor in contributing to growth is to be realized and they are to benefit from it.

Notes

1. The same messages would have emerged whatever social indicator had been chosen. Similarly, Purchasing Pow-er Parity (PPP) gross domestic product (GDP) would be more appropriate but would not alter the general picture, and so was not used in order to increase the sample size.

2. Technical note: The scatter plot shows that the relationship between life expectancy and the log of income is clearly nonlinear. The fitted line shown, from a double-log function, is in fact mildly convex. From the scatter a concave function may have been expected, but the curvature is "pulled the other way" by the small group of relatively high-income, low life expectancy African countries. The basic message would not be changed by reestimating the curve excluding these countries to get a concave line.

3. The four African countries lying above the line are, in ascending order of income, Madagascar, Ghana, Cape Verde, and Mauritius. The Seychelles is the highest income African country and lies on the line.

4. In a similar analysis (based on the Human Develop-ment Index) Moore and others (1999) find population density, mineral and aid dependence, and (with a perverse sign) good governance to significantly affect a country's success at turning income into social indicators—but an Africa dummy remains significant (and one for only West Africa even more so).

5. Social security systems are also important but virtually undeveloped in Africa. Exceptions are Botswana, Namibia, and South Africa, where poor families rely on the pensions of elderly relatives to provide a regular income to meet the basic necessities of daily life.

6. Both cross-country and household-level regression analyses of the determinants of infant and child mortality consistently find female (or maternal) education to be a significant factor (see the review in Hanmer and White 1999).

7. The "modern" private sector is specified, since traditional medicine remains important in Africa, and is frequently the first port of call. Households may also spend considerable amounts on private modern medicine, mainly the purchase of drugs, so that health care costs can represent a sizeable proportion of the household budget of poor families.

8. In addition to the issue of data quality, there is substantial regional variation with mortality rates higher in West Africa than those in southern Africa.

9. Although success in combating AIDS may have reversed this trend in urban Uganda.

10. Uganda's success had been too recent to show up in the data available for this report but is documented in Harper and Marcus (1999).

11. These data and most others in this paragraph are from Colclough and Lewin (1993).

12. A DALY is a disability-adjusted life year, which measures the burden of disease as years lost from either premature death or disability.

13. Table A.12 of the appendix reports these data for all countries for which they are available.

14. There is an assumption here that spending per pupil is the same across the country; in fact, it almost certainly will not be in a way that will further disadvantage the poor, as poorer regions will have less resources.

CHAPTER 10

Household and Population Dynamics: Good and Bad News for Poverty Reduction

Household Structure and Poverty

The changing nature of social relations embodied in the household is central to an understanding of African poverty. Four key features of the household are important. First is what constitutes a household. European models of the household are not readily applied in some African settings, and attempts to do so can give misleading results. Second, the importance of household structure: different household structures provide support for different individuals. While those excluded from the family support system will typically be among the poorest of the poor, those included in it are not necessarily protected unless they can effectively operate in the system of bargaining and mutual reciprocity that characterizes social relations (see chapter 8). Third, while household size is typically taken as a correlate of poverty, it is in fact household composition that matters, as reflected in the child/adult ratio and the dependency ratio more generally; the female/male ratio can also be important. Finally, there exists a "household life cycle"; household members are more likely to be poor at some stages of this life cycle than at others.

In many African languages the word for poor means literally the lack of support: *umphawi* in the Chewa language of Malawi means one without kin or friends. A participatory survey in Mali showed that most people did not think of themselves as poor—those without families were poor. In many societies, though not all, groups such as barren women, the elderly with no surviving children, and orphans will be particularly at risk. A nineteenth century traveler recorded that "a poor person who has no relatives will seldom be supplied even with water in illness, and when dead will be dragged out to be devoured by the hyenas, instead of being buried" (Illiffe 1987, p. 58). While undoubtedly important, the security provid-

ed by the family must not be overstated and is often provided in return for service: in the words of a Bemba (Zambia), "no one would know the difference between a slave and a poor relative" (Illiffe 1987, p. 57). As documented in chapter 8, poverty can remove individuals outside of usual support systems, and at times of widespread poverty these systems collapse. Thus a recent study among the Chagga in Tanzania records how a child may die of malnutrition while living in the compound of a wealthy relative if the mother is considered an outcast (Howard and Millard 1997). Collapse may occur in times of conflict or famine, or when official interventions undermine livelihoods: members of the Ik would formerly share meat, but now, forbidden to hunt by the creation of a nature reserve, they take any kill into the bush to eat alone (Turnbull 1973).

African politicians, such as Kaunda in a statement on humanism, have held up the care of the vulnerable inherent in African social systems as a sign of moral superiority over more developed countries. In fact, different household structures provide support for different individuals. Two ethnic groups with a bilateral tradition—the Hausa and Amhara—have produced among the highest proportion of beggars on the continent. Although the universality of the nuclear family is a matter of contention, a sizeable body of opinion holds that more extended family structures provide social safety nets to prevent family members from falling into extreme poverty. This extended family goes beyond the bounds of the immediate household, so that remittances form a large part of the income of many households: participatory analysis repeatedly finds the poor being identified as those who rely on others for food in the lean period.

Surveys typically find that large households are disproportionately represented among the poor. This finding has been questioned on methodological grounds related to possible economies of scale in household production and consumption. The view of an automatic link between household size and poverty is also not supported by evidence from Participatory Poverty Assessments—there are some communities in which well-off households are the large ones (partly as "unsuccessful families" break up). But more important than these methodological disputes is a recognition that large households differ considerably from one another: it is household composition that matters rather than size per se. This point can be simply expressed by saying that a rural household of 10 with two adults and eight children aged less than 10 will very likely be poor, whereas a household with four or five able-bodied adults is far less likely to be so.[1] The dependency ratio is thus an important poverty correlate. The presence of young children, elderly dependents, or disabled family members all, by adding a nonproductive mouth to feed, reduce the family's mean consumption. In Tanzania households with a disabled family member had mean consumption 20 percent less than the average for the country as a whole (Cortijo and LeBrun 1999). This point does not deny the possible importance of economies of scale in household consumption, so that normalizing by family size may give misleading results.

Families with high child/adult ratios are more likely to be poor, but it is also the poor who are likely to have such ratios. Among better off families, women are more likely to be educated and have access to paid employment, so that the opportunity cost of their time is higher. Moreover, richer families may "substitute child quality for child quantity," and provide them with the education to also obtain formal employment. Hence the demographic transition—described below—that manifests itself in declining child/adult ratios at the household level will occur first among the nonpoor.

Different forms of household structure can affect household size in ways that might be expected to be related to poverty. For example, polygamous households might be expected to be poorer as one man's assets are spread over several wives and their children—and junior wives and their children are seen as being particularly at risk. But, on the other hand, it is richer men who will be able to attract multiple wives. Once again, since the household contains a high proportion of adults, it is not as likely to be poor. Female-headed households are often—although not always—disproportionately poor; but if such households include those with an absent male who is remitting income, then they can be among the better off. But if the household lacks an able-bodied male, it is disadvantaged by a female/male imbalance, and perhaps doubly so if the child/adult ratio is also high: lack of able-bodied (male) labor is the key characteristic of the poorest. In Tanzania, female-headed households with no supporting male have a level of mean consumption that is barely half that of other female-headed households (Cortijo and LeBrun 1999). The security afforded to a widow by the tradition that one of her sons is responsible for her well-being is rather negated by the loss of her right to the property that was her husband's, or widespread land grabbing where such a right exists.

An individual's exposure to poverty also depends on the interaction of family structure, livelihood strategies, and the stage of household life cycle. An agriculture-based household with many young children will have low mean consumption, but this will increase as the children can be productively employed in household production or in the period in which they migrate but have no family of their own. Through remittances, elder children pay for the education of their younger siblings. In poorer families such migration is more a matter of necessity; one mother lamented her eldest son having to leave school so he could go away to earn money so she could buy food for the youngest child—"killing the old to save the young" (Howard and Millard 1997). A poverty trap is thus created in which the children of the poor are denied access to education by the need to feed the family. The parents' consumption will be maintained if grown children successfully establish their own production. For an urban household children may be a burden on the household for longer, unless this burden can be spread among relatives, so that young children are sent to live with grandparents or others may go to another relative nearer school.

Since poverty depends on household structure, poverty trends will be affected by changes in these structures, which are very largely driven by the demographic transition.

The Demographic Transition Is Under Way

The demographic transition is the change from high levels of fertility and mortality to low ones, so that population growth tends to low levels, or even zero, as fertility rates approach the replacement rate. Typically people start to live longer and infant and child mortality drop before any decline in fertility, so that a period of rapid population growth is experienced. Socioeconomic development, and lower under-five mortality itself, then set in train a trend toward lower fertility. The now developed countries underwent the demographic transition over several decades starting in the last century. Most developing regions are now well under way with the transition (table 10.1) although Africa has been an apparent exception with birth rates both well above those of elsewhere and having the lowest observed decrease. Such figures have led some commentators to talk of a "delayed demographic transition" in Africa and speculate upon cultural factors—such as beliefs about ancestors living on in current generations and lesser social sanctions against pre- and extramarital sex—which act as a barrier to reduced population growth. But the most recent evidence, mainly collected in the three rounds of Demographic Health Surveys, shows large declines in fertility in some countries over the last two decades and modest reductions in several more.

Population data are scanty before 1960, so that demographic trends before the last three decades are necessarily a matter of some speculation. Nonetheless, it seems likely that, while mortality decline was being recorded since at least the 1940s, fertility was actually rising, which is consistent with evidence that fertility rose in other regions before the onset of fertility decline, and with economic models of the household that predict higher fertility as a result of income rises at low-income levels. The available data confirm that increases in fertility were being observed in some countries into the 1970s; for example, a rise in Angola from 6.4 in 1960 to 8.0 in the early 1980s, from 4.9 to 6.1 in the Central African Republic from 1959 to 1988, and in Mauritania from 6.5 in the early 1960s to 7.2 a decade later (see appendix 1). Higher fertility may be attributed to the erosion of traditional attitudes supporting breast-feeding and postpartum abstinence for two to three years and increased availability of medical treatment for causes of infecundity, such as venereal diseases. Breast-feeding may have a natural contraceptive effect, in addition to which in many African societies it is believed bad for a pregnant woman to breast-feed, so that sex is

prohibited during this period (a period of postpartum abstinence of up to two years is not uncommon). Western medicine rejects these views, perhaps unwisely as, while it is not that the milk of a pregnant woman is bad, it is so that child health suffers from close child-spacing, and missionaries, particularly the Catholic church, explicitly attacked such beliefs. For these reasons the relationship between female education and fertility in Africa is an inverted U shape: education initially leads to higher fertility as traditional beliefs are abandoned but later to declines as educated women are more likely to have the characteristics associated with lower fertility (namely, formal-sector employment, later marriage, and access to modern contraception).

Two further factors, HIV/AIDS and conflict, may be expected to further accelerate the fertility decline, though their effects may be less than commonly believed. AIDS will reduce fertility as it encourages contraception and abstinence, and very directly as women die before completing the reproductive period of their life. But while fertility reductions may occur on account of AIDS, it is less clear that it will promote the transition to yet lower fertility. This transition occurs as the age structure shifts to reduce the dependency ratio and there is an improved capacity to save. But the impact of AIDS on the age structure is limited, and any beneficial effects on savings are outweighed by the high costs borne by the families of AIDS victims. Conflict may have a short-term effect on fertility as young couples are separated and partners killed, but there is every possibility that reunited couples, or remarried widows, will still attain their target level of fertility.

In countries with "fair" data, moderate to large reductions in fertility (1.5 or more) have taken place in the last two decades in Botswana, Côte d'Ivoire, Kenya, Rwanda, Senegal, South Africa, and Zimbabwe, and moderate declines (0.5 to 1.5) in Benin, Burkina Faso, Cameroon, Ghana, Malawi, and Tanzania. Clear, though rather smaller, declines

Table 10.1 The demographic transition: birth and death rates by region

	Crude birth rate		Crude death rate		Population growth	
	1980	1996	1980	1996	1980–96	1996–2010
East Asia and Pacific	22	19	8	7	1.5	0.9
Europe and Central Asia	19	13	10	11	0.7	0.2
Latin America and Caribbean	31	23	8	7	1.9	1.4
Middle East and North Africa	41	29	11	7	2.9	2.1
South Asia	37	27	14	9	2.1	1.5
Sub-Saharan Africa	47	41	18	14	2.8	2.5

Source: World Development Indicators 1998, tables 2.1 and 2.2.

are also apparent in Namibia, Niger, Madagascar, Uganda, and northern Sudan. Although the data are weaker, Ethiopia and Swaziland also seem to have experienced large declines and Eritrea, Gambia, Lesotho, and Mauritania smaller ones. Mali is the only country with fair data showing no perceptible fertility decline. These trends are most marked among educated women and those living in urban areas; indeed fertility is falling quite sharply among these groups even in countries in which the overall trend is quite weak. Thus fertility declines first among groups that are less likely to be poor.

Various mechanisms link lower fertility to poverty reduction. There are many arguments at the macroeconomic level as to why lower fertility will boost growth and improve income distribution. For example, lower dependency ratios will increase savings, and reduced labor supply will increase real wages. Econometric analysis supports the link between lower fertility and poverty reduction, particularly in the high-fertility/low-income setting that characterizes most African countries. A cross-country analysis suggested that, in Africa, a reduction in the total fertility rate of 4 per 1,000 may be expected to reduce the incidence of income poverty by more than 7 percent.[2] These macroeconomic benefits will be felt by poor families even if their own fertility levels at not falling. But many of the household level gains depend upon fertility decline among the poor themselves. At the microeconomic level larger families tend to be poorer, and family size has a strong inverse relationship with child welfare. Poor households with many children cannot afford to adequately clothe and feed them let alone send them to school. Child mortality is higher among larger families, as is maternal mortality, especially for older mothers giving birth to high birth-order children. Reducing fertility will thus decrease mortality, which in turn will further reduce fertility.

While there is clear evidence of the start of the demographic transition, two important caveats apply. First, contraception appears to be used for child-spacing rather than limiting family size: this conclusion can be drawn both from mothers' expressed preferences and observing the structure of births. Second, and related to the first point, fertility rates remain high by international standards, and there is no immediate prospect of them declining to replacement levels. On the other hand, the fact that fertility levels remain high means that there is scope for further reductions and the consequent beneficial effects on poverty. So which factors have been responsible for falling fertility and are these amenable to policy intervention?

The demographic transition has typically been led by socioeconomic development, and rising incomes in particular. But many countries in Africa have experienced prolonged economic decline, leading some to speculate that the region is experiencing a "crisis-led transition." While this latter argument must be rejected in the face of overwhelming evidence in support of a positive relationship between transition and economic performance, it is clear that the source of the African transition has been factors other than growth. The most likely causes are lower under-five mortality and female education. Associated with these two factors are later age at marriage and increased contraceptive use.

Despite speculation about the increase in births outside of marriage, there is in Africa, as elsewhere, a strong relation between mother's age at first birth and age at marriage: teenage fertility is highest in Niger where the median age at first marriage is 14.9 (among the lowest in Africa), but much lower in Burundi where the average at first marriage is 19.5 years. Comparison of the age of first marriage of women aged 20–25 with those now aged 45–49 demonstrates an upward trend. In Tanzania, for example, 60 percent of 20–25-year-olds were married by age 20, whereas 70 percent of 45–49 year olds were; for Senegal these figures are 60 and 83 percent, respectively, and for Côte d'Ivoire 59 and 68 percent.

While there is some truth in the view that "development is the best contraceptive," it alone will not prevent conception. There is a clear relationship between fertility and contraceptive use: countries with lower fertility have higher contraceptive use (contraceptive prevalence rates, figure 10.1). Contraceptive supply cannot lead the fertility decline, but for it to take effect they must be available.

Figure 10.1 Lower fertility is linked to adoption of contraception

Total fertility rate (children per woman)

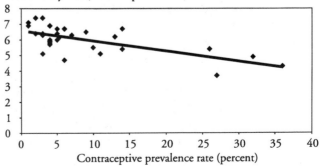

Contraceptive prevalence rate (percent)

Source: Lipton (1999, p. 10).

Figure 10.2 There remains a large unmet demand for contraception

Percentage of women of reproductive age

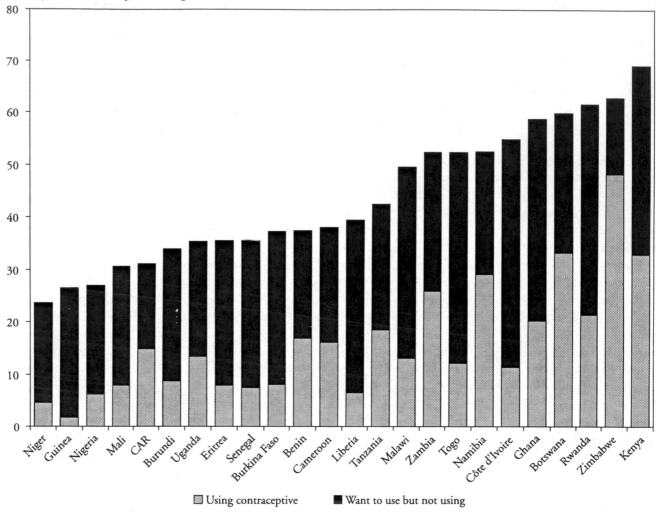

☐ Using contraceptive   ■ Want to use but not using

Source: Cohen (1998, p.1, 443).

Yet in Africa there is a large unmet demand for contraception: in Burkina Faso, Burundi, Côte d'Ivoire, Eritrea, Guinea, Mali, Nigeria, Senegal, and Togo, only one-quarter of women wishing to use contraceptives are actually doing so (figure 10.2). Increasing contraceptive availability is a major action government can take to facilitate the demographic transition and reap its poverty-reducing effects.

Contraceptive use is strongly related to female education: a study in the early 1990s found that contraceptive prevalence only rose above 10 percent in countries with mean female education of at least four years (Working Group on Factors Affecting Contraceptive Use 1993). But for women to use contraceptives they must be available. Contraceptive prevalence rates of less than 10 percent are observed, at least in part, as contraception is not readily

available to the vast majority of African women. Reproductive health services make a difference. Pilot project have frequently raised prevalence rates to above 20 percent in project areas in countries with low prevalence, and survey data show prevalence to be related to accessibility. Accessibility can be defined as distance to facilities (the contraceptive prevalence rate is higher amongst women living within five kilometers of a clinic), but also has a cost component, with the accessible alternative being defined as costing no more than 1 to 2 percent of household income, which in the early 1990s was not true for 19 out of 23 countries in Africa. Three countries with the highest rates of contraceptive use—Botswana, Kenya, and Zimbabwe (figure 10.2)—have well-established reproductive health systems providing subsidized services.

There have of course been programs to provide reproductive health services for many years, and it is important to make plans for the future, bearing in mind the lessons of the past. Programs have been plagued in part by weak government commitment, inadequate resources, and consequent lack of capacity. Reproductive health services will fail to have an impact if they focus unduly on women. As is vividly clear from the following account from a Chagga woman in Tanzania, many women do not have control over reproduction:

> I had been unsuccessful in keeping my door closed, and my husband gave me nine children. So I went to the clinic for some assistance to stop having more babies without informing my husband. They gave me prescription pills and I locked it in my personal box, but he found it and exploded. Right then he took me to bed, and that's why I stand before you, pregnant for the tenth time. (Howard and Millard 1997, p. 120)

Although reproductive health services are not that expensive, it is an area that requires continued donor support for some time to come.

Changing Household Structures and Demographics Provide a Case for State Intervention

The evidence presented in this chapter provides good and bad news for poverty reduction. The good news is that the demographic transition is under way, and that this trend will produce both macro and micro benefits that reduce poverty. But the micro benefits go first to the nonpoor, and there are impediments to the poor reducing family size. These impediments include lack of contraception and resistance to family planning, particularly by men. Countries that have gone the furthest with the demographic transition are those that have provided strong state support to family planning.

While the demographic transition is good news, it may be expected to further increase the vulnerability of the poor by limiting traditional safety nets for the poor. As already seen in chapter 8, these safety nets can handle idiosyncratic poverty but do not always do so, failing at times of widespread hardship. The policy implications of these facts differ, but once again imply state action if poverty is to be reduced.

Notes

1. However, this picture is further complicated by differential consumption requirements, which may be partly determined by cultural norms.

2. Two recent papers demonstrating the link between demographic change and macroeconomic performance are Eastwood and Lipton (1999) and Bloom and Canning (1999). The results quoted here are from the former study. The latter argues there is a virtuous circle between reducing fertility and higher growth, which can be triggered by an exogenous intervention. The critical variable in their argument is the ratio between workers and dependents, which remains less than 1.2 in Africa compared to around 2.1 in East Asia.

CHAPTER 11

Women's Unequal Position Pervades the Poverty Problem

Poverty is not gender neutral. Research has demonstrated the disparities between men and women in access and control of land, credit, technology, education, and health (see chapters 8 and 9). Women's inequality in household decisionmaking and community and public participation is a well-documented fact. Table 11.1 presents evidence from selected countries on the scale of the problem: literacy is lower among women, they have less control over economic resources, and they are scarcely present in government.

Gender inequity in Africa operates alongside conditions of dire poverty and ill health. Women face multiple tasks and competing priorities as well as daily rearrangement of their priorities to ensure their survival as well as that of their children. The 1998 Poverty Status Report, *Gender Growth and Poverty Reduction in Africa*, argued that there are synergies between positive outcomes for women's well-being and pro-poor economic growth, estimating that the various disadvantages that women face reduce economic growth by nearly a full percentage point (0.8 percent) each year, with a concentration of loss in agriculture where women's labor is especially important but is often held back by the combination of farming work, childcare, and household duties.

This chapter draws together the gender issues from this report. The fundamental aspect of gender relations within the context of extreme poverty is based on the survival strategies of individuals, households, and other social groups. Within each of these groups, men and women are involved in bargaining over resources and obligations (Aggarwal 1997). Consequently, the central focus of the debate on gender and poverty should move further than the discussion of the subordination of women. Nonetheless, it is important to state women face constraints that derive from cultural attitudes and religious values that give women low status in society and relegate their work and needs to

second place. In September 1999 the supreme court in Zimbabwe ruled that women are inherently inferior to men, citing "the nature of African society" as the basis for its decision (*The Guardian*, September 25, 1999).

The household is an inappropriate unit of analysis in the measurement of poverty on account of intrahousehold variability in access and control of resources. Such data by themselves will not permit an understanding of the dynamic complexity of gender relations. One consequence of this is that, despite the fact that the dimensions of poverty are similar among men and women, their priorities differ significantly. For example, as major

Table 11.1 Women are disadvantaged in social, economic, and political life

	Female literacy (as a percentage of male)	Real GDP per capita (as a percentage of male)	In government positions (as a percentage of total)
Benin	44	70	15
CAR	53	63	5
Côte d'Ivoire	66	37	7
Djibouti	56	..	1
Malawi	60	73	4
Mauritania	56	59	5
Mozambique	44	70	13
Namibia	97	52	11
Niger	33	59	11
Sierra Leone	42	42	6
South Africa	98	45	7
Tanzania	76	90	10
Togo	56	50	3
Uganda	71	69	9
Zambia	81	64	8

Source: UNDP (United Nations Development Program), *Human Development Report 1999.*

caretakers of family health and welfare, women place greater importance on food, water, fuel, and health, while men stress the importance of economic activities (often visible productive assets such as cattle) that are not related to the immediate needs of their families. Hence, these priorities reflect significant differences in the ways men and women allocate their meagre resources. Decisions on family resource allocation therefore become a serious issue when the priorities of men and women differ and women lack the bargaining power to control decisionmaking over the majority of household resources.

Social Trends in Gender and Poverty

Gender-based poverty is a major feature of the African scene, one that is strongly connected to the high incidence of child poverty, and has adverse implications for the care of the elderly. The position of female-headed households with no economically active male (either present or working elsewhere) is the most severe. The lack of able-bodied male labor is a key characteristic of many of the poorest Africans. However, women who manage households for absent males can also be badly hit, especially if the males do not send regular money, perhaps as a consequence of starting a second family.

Environmental and civil conflicts also cause displacement of people just as does the breakdown of traditional family structures (increasingly high separation and divorce rates). All these circumstances deprive many rural households of male adult workers. Some parts of eastern and southern Africa are afflicted by diseases such as AIDS or by civil unrest and rebellion, as in central and western Africa. Women (wives, grandmothers, and sisters) must then assume complete responsibility for raising, feeding, and educating young children.

Female household heads tend to be younger and less educated than their male counterparts. They also have less land to work as well as less capital, inputs, and farm labor to work it with. Widows may have their land taken from them, so that they are forced to become dependent. Even where they retain control over land, the lack of a male household member denies them access to social networks necessary for certain types of production: female-headed households thus have to make adjustments to cropping patterns and farming systems that can result in decreases in production and, in some cases, shifts toward less nutritious crops. Not surprisingly, these households often suffer from increased malnutrition and food insecurity (Food and Agriculture Organization of the United Nations—FAO 1999). More generally, the sexual division of labor can reduce agricultural production, meaning that women's needs, such as improved water supply, go unmet as men accord them lower priority.

Economic Trends in Gender and Poverty

Some argue there is a feminization of poverty in Africa,[1] contributed to by factors such as limited skills and knowledge, unfriendly market structures that concentrate women in lower paying and time-consuming work and restrict their access to capital and credit, traditional family structures perpetuating gender inequality through patriarchal norms of property ownership and inheritance, discrimination in the public domain, nonrecognition of the value of women's work, the permanence of debt, weak and unequal trade and economic reforms, and the rise of fundamentalism of a religious, ethnic, or military kind.

Economic, demographic, and political trends are changing the rural landscape and affecting activities carried out by women. Agriculture is increasingly vertically integrated, coordinated, and responsive to market forces. Policies of economic liberalization and privatization aim to create a macroeconomic environment favoring economic growth. However, the gains from growth can be unequally distributed, and rural women can number among the losers since they are ill-equipped to benefit from the introduction of changes in agricultural processes and the rural economy.[2] They have less capacity than men in terms of education and training, less time to devote to productive resources, and less command over important resources such as land and capital. In some parts of Africa, the sexual division of labor precludes women from growing crops for sale, although women remain responsible for the bulk of agricultural labor. But this does not mean that men are unproductive; they operate in social space from which women are normally excluded and is essential for production and distribution to function (Kabeer and Whitehead 1999). Hence men are active in, and may well chair, "women's groups" set up in rural areas—and both men and women see this as natural, since men have knowledge of the official world of bureaucracy (see Crewe and Harrison 1998, for discussion of a Zambian case, and the more general discussion by Coquery-Vidrovitch 1997, of why women are dependent on men). The gender bias here is deeply rooted; it is not only ignorance of English or illiteracy in their own language that excludes women from these roles but also social norms concerning appropriate roles.

Women also have less incentive with regard to control over income from their labor as well as economic assets, to respond to economic signals. For example, modernization and mechanization can improve farm productivity and income, but they can also reduce the need for manual labor and therefore reduce options in rural communities. In poor households, the impact of technical change on men and women is frequently different, depending on whose tasks are mechanized, how workloads are affected, and who loses opportunities for paid work.

To sum up, one can state that poor women are confronted with three main obstacles:

- Discriminatory laws, policies, and practices that impede their access to productive resources (land, water) and institutional support (training, credit, services)
- Women's exclusion or marginal participation in organizations or in representation in public and political institutions
- Low investment in women's economic, managerial, and technical capability

To reverse this negative process, governments and development agencies are increasingly focusing on programs to empower women. However, programs designed to alleviate the conditions of poverty through increasing the capacity of women have often been unsuccessful, providing minimal benefits and adding new responsibilities to already overworked women. In rural households where girls are fully engaged in helping to take care of younger siblings and in the transport of water and fuelwood, families cannot afford to relinquish this important contribution that the girl child is making to help the family survive; without addressing these concerns, attempts to expand girls' education will be frustrated. Similarly, literacy programs have also been touted as vehicles to empower women, but literacy of itself can do little to help women and families with their immediate needs. Consequently, it would seem naïve to ask women to spend their limited time attending literacy classes without finding ways to lessen their burden. These examples reinforce the message of this report that poverty must be tackled on several fronts.

The empowerment of women cannot be achieved without representation. But the debate on gender takes place predominantly in urban centers and institutions of higher learning where poor rural women have little or no opportunity to express themselves. Are urban women's concerns representative? Even results from Participatory Poverty Assessments carried out in rural areas are often unrepresentative because the voices heard are often those of local elites and not-so-poor men who have more time available to contribute to such exercises. Both urban and rural women need to participate in decisions that affect their livelihoods. Women are unlikely to improve their levels of well-being while they are still marginalized and excluded from decisionmaking processes.

The Importance of Intrahousehold Relations

In the African context, the household should not be understood to mean the same as in the Western context. But it is one of the social units around which survival strategies are organized. In rural areas characterized by low productivity, agricultural production requires the participation of each member of the household, and gender relations in the household and in society play a critical role in shaping household strategies and determining their response to market incentives. In urban areas women have increasingly assumed the role of breadwinner, as men cannot find adequate paid employment. To some extent then households are comprised of individuals with common interests, but that does not preclude the importance of bargaining in the household over respective roles. The fulfillment of each of these roles ensures the survival of the entire household. Conflicts are often overshadowed by the most immediate goal of survival, though unsuccessful families can cease to exist.

Poverty Reinforces the Subordination of Women

As currently configured, women's projects do not question the status of women in their households and in the larger society. The improvement of women's income does not necessarily guarantee a change in their subordination. It is time to balance the process of empowerment through initiatives that support women in the domain of laws and culture. Both genders should be aware of the need to reexamine the values that justify some practices whether they are traditional or modern.

African poverty is deeply embedded in social attitudes and structures, and female poverty is manifested according to cultural context more so than male poverty—"they are less able to turn labor into income, income into choice and choice into personal well-being" (Kabeer and Whitehead 1999). The fight against poverty requires a concerted effort to understand the cultural mechanisms that create uncertainties and dependency. Unequal relationships between men and women create high levels of dependency and low levels of self-esteem among women who lack the power to make decisions. Based on such understanding, programs must design ways to overcome such disparities, which means addressing both men and women. For example, issues related to reproductive health should not be the sole responsibility of women but that of men, too. Empowering women to make informed reproductive health decisions must be accompanied by equal emphasis on men's role as the primary decisionmakers in matters related to reproduction. Even when women are "empowered" to make decisions, these must have the support in the household, especially of men. Unless this occurs, women have to bear the consequences of decisions they make without the support of their husbands and partners. Hence efforts towards lowering fertility must be directed toward men as well as women. Women's voices should be heard in the public debates through their opinion leaders in cabinets, parliaments, and civil society organizations.

The personal behavior of both men and women within the family—on the education of children, emerging roles and images, and self-esteem—is no longer determined in the private realm only; in fact, the traditional dichotomy between the public (male) and private (female) spheres is gradually disappearing. Today, traditional norms in African societies coexist with modern values and behavior, which often contradict each other. Such contradictions are manifested in the absence of a coherent set of values and beliefs to guide parents and children, mothers and fathers, to meet the challenges of the new millennium. The development agenda continues to superimpose ideas and strategies that are noble yet unrealistic to the ways in which families are organized. This critical socialization process should be the concern of any person or organization involved in the process of the transformation of African societies. The fight against poverty is not a mere program or project. It is at the heart of the development problem of Africa in the era of globalization.

Gender has entered the debate on poverty reduction, but due to its cross-cutting nature it is difficult to estimate how much has been achieved in policy implementation. Policymakers have been known to resort to tokenism with grand gestures that have little effect on the actual lives of rural women, while other policies are having an adverse impact on women (as noted above in the context of adjustment policies). Gender inequality cannot be solely tackled through the improvement of economic performance because of its socially embedded nature, but it can be addressed through narrow targeting that aims to deliver benefits to particular social groups such as rural landless women. If schemes can be context specific, both

politically and socially, they have a higher chance of success. But again, evidence shows that narrow targeting can lead to exclusionary practices, and because of this there is often a lack of political support because they are of no benefit other than to those who are directly targeted.

The Challenge of Poverty-Sensitive Policy and Planning

The challenge today is the modernization of very poor societies when knowledge, services, technologies, and democracy condition the market. Human resources development comes to the forefront of the challenges and opportunities. What is the vision for the new men and women that African societies need? How will they become productive and efficient workers? How will they empower themselves to become real citizens? What governance structures are required to allow all this to happen? Africans will have to create a new lifestyle that is sustainable, a balance between rural and urban. The new approach toward gender equality and development should learn lessons from the past. Development approaches of the last three decades have been frustrated by the intractable poverty in Africa. The reasons for the failure of such programs to remedy the situation are numerous. However, one constant factor that has been an impediment to progress in Africa has been the lack of appreciation of the survival strategies that are already in place in households. A program or an activity cannot replace the delicate balance that holds household members as a unit to provide basic necessities. Culture, beliefs, and values where accountability to the common good is paramount carefully support this balance. Activities such as empowerment threaten this balance if directed at a specific member, even for those who can benefit from it. While development programs have the flexibility to design their programs toward specific beneficiaries, it is naïve to think that households will reorient the ways they work, relate, help, and cooperate for daily survival. Terms such as long-term sustainability hold no meaning to those who are faced with immediate survival. Consequently, it is no wonder that those women beneficiaries who are supposedly waiting to be empowered are reluctant to abandon their collective security for individual empowerment, which holds very little meaning.

It is matter of high priority to enhance the capacity of governments, civil society associations, nongovernmental organizations, and international partners to collect primary data and to analyze and use gender disaggregated data for formulation of gender-responsive policies, strategies, and programs. Institutionalization of gender-sensitive planning will allow capture and response to new global trends and emerging issues. More specifically, the challenge is to help poor women take advantages of the new dynamics that the current macroeconomic trends are supposed to create. This involves promoting a systematic strategy directed towards the following:

- Raising the level of skills and productivity of women workers (rural and urban) through public and private investment in basic education and literacy, skills programs, and vocational training
- Eliminating legislative, administrative, socioeconomic, and attitudinal barriers to women's access to assets (land, capital, technology) through changes in legislation and proactive economic and social policy, institutional restructuring, and socioeconomic and gender analysis training
- Building and empowering women's organizations and enhancing their participation in mainstream policy and decisionmaking bodies

- Changing the mindset and operational procedures of institutions both public and private to increase their responsiveness to women's needs
- Building support for mechanisms that will allow men to be more responsive to the changes, to cope with their new responsibilities

Notes

1. A caveat is in order here since "feminization" implies a dynamic process. Data at any single point in time provide a static picture illustrating clear gender disparities. In some respects, such as school enrollments, these disparities are narrowing. For others, the belief is that they are widening, although data are hard to come by.

2. There can be exceptions to this general statement. In West Africa trading networks are dominated by women, some of whom have become very wealthy as internal trade has been liberalized. Even here, however, many women at the bottom end of the chain eke out a living on tiny margins.

PART III: *Poverty Reduction Policies*

Part III of the report discusses strategies for combating poverty. Chapter 12 outlines elements of an antipoverty strategy, which the following chapters address as (i) national policies, (ii) poverty monitoring, and (iii) the role of donors.

CHAPTER 12

Outlines of an Antipoverty Strategy

Promoting Social and Political Change for Poverty Reduction

Part II of this report demonstrated that poverty is deeply embedded in African social structures, and that political systems have militated against rather than promoted poverty reduction. Sustainable poverty reduction will only be achieved through social and political change. This is not to say that things cannot be done with the support of outside agencies to address proximate causes of poverty. They can, but they will only have short-term effects unless the underlying issues are also addressed, which can only be done in the domestic political context. Thus while part III lays out the elements of a poverty reduction strategy, it does not offer a blueprint. Each country's strategy must be borne out of a process of consultation and resulting government commitment to agreed-upon poverty reduction goals.

It follows from the analysis of chapter 5 that poverty reduction requires increases in the rate of economic growth and improvement in income distribution. But, in the end, poverty reduction is ultimately a political act. Governments that are not politically committed to poverty reduction will always find other areas and projects on which to spend the surpluses generated by the economy. But experiences from across Africa show that where governments have the will to act, they have the capacity to achieve results (see box 12.1; Greeley and Jenkins 1999). However, poverty reduction need not always derive from altruism; it is important for sustainable development and can even be so for political survival, and may become more so as political systems are liberalized. The disruptive political changes of the past decades have partly stemmed from the dissatisfaction of the common people.

Most African governments have had poverty reduction on top of their policy agendas. But practice has fallen far short of the ideal, even where, as in, say, Mozambique and Tanzania in the past, the government has been genuinely committed to social change. Effective steps toward poverty reduction require more concerted efforts than in the past and call for a method that enables the poor to sanction government. Unlike India, where poor people have established political parties that contest the elections, the African poor have little means of exercising their collective power. In this regard the new emphasis on decentralization as a means to greater rural participation might prove a useful means of getting the voices of the poor heard, although doubts have also been expressed about this. More generally, the growth of civil society, including a free press, will create mechanisms that hold government accountable in ways that can protect the poor, as the antifamine contract has in South Asia (see chapter 7).

Policymakers' unwillingness to concede to the seriousness of the poverty problem also meant that the capacity for evaluation, policy prescription, and monitoring has been poorly developed. As the process of internalizing poverty reduction policies gets under way in most African countries, it will be necessary to develop capacities in all areas of poverty analysis. The credibility of African governments will be enhanced when they have set themselves realistic poverty reduction goals and initiated monitoring programs by which they may be held accountable for progress, or lack thereof, toward these goals. The creation of such systems requires training, implying a role for donor support. Not only do countries need to monitor and analyze all aspects of household composition, determinants of poverty, and access to services, they also need to develop the competence needed to evaluate

---

Box 12.1 Government action to improve well-being: AIDS prevention in Senegal

While HIV/AIDS has taken hold in countries across Africa, in Senegal the prevalence rate has remained at less than 2 percent over the last 10 years. Forestalling the spread of the epidemic has been achieved through changes in sexual practices brought about by a concerted government campaign.

Unlike some other African countries, the Senegalese government has been the driving force behind tackling AIDS at home, and led the way for the Organization of African Unity's AIDS declaration in 1992. Most of the country's population is either Muslim or Christian, so religious leaders were brought into the program at an early stage, gaining their acceptance of the messages to be conveyed.

Surveys show a very high knowledge of AIDS, how it is spread, and how to prevent it. And this knowledge has trans-

lated into changed behavior. Women are postponing the age at which they first have sex—the median being nearly 19 among 20–24-year-olds compared to under 17 for 40–44 year olds. Data on condom use are hard to gather for the population as a whole, but sales have risen from 800,000 in 1988 to seven million in 1997. The vast majority of sex workers report that they use condoms with all paying partners. Such high levels of condom use are unknown elsewhere in Africa, with the exception of Uganda, where a combination of observing the effects of the disease firsthand and government efforts have raised AIDS awareness and preventative practices.

Senegal's success in combating AIDS clearly shows that African governments can have the capacity to implement successful programs if they have the commitment.

Source: UNAIDS (1999).

---

the impact of macroeconomic policies on the income generation and livelihoods of the poor. There have been steps in this direction in the 1990s, with the development of poverty monitoring systems. Such systems can also be developed on a sector basis, a good example being performance agreements in the Ghanaian health service, including targets for both service delivery and improvements in output indicators (Booth 1999). Building a political consensus around poverty reduction targets is at the heart of the rights-based approach to poverty reduction, in which improved living standards become a right citizens can claim from a country's leaders.

As more and more African governments begin to acknowledge the importance of poverty reduction, they need to begin changing their structures and priorities. The most crucial of these relate to the national budget. A poverty-reducing government will not be credible if it continues to sustain a budget structure that favors, for example, military expenditure as opposed to health and education or rural development. However, even countries with higher social-sector expenditure have not always been able to have a real impact on service provision in the countryside, since spending has been skewed to services less utilized by the poor, and the bulk of the resources were spent within line ministries, with little reaching the local level. The public sector thus also needs to develop systems that can deliver resources efficiently to the local administration, and at that level to make sure that the target groups are reached. Few governments have developed social safety nets, but there is ample scope for targeting the most vulnerable groups. The special position

of children for whom poverty has irreversible consequences, particularly orphans created by the ravages of conflict and HIV/AIDS, requires special emphasis here.

The harder challenge is confronting the social inequalities that perpetuate poverty through discrimination against marginal groups by reasons of age, sex, disability, or ethnicity. As has been done in India in the case of the caste system, legal measures can make some progress toward redressing the situation. For example, women's rights to access to land on an equal basis with men can be legally enshrined. On the other hand, legal measures alone will not be sufficient, as the continuation of slavery shows.

While women are hardly a homogeneous group, they are disproportionately represented among the poorest groups of the country, who can be subject to many types of deprivation. While many African countries are formulating gender-friendly policies, the recent experience of South Africa indicates that serious implementation of gender-sensitive programs will only begin when women in their own right become policymakers, as well as community leaders. However, as Pregs Govender, an African National Congress Member of Parliament, warned, when "women begin to engage in economic debates, they will initially have to run the gamut of dismissive responses which put issues such as poverty or lack of child care or loss of parental rights outside the arena of economic debate because the latter is concerned with the much more serious and significant macro level" (see Govender 1998). Although female involvement in politics and decision-making is crucial to reversing the gender imbalance and related poverty, the means of implementation must evolve within the political structures and environment of each country. It cannot be assumed that formal democratization will go far enough in empowering disempowered groups such as rural women, so that mechanisms need to be in place to ensure their voice is heard.

The Primacy of Pro-Poor Growth

Past experience and an examination of fundamental growth determinants in Africa suggests that most countries are unlikely to sustain the growth rates required to reduce poverty if growth is distribution neutral. While there is no clear picture of the extent to which growth has been pro- or antipoor, this statement alone is sufficient to suggest that there should be a concern with distribution. Growth is central to poverty reduction, but so is ensuring that growth is inclusive. It is thus important for governments to re-create and promote policy environments that are supportive of the expansion of sectors that increase the income-generating capacities of the poor. There is general agreement that credible poverty reduction cannot be pursued in an environment of macroeconomic instability, or of serious fiscal and external payments imbalance. The postindependence experience, including the era of economic reform, indicates that countries that pursued sensible policies, including those that reduced inflation, created incentives for increased domestic investment, and encouraged economic efficiency by promoting market-based economic activities, were best placed to generate sustainable economic growth. While growth increased in the 1990s, however, the impact on some of the poorest groups may have been small (though the evidence remains scanty), with even signs in some countries of further deprivation of the weaker groups, either as growth has not been sufficient to offset other adverse trends or poverty-inducing effects of policies themselves. Important groups of the poor are likely to be bypassed by growth, which means that government must pay attention to the pattern of growth and provide safety nets. If it is to reduce poverty, growth must be inclusive growth.

Hence current policies for promoting growth are not sufficient. First, the structural impediments to sustained growth need be addressed. Second, the pattern of growth should be a matter of policy concern, requiring reformulation of some policies and addition of others. Third, supplementary interventions are required to reach the substantial numbers who will not benefit from growth. The last two points follow from the fact that distribution must improve if poverty reduction is to be achieved.

However, little thought has been given by policymakers even to the meaning of pro-poor growth, let alone how it is to be achieved. What, then, are pro-poor growth policies?

The impact of growth on the poor depends largely on the extent of their participation in the economy, reflecting in turn on their ownership of assets, the supply and demand of their factors of production, as well as their access to markets for inputs and outputs. However, in many countries the poor have withdrawn from the modern economy. While this withdrawal, often forced, could imply short-term advantages, notably escaping "taxation without services," households that have entirely withdrawn from the mainstream tend to fall deeper into poverty. Their reincorporation into the economy will depend in large part on improving their access to assets of all kinds. A related argument is that policies should pay attention to the vulnerable as well as the poor—action should be taken to prevent those dependent on fragile livelihoods from falling into destitution.

Enhancing the assets of the poor includes investing in physical and human capital. Labor-intensive public works are among the doubly blessed measures that directly increase the incomes of the poor while at the same time laying the basis for growth. Access to affordable healthcare is also important for the productivity of the farmers and other poor groups. However, as in the case of education, this presupposes a more dynamic economic environment—including good access to markets—in which investments in human capital, that is good health and better education or information, are worthwhile. Given limited employment opportunities, there is also a requirement for improved access to other factors of production, notably land and capital. That is, action on one front alone will not be sufficient: there is not a single bottleneck holding back poverty reduction but rather an interacting range of factors. Both governments and donors have failed to confront issues of asset redistribution, which is a possible fast-track to sustained poverty reduction. Development of rural infrastructure is an important example of an asset that can benefit the poor in many ways: employment creation through public works, improved access to markets and services, and greater availability of goods. Biases in both government and donor spending have shifted infrastructure development away from such activities.

The role of the private sector in African economies in the past decade has been greatly enhanced by economic liberalization. The donor community has also emphasized the importance of encouraging the private sector in all areas, including provision of services and infrastructure development, as well as the provision of transport services. Since it is believed that with time the bulk of the African economies will be in private hands, it is imperative to begin defining a role for the private sector in poverty reduction. However, the expanding formal private sector is in many countries vehemently opposed to labor unions and minimum wage legislation. The sector also opposes all fiscal adjustment that has tax implications on its activities. Still, in the emerging framework, which in some countries is seeing the beginning of the growth of a middle class, the poor might yet find champions among the business classes, even if more for reasons of profit than altruism.

Making growth more inclusive will benefit many of the poor. But some, such as the elderly, disabled, and many single women, may be left out of this process, so that consumption transfers will be a part of a poverty-reduction strategy.

But government actions are only a part of the lives of the poor, and most of the effort in reducing African poverty will come from the poor themselves. Thus government actions should reinforce rather than counteract the coping strategies adopted by the poor. The policy measures mentioned here can largely be seen in that light—for example, improving access to markets and services and providing a secure environment. But some governments continue to take steps to the detriment of the poor—action against street traders is a common, visible manifestation of this, but other constraints are also placed on the workings of the informal sector.

The Need for an Integrated Approach

Since the different dimensions of poverty reinforce each other, many poverty-reducing policies are complementary to one another. Good health, education, and water supply go hand in hand, and all of them, along with infrastructure and credit, facilitate higher incomes. But there is, of course, a social base to social exclusion that reminds us that poverty reduction will be part of a longer run process of social change.

It is a mistake, therefore, to think that the priority is "to get growth going" before having the luxury of turning attention to these other issues. It is in part precisely because growth is so important that these other things matter so much. Without increasing the basic capabilities of the poor, the prospects for sustained growth are not encouraging. The need is for balanced development.

Stressing the importance of an integrated approach often goes under the label of sustainable livelihoods. But many will see echoes of the integrated rural development projects of the 1970s and early 1980s, or even of the community development movement in the 1950s (and earlier in Africa, being promoted by both British and French colonial governments in the 1940s). These approaches are widely perceived to have failed. Learning from the mistakes of the past is crucial in succeeding today. A primary lesson is to be wary of grandiose schemes, particularly ones that have little basis in reality. The current fashion for Poverty Reduction Strategies may be helpful in focusing attention on poverty reduction. They may not be helpful if they promote the idea that a simple planning exercise will really tackle the problem. There is indeed a need to tackle the problem on many fronts, whether or not that requires unifying them into a single strategy is a moot point.

The Role of Donors

Donors need to behave rather differently than in the past in two ways. First, they must take seriously their own commitment to poverty reduction and so improve their rather poor record at devoting resources to this end and in having a positive impact on the poor. Second, the formulation of poverty-reduction policies must be a matter for national governments, so that donors must provide the space for these policies to be formulated and discussed and plans prepared for implementation. Important areas for donor involvement will remain, of which debt relief is one that deserves to be singled out.

Conclusion

The antipoverty agenda outlined here is based on the simple precept of inclusion. To realize sustainable reductions in poverty, the poor must be included in the growth process, which has to be broad enough to include sectors where the poor derive a livelihood. However, owing to sickness and poor nutrition, the poor might not be in a position to raise their productivity, even if the market incentives were to improve, pointing to the necessity for better service provision in the countryside. However, African experience shows that policymakers' capacity for commitment is inadequate, and that there is need for constant political challenge as well as pressure. It is thus useful to see poverty reduction as a political act that reflects the government's capacity to respond to the needs of the majority of the population. However, poverty is dynamic and multifaceted, demanding that governments also evolve capacities for its monitoring in order to reach relevant policy prescriptions. Finally, while it is tempting to see poverty reduction as solely a public sector activity, the view needs revision in light of the expanding role of the private sector in the African economies.

CHAPTER 13

National Policies for Reducing Poverty

The Policy Challenge

The problem of mass poverty is an acutely difficult one for African policymakers as well as for donors wishing to support their efforts, for the eradication of poverty is not readily achieved through the conventional instruments and modalities of policy, and quick results will be particularly hard to achieve. Indeed, poverty is not a single affliction but represents a range of problems. There are two sources of difficulty, one arising from the nature of the problem, and another arising from the limitations of what the state can achieve in the circumstances of many African countries.

The difficult nature of the problem

The description of poverty in chapter 3 provided an insight into some of the difficulties. Some stress is placed there on the multifaceted and socially relative nature of poverty, factors that necessitate flexible and inclusive approaches to its reduction. Social analysts stress the importance of the social context in which poverty occurs and the differences among poor individuals or households, even within a given community. In the extreme case, they contest the validity of aggregations and general policy recommendations. Even if such a position is seen as too extreme, there remains the large kernel of truth that governments and their advisers are grappling with a complex array of dilemmas that take different forms in different places and at different times and, therefore, call for much more information—and capacity to utilize it—than will normally be available. The multifaceted nature of the poverty problem presents a web of factors that cannot be penetrated by interventions focusing on a single item or emanating from just one level of government.

In most African countries, lack of information and means to appreciate the full extent and nature of poverty remains a serious impediment to poverty-reduction efforts. Hence chapter 14 discusses recommendations for data collection, research, and monitoring. The need is not just for more information about the specifics of poverty in a given country but also about how the poor participate in the wider economy and the degree to which they are able to influence the policies that affect them. It is *individuals* who are poor, so policymakers need to understand how the policies they can deploy work their way through to poor people. This need is all the greater because many of the structurally poor are economically marginalized, operating on the fringes of the modern economy, touched more by state failure, for example, lack of social services, than success, with adjustment-induced improvements in economic performance bringing few immediate benefits. Or, as also addressed in chapter 3, they may not be economically active at all: the dependent poor, including orphans, poor widows, the aged generally, and the disabled. Many of these rely on relatives for survival, often female, but many others, such as street children, beggars, and AIDS victims, have slipped through traditional safety nets. These are people for whom it is difficult for the states to reach.

The socially entrenched nature of important aspects of the poverty problem, particularly as it serves to disadvantage women, is also critical. This fact draws attention to a limitation on what it is realistic to expect to achieve through the state. What usually happens when policy gets much ahead of social practice and opinion is that large discrepancies emerge between what the law (or the president) specifies should happen and actual practice. Recent African experience is littered with well-meaning attempts at social engineering that were ignored in practice. While a large number of countries have in recent years adopted legislation and other measures to protect women and children and other vulnerable categories, they have few means of enforcing them. The persistence of slavery has already been cited as another example. Instability of governments and policies, and weak executive capabilities, undermine the credibility of announced measures.

Although poor policy implementation is often blamed on inadequate resources, lack of political support for poverty reduction has been the real culprit. In Sub-Saharan Africa, countries that have been able to tackle the AIDS pandemic, reducing the rate of prevalence, notably Uganda and Senegal, are not among the continent's richest. Moreover, although no African country has been able to establish a firm record on poverty reduction, countries that are making strides in the right direction are characterized by a higher level of political commitment than their poorly performing neighbors. The main requirement for poverty reduction in Africa is thus for poverty reduction to be placed firmly and seriously on the political agenda. There are limits to the role the donor community can play in this process, though the International Development Targets may have a part to play in holding governments accountable for their performance (see section on setting targets below). While these political changes are essential, it is important not to forget the limitations to what the state can achieve.

The limitations of the state

The difficulties just described should be set against the limited capabilities of the state in Africa: a result of the narrowness of the tax base relative to the manifold claims on revenues (including those of external and domestic creditors). They are also limited by shortages of skills and social capital. The power of decentralization is partly constrained by limited capacity at the local level (chapter 7), but analysis of poverty-reduction policies more generally in Ghana (Booth 1999) has stressed the importance of effective government, which must be able to do anything, and moves toward such a position are a vital step toward more specific attempts at poverty reduction. Enhancing institutional capacity is a critical part of tackling poverty. Presently governments are often overwhelmed by the scale of the tasks they confront, sometimes compounded by the excessive demands of a multitude of aid donors. Hence governments in Africa have revealed limited capacity to deliver education, health, and other services of a sufficient quality and in appropriate forms to benefit the poor.

There is a particular problem with targeting. Slight resources and often growing inequalities indicate the desirability of targeting interventions on poverty groups. Depending on how the poor are defined, efficient targeting makes heavy informational and administrative demands. It also has a larger drawback: the political sustainability of narrowly targeted services, excluding the nonpoor from benefits, is often fragile. This is a particular example of the more generic problem of the limited constituency for pro-poor measures (see chapter 7).

Political cultures may get in the way by other routes. In many African countries the established modalities of government are generally top-down, with little recent tradition of strong local governments and effective grassroots initiatives. Against this, many argue that the best antipoverty interventions for reaching the poor are bottom-up, incorporating local participation and ownership. However, experience has shown that even grassroots initiatives, for example those in primary education cited by Hoppers (1989) and Fuller (1989) for Zambia and Malawi, respectively, are often undertaken by the better off, even in rural areas. Moreover, the participatory approach itself remains controversial, with its advantages needing to be set against the dangers of undermining the development of representative local political structures.

These considerations need not imply a fatalistic retreat into laissez-faire. Rather, it poses a challenge to policy makers to overcome the difficulties described. There is still much that governments can do, as becomes clear below. But it is important, too, to be realistic about what can be achieved and how rapidly. Once again, the importance of mobilizing a large constituency of support for antipoverty measures is underlined. So too is the message that governments and donors should work in a sustained way at local levels, with communities and civil society.

The need to fill gaps in knowledge

At various points in this report, gaps in knowledge have been identified. Filling these gaps is one crucial element to devising effective poverty-reduction strategies. The most pressing areas are the following:

- Determining the extent and nature of transitory poverty
- Understanding better the workings of labor markets, particularly in rural areas
- Assessing how changes in land tenure systems will affect the poor

- Developing guidelines for effective targeted programs
- Identifying the trade-offs between growth and distribution. In other words, determining how growth can be made more pro-poor without sacrificing a high rate of growth.

Two Initial Truisms

There can be no solution to African poverty without sustained accelerated growth. Chapter 5 illustrated the past slowness of African growth and the grave implications of this fact for the extent of material poverty. Given the severe limitations on what can be achieved in the face of widespread poverty by redistribution of existing income and assets, improved growth is essential for satisfactory poverty reduction. There are cases of rapid growth in Africa, notably Botswana, and Ghana and Uganda have also achieved periods of sustained growth at reasonable levels, and these successes can be linked with reversing the tide of rising poverty. Each of these three countries had a government with a serious political commitment to growth.

In the 1970s African growth managed to stay ahead of population growth, albeit only slightly. But in the 1980s the average rate fell back to around 2 percent, reducing per capita incomes. There has been some recovery in the 1990s, but this has not spread to all countries, so average growth remains at around 2.5 percent, or about the same as the rate of population growth. Various estimates, such as those by the Economic Commission for Africa, indicate that, with unchanging income distributions, gross domestic product growth needs to reach around 7 percent to achieve the international target of a 50 percent poverty reduction by 2015, or even simply to prevent further increases in absolute numbers of the poor.

While there are grounds for some optimism on the basis of a handful of success stories and the modest upturn in growth in the 1990s, there are two clear implications from the analysis of Africa's growth performance. First, there remain significant structural impediments to growth, such as the continent's weak infrastructure base, as well as also political factors, which need to be addressed as part of growth-promotion policies. Second, growth is extremely unlikely to attain the required levels. The second point leads us to the next truism.

There can be no solution to African poverty without attention to income distribution. The constraints on growth acceleration imply that growth cannot solve the problem at a satisfactory pace without attending to the distribution of benefits. This fact is compounded by the negative effects of the large and, in some cases, apparently grow-

ing existing inequalities, which not only reduce the poverty-reduction effects of growth but also tend to retard the pace of growth itself. That highly skewed income distribution is bad for growth, and thus for poverty reduction, is illustrated by a number of African experiences. In the boom decades of the 1960s and 1970s, many African countries, including Côte d'Ivoire and Nigeria, were able to raise their rates of capital formation to "tiger" levels, but failed, in spite of initially high growth, to reach the prosperity of the East Asian countries with which they were at par at the end of the 1950s. The latter had been able to include more of their populations in the growth process by enhancing their human capital via improvement of social services, boosting agriculture via land reform, and ensuring a degree of political accountability. The bulk of the African investment was in "enclaves," plantations and oil production, and urban-based industry so that the resulting benefits of infrastructure expansion, growth, and rapid income increases were poorly distributed among sectors and the population. In few cases, the many projects undertaken in the expansive years had a lasting effect on poverty reduction. In some cases, the expansion of the "modern" economy hit directly at rural agriculture, with some peasants retreating entirely into subsistence. Poor distribution of benefits ultimately led to fragility of the growth process. With the recent recovery and resumption of per capita growth in some countries, governments are attempting to make the growth impact broader and more inclusive by undertaking administrative and land reforms, and improving marketing structures and rural access to services. However, for growth to be poverty reducing, policy implementation must be more effective in the future.

It is thus important to reiterate the point made in chapter 5 that measures to address distributional issues are required for African poverty reduction. The dissection of the nature of poverty reveals a number of groups seriously at risk of being left out of general economic expansion. Hence the possible gains of economically dependent poor (children, aged, handicapped, single women) are contingent on sharing mechanisms, social structures, and distributional trends. But even some of the economically active poor are at risk, and are particularly likely to be so if unfettered market forces remain the mainstay of development strategy, including many among subsistence farmers, pastoralists, and informal-sector workers. Thus satisfactory poverty reduction also depends on the pattern of growth, particularly with respect to its employment-creating qualities, and the safety nets put in place to protect those most at risk. These arguments are strengthened by the growing evidence that the poor distribution has in itself been a major factor behind the continent's flawed growth record. Many of these factors point to the importance of the agricultural sector, which can provide labor-intensive growth, generating higher incomes for many of the poorest. There is not a choice between growth and distribution: both are essential.

Other Principles of a Poverty-Reduction Strategy

This chapter outlines other principles for a poverty-reduction strategy. The first, which the donor community particularly needs to take to heart, is precisely that there cannot and should not be a blueprint for poverty reduction. The other principles discussed are that ownership should extend beyond central governments, the importance of a comprehensive strategy, and the need to address causes of poverty.

There can be no blueprint for poverty reduction

Earlier chapters illustrated the wide variety of countries' initial situations, histories, economic and social structures, resource endowments, incidence and nature of poverty, growth records, and so forth. The great variety in the level and composition of poverty imply a similar variety in country poverty-reduction strategies with respect to specificity and local ownership. The only way to ensure such a variety is the basis for the second principle: wider society needs to be engaged, and a coalition of support needs to be built.

Local strategies require local knowledge of both the nature of poverty and of political conditions. A second equally important reason for local design is that poverty-reduction strategies will only make a lasting difference to poverty if there is local ownership. Local ownership does not mean holding a few meetings for government to disseminate a strategy agreed upon between top-level officials and donors. Ownership must extend beyond government to elements of civil society, meaning more than the usual round of donor-financed nongovernmental organizations. The poverty-reduction strategy is preferably developed through a system of consultation and debate, which builds a political consensus around its main elements. There have been only slight moves in that direction—poverty reduction has been absent from African political discourse, suggesting there is still far to go in this regard. However, donor impetus for poverty reduction must not be taken as a substitute for domestic action: it cannot be so and, at best, will result in ineffectual attempts

at reducing poverty. Donors should not use aid to make governments accountable to the international community but to facilitate platforms for domestic accountability. Thus the third principle is that poverty reduction is helped if government structures are in place to hold government accountable for its actions, including its record on poverty reduction.

The fact that African political systems developed in ways that made governments increasingly unaccountable is a primary factor behind the failure to reduce poverty. Comparisons with the South Asian experience suggest that the persistence of famine in Africa is a direct consequence of nonaccountability and the absence of a more open civil society. The promotion of the International Development Targets thus draws on the notion of a rights-based approach to poverty reduction to hold governments accountable for progress toward these targets (or their domestic equivalents).

Of course, committing to meeting targets is just a first step. It must be followed up by actions to reduce poverty. The fourth principle emerges from the complexity of the poverty situation in different countries: the importance of governments' developing comprehensive antipoverty strategies, that is, of an integrated, or comprehensive, approach.

There is no single cause of poverty and any single intervention is likely to fail. At the most basic level, governments need to pay attention to both growth and distribution. The pattern of growth can be affected both by altering current policy packages and by additional interventions, such as investment in infrastructure and provision of rural credit, to spread growth more widely (and multiplier effects would lead us to expect that if growth is spread more widely it will be thicker rather than thinner). For the poor to benefit from additional interventions and to access markets requires changes in the political and legal framework. The argument here is not necessarily that government needs to publish a single strategy document (though this may be one way of signaling commitment and certainly seems a condition for attracting donor support at present), but that poverty reduction will be achieved by policies that tackle the several causes of poverty.

Two specific examples of the need for a comprehensive approach are provided by the analysis of gender, on the one hand (chapter 11), and economic reform (chapter 6) on the other. The pervasive and embedded nature of the gender dimension of the poverty problem shows that it manifestly cannot simply be solved by government dictate, although legislation of women's rights can help, and even less by donor interventions. Chapter 6 argued that reforms have not done enough to address the causes of poverty, and that they can be modified in this respect. However, such modification will not in itself be sufficient, and there will remain a need for add-on safety nets for the dependent poor and some of the most vulnerable.

The above list of the different elements of a poverty-reduction strategy may be restated as saying that no poverty-reduction strategy is likely to produce satisfactory, lasting results unless it addresses the causes of the country's poverty.

Although alleviating symptoms has its place, it can only touch the surface. The causes of African poverty are long term and structural. Lasting poverty reduction can only be achieved by addressing these causes. Tackling the roots of low growth is one element as is tackling the most antipoor income distribution in the world, but there are also social and political dimensions to poverty that need to be addressed.

A Checklist of Policy Possibilities for a Poverty-Reduction Strategy

Although no blueprint is put forward, a checklist is suggested of items that should probably be featured in a country's poverty-reduction strategy. These are the following: promoting faster growth; making growth more pro-poor and addressing inequalities; promoting twice-blessed policies, which both reduce poverty and enhance growth (addressing gender biases, constructing infrastructure, and renovating social services, including population policy); and addressing other causes of poverty, namely, vulnerability, instability, uncertainty; HIV/AIDS; and conflict.

Promoting faster growth

Adjustment policies have been pursued in parts of Africa for nearly two decades. Although the general comment that they do not work begs the point. Since they rarely are fully implemented, continuing poor growth performance indicates a need for better policy implementation as well as augmentation by other measures. While a return to the days of the control regime are not advocated, it is necessary to recognize the fact that the successful developing countries in the last 50 years combined market forces with a measure of intervention to power their development. So what should pro-growth policies consist of?

There should be measures to take greater advantage of trade opportunities, including greater openness and export diversification, which are to be achieved in part through exchange rate competitiveness. There should also be measures to encourage greater saving and investment (public and private), which can in part be done by lifting controls. Moving toward addressing the structural basis for poor growth should also include measures to reduce perceived uncertainties and raise expected private returns, thus encouraging domestic capital formation, for instance, through public provision of infrastructure and support services. At a structural level are also measures to enhance human capital, technological capabilities, and factor productivity. There is also the need for an appropriate legal and institutional framework, with enforceable contracts, predictability, and time consistency of policies, and the development of institutions for social harmony.

None of this negates the need for the maintenance of macro stability. But this needs to be done without undermining the formation of physical or human capital by cutting into the government's social spending. Against this, governments must avoid crowding out of private sector credit by controlling the size of their budget deficits. African governments thus have a tightrope to walk between inflation control and developmental expenditure. It is a walk they must take, however.

Finally there is a need for a reduction of external debt overhang (see chapters 5 and 6), which is an area in which donors can play a role.

Making growth more pro-poor

The pattern of growth can be affected by the alteration of existing policies and additional interventions, spanning a range of sectors. The policies here are those that can affect the distribution of growth, and under the next point are those that promote both growth and poverty reduction (though this distinction is not a hard and fast one).

The one that has received some attention is the correction of antipoor biases in social spending: there is no doubt that addressing the basic capabilities of the poor by improving the health (including water supply) and education status is a central element of a pro-poor growth strategy. However, achievements have been somewhat limited.

But there are other important areas that have received little attention; for example, the distributional impact of tax changes, privatization in the absence of a regulatory framework, and the possible poverty-creating effects of some liberalization measures such as input subsidy removal and the creation of land markets. There are other areas of anti-poor bias in government spending, such as the neglect of rural infrastructure and the distribution of agricultural extension services, including their bias against women that need to be redressed. Public works have been underused in the African context, and infrastructure development has been excessively capital intensive in countries in which more labor-intensive approaches would provide an ideal opportunity for putting cash into the hands of poor people.

In order for the economically active poor to benefit from measures such as improved infrastructure and extensions, it is necessary to enhance their diverse assets: improving education and health; improving property rights, for example, security/clarity of property rights to land and access to land, by land reform; improved access to credit through the extension of microfinance schemes, and promoting the productivity of smallholder agriculture (research and extension; reducing gender biases for a more rational use of resources; improved infrastructure and marketing arrangements). Greater attention should also be paid to stimulating job creation, for instance, through measures to encourage relative expansion of labor-intensive sectors and industries and in government and donor-supported construction activities; encouraging greater linkages between small- and medium-sized enterprises and larger enterprises; and more support for urban informal sectors.

Finally, there is a need for the provision of measures to spread benefits to the dependent poor, especially those at risk, of which children require special priority. School feeding and targeted food supplementation programs are feasible examples even in poor countries, the former having the extra advantage of creating an additional incentive for parents to send children to school.

Centering poverty reduction strategies around twice-blessed measures

Although specific trade-offs are likely to arise, there is also a range of policy possibilities that are twice blessed in the sense that they promote both growth and a more broad-based distribution of benefits. These include the following:

- Actions to reduce *gender-based poverty*. Although this goes deep into social structures, there is a range of specific measures that can be undertaken, elaborated in the 1998 *Poverty Status Report*. Such measures are twice blessed because, as the report shows, gender bias leads not only to inequities and avoidable pover-

ty but also to the inefficient use of resources and retarded economic expansion, particularly in agriculture.

- Actions to raise *productivity in small-farm household agriculture*. These will help directly raise the incomes of many of the rural poor, boost overall agricultural growth, and stimulate the growth of off-farm sources of income.

- Improved access by the poor to *education and health*, allowing better use of a country's human capabilities, improving the income-earning potential of poor people, widening their range of choice, improving the quality of their lives, and reducing their social exclusion. There are some core measures, such as malaria eradication and reproductive health services, that have clear and strong links to poverty reduction and growth at both macro and micro levels.

- Improvement of the economy's basic physical infrastructure, particularly the network of rural roads, increasing the responsiveness of the rural economy to economic opportunities (supply elasticities), raising farm-gate prices, lowering costs and raising marketed agricultural output, and reducing the poverty-increasing effects of remoteness.

- Public works that directly transfer resources to rural communities through payments to the poor and create the important infrastructure mentioned above.

- Measures to encourage/facilitate *reduced fertility and slower population growth*, satisfying the unmet demand for family planning services, striking at one of the most powerful correlates of poverty and a strongly negative influence on economic growth in Africa.

Addressing other causes of poverty

The lines of action proposed above would address various of the causes of poverty but not all. They should be augmented in various ways, including the following:

- Actions to reduce the extent of *transitory poverty*, which was shown in chapter 3 to be a probable large part of total poverty. This draws attention to the desirability of greater economic stability (linking in with earlier advocacy of sound macro management) but also to such variables as reduced reliance on rain-fed cultivation methods and other food security policies, early warning information systems, water management strategies, improved transport, and communications systems.

- Action to *bring the HIV epidemic under greater control*. This actually belongs as a twice-blessed measure, because HIV is both a large source of poverty and also a grave burden to economies' growth potential, particularly in eastern and southern Africa. A few African governments have shown that, working with local society, real progress can be made, but other governments have been reluctant to acknowledge the extent of the problem and to act.

- Action to *minimize the extent of conflict*, which also is both a huge brake on the possibilities of economic growth and a source of much poverty.

Finally, it is necessary to be brought back to politics. There are no new ideas in this section. There is no big idea waiting to be discovered that provides the key to eliminating poverty in Africa. The measures described here are known, but have been implemented only partially or not at all. Both governments and donors have allowed other interests to impede implementation of pro-poor policies. Public commitment to poverty reduction is a first step toward taking the actions required to reduce it. Hence the importance of development targets.

The Need to Set Targets

Although poverty-reduction targets should not be carved in stone, they are useful in focusing domestic efforts and garnering international support. While setting targets has been a feature of international development efforts in recent years, there are always the questions of feasibility and enforcement: many internationally agreed upon development targets have come and gone with little progress toward their being met (or even movement away from them). In 1996, a group of 21 donor governments who make up the Development Assistance Committee of the Organization for Economic Cooperation and Development adopted the International Development Targets that set dates at which certain goals relating to a whole array of poverty indicators will be met (box 13.1). These targets have since been embraced by the donor community, with some donor countries and institutions including them explicitly in their aid programs and policies.[1]

However, while donors agree on the feasibility of these targets, the most important determinant of success remains the attitude of developing country governments. Two questions arise in this regard: How will success in meeting targets be ensured among developing countries, notably in Africa? Can recipient governments be called to account (and by whom) in the event of failure to meet them? For attempts at enforcing targets to not disintegrate into simple conditionality, it will be important for African governments to evolve their own concept of poverty around which they are willing to design economic programs. While donors could influence recipient programs in various ways, sustainability requires that the concept evolve from domestic political processes. In this regard the so-called partnerships approach currently advocated by the donor community is attractive: donors and recipients would agree on the targets to be achieved by their development collaboration, with the understanding that there will be a parting of ways when they are consistently not met. This issue is pursued in chapter 14.

Conclusion

A poverty-reduction focus implies a serious policy challenge to African policymakers not only owing to a paucity of resources but, more crucially, owing to a lack of political commitment. It is twice-blessed policies, that is,

---

Box 13.1 The international development targets

- The proportion of people living in extreme poverty in developing countries should be reduced by at least one-half by 2015.
- There should be universal primary education in all countries by the year 2015.
- Progress towards gender equality and the empowerment of women should be demonstrated by eliminating gender disparity in primary and secondary education by 2005.
- The death rates for infants and children under the age of five years should be reduced in each developing country by two-thirds of the 1990 level.

- The rate of maternal mortality should be reduced by three-fourths by 2015.
- Access should be available through the primary health care system to reproductive health services for all individuals of appropriate ages, no later than 2015.
- There should be a current national strategy for sustainable development, in the process of implementation, in every country by 2005, so as to ensure that current trends in the loss of environmental resources are effectively reversed at both global and national levels by 2015.

those generating the conditions for renewed growth while ensuring greater participation of the poor in economic activities through egalitarian distribution of its benefits, which can ensure sustainable poverty reduction. Luckily, few of the required measures, such as improvements in basic health and education, land reform, and improved roads, are quite beyond the means of African countries.

The extent to which the donor community can help bring about poverty policy change in African countries should not be exaggerated. Sustainability of efforts can only be ensured by the evolution a solid domestic constituency in Africa in favor of poverty reduction. Accountability of governments is important and donors should strive to be supportive without preventing this process from taking place. The role of donors is discussed in more detail in chapter 15, but first the role of poverty monitoring is examined more closely.

Notes

1. The International Development Targets are being embraced by donors in a way that the 20/20 initiative was not. The targets are, for example, explicitly adopted in the U.K. 1997 White Paper on International Development. The World Bank is incorporating the targets into its Country Assistance Strategies to guide policy dialogue, and in February 1998 the World Bank, United Nations, the Organization for Economic Cooperation and Development, and developing country governments met to agree on 21 indicators by which progress towards the targets can be measured.

CHAPTER 14

Find Out More and Monitor Progress

Why monitor poverty? Data from poverty monitoring systems may serve three purposes: recording, research, and response. First, the monitoring function of recording progress in poverty reduction must hold government accountable for its performance. A main foundation for poverty monitoring is the poverty-reduction goals that government sets itself. Although the International Development Targets (IDTs) provide a useful context for such an exercise, actual goals should be homegrown ones to which there is a genuine government commitment and for which government can be held accountable for progress toward these goals. Second, there must be a generation of data that allows poverty analysis (research) to take place. This function includes evaluation of the impact of policies and other interventions, although this activity is not the direct responsibility of the poverty-monitoring unit. And, finally, information can be collected that allows government to respond to current and emerging poverty problems. From the point of view of poverty reduction, collecting indicators that allow a rapid policy response is the most important component of a poverty monitoring system.[1]

The data requirements for each of these three purposes are somewhat different. Recording progress relies on outcome indicators for the recent past, such as mortality data and income poverty. Poverty analysis relies upon information on a wider range of variables covering inputs and process. Indicators for government response should include some of a predictive nature, what economists call "leading indicators," which allow anticipation of problems before they arise. The best known examples of such leading indicators are famine early warning systems (EWS). Although poverty monitoring systems are in place in a number of African countries, they are not yet at the stage of EWS, the development of which holds some lessons for the less developed art of more general poverty monitoring. A discussion of EWS is, of course, also important in its own right as food security is an important dimension of poverty.

Early EWS focused on food availability. However, during the 1980s it was increasingly recognized that famine results from entitlement failure rather than the lack of food per se. Hence the focus began to shift from food production to livelihood monitoring systems. Such a development has made EWS more responsive, identifying likely famine situations earlier and being sensitive to a broader range of food insecurity situations than full-scale famine. More recent approaches to EWS promotes "saving livelihoods rather than lives" (Buchanan-Smith and Davies 1995), for it identifies the vulnerable before they are driven into destitution. In the context of countries with potential food insecurity, which is most if not all of Africa, EWS can play a critical role in a poverty-monitoring system. Indeed, where such systems are well oriented to local livelihoods, poverty monitoring systems can be developed by augmenting existing channels of data gathering.

However, collecting indicators that can potentially inform life-saving poverty interventions is not the same as saying that such interventions will take place. The lesson of EWS is again instructive in this regard (see box 14.1). Poverty monitoring should not stop at developing data collection systems but encompass the institutional framework to respond to the signals given by the data.

It is often said that little is known about poverty in Africa and available data are of poor quality. Many data are simply unavailable, but those that are available may be simply misleading. The columns of numbers filling the tables in the appendices of many international reports, such as the *Human Development Report* (HDR), are estimates. Sources presenting time series, such as the World

Box 14.1 Better monitoring must go hand in hand with the development of systems for an adequate policy response: lessons from the experience of the Famine Early Warning Systems (EWS)

Failure to respond to famine in the Sahel and the Horn of Africa in 1984–85 was widely attributed to the absence of adequate early warning to alert government and the international community. In the second half of the 1980s considerable resources were devoted to the establishment of an EWS, which has been refined from a simple focus on food availability to multi-indicator systems that can monitor changing entitlements. By 1990 donors and government were better informed of the likelihood of famine than ever before.

A study of five countries that experienced famine in 1990–91, Ethiopia, Sudan, Chad, Mali, and the Turkana District in Kenya, found that in all cases the EWS did indeed give timely signals as to imminent problems. But the response was too little, too late. The delay between the signals from the EWS and a decision being taken to act was up to six months, and it took a further six months or more for deliveries to arise. The lag between identification of the problem and response to the problem was thus a year or more.

Analysis of these five cases reveals that the international community can, political circumstances permitting, respond to famines once they are under way. But they are ill-equipped to react on the basis of genuine early warning that would allow action to prevent mass starvation. Although they have

established systems that alert them to the threat of famine, both donors and governments have failed to develop appropriate institutional systems facilitating an appropriate response to this information.

Donors are reluctant to accept government's own assessments, preferring the more "independent" voice of international agencies, although the information in the international EWS is only as good as that in the national EWS on which it is usually based. Agencies wait to react until there is a large degree of certainty, whereas the earlier the information the more it is necessarily based on probabilities. Hence a crisis has to be under way before a response is forthcoming. But by that time the victims of famine are beyond the stage at which interventions can seek to sustain livelihoods rather than lives. Besides, in most agencies emergency aid and development aid are organizationally separate, with the former geared to the provision of food. All these problems are exacerbated by systems that are excessively centralized, with decision-making neither involving nor accountable to those who will suffer if the response is inadequate.

The experience with the EWS illustrates the necessity of putting in place systems to respond to data, rather than merely to collect it.

Source: Buchanan-Smith and Davies (1995).

Bank's *World Development Indicators* CD-ROM, rely on techniques such as linear interpolation. For domestic poverty monitoring-systems it is important that locally produced data with local ownership are used in tracking progress toward targets, but international discussions and documents rely on these international sources. Even country-specific reports by donors often rely on these "international data" rather than "national data." Many World Bank reports have literally photocopied the relevant pages of *Social Indicators of Development* to include in country reports. Such practices echo donor mistrust of local data, a problem that has bedeviled the EWS.

One manifestation of these practices is that rather different numbers can be given for the same series. Maternal mortality, which for Ghana jumped from 400 to 1,000 from one issue of the *World Development Report* (WDR) to the next, is often mentioned in this regard.[2] Mauldin (1994) showed that, although they both used the same source, the WDR reported data for 56 developing countries and the HDR for 55 of these 56 and a further 48. Counting differences of less than 50 points as the same, HDR gave higher values than WDR for 26 countries,

lower for 12 and about the same for 17. Some differences are substantial, for example, Benin at 800 and 161, Mali at 850 and 2,325, and Malaysia 120 and 26. The correlation coefficient between the two sets of figures is only 0.7, dropping to only 0.4 for high-morality countries. Both sources use the World Health Organization's *Maternal Mortality: A Global Factbook*, which presents a range of estimates for each country. In some cases the respective reports pick one of the estimates, while in other cases they report an average, and still in other cases it is unclear where the number comes from. Nor is it clear why some countries are omitted. Maternal mortality data have improved in recent years as the health-facility-based statistics have been replaced by more reliable (and higher) estimates from survey methods. But table 14.1 shows maternal mortality data from the early 1990s, illustrating that marked discrepancies may remain.

But the nonavailability of data should not be overstated. There are a wide range of surveys that can yield relevant information for poverty monitoring, and several countries have made considerable progress in establishing poverty-monitoring systems. The most usual sources are

Table 14.1 Poor data quality can give misleading results: maternal mortality from different sources (deaths per 100,000 live births)

	DHS	WDR	WDR as a percent of DHS
Central African Republic	1,451	700	48
Madagascar	663	660	100
Malawi	752	620	82
Morocco	380	372	98
Namibia	395	—	—
Niger	672	593	88
Senegal	566	—	—
Sudan	569	370	65
Zimbabwe	393	280	71

— Not available.

Sources: DHS (Demographic Health Surveys) (1997); World Bank, *World Development Indicators.*

household income and expenditure surveys, of which there have been more than 70 in Sub-Saharan Africa since the mid-1980s in 35 countries. But labor force, agricultural, manufacturing, informal-sector and administrative surveys, as well as the population census may all yield useful information, as will more obvious sources such as the Demographic Health Surveys (DHS), nutrition surveys, and, as already indicated, data collected as a part of famine EWS. Finally, the recent development of the Core Welfare Indicators Questionnaire (CWIQ) (box 14.2) promises to make more data available more quickly. The problem is only in part, if at all, that data are not available, but they are not being captured and analyzed in a way that makes them usable (or at least used) by policymakers.[3]

These sources may all be described as quantitative in nature. This need not mean they are restricted to solely economic concerns, since the 1996 Living Standards Measurement Survey (LSMS) in Zambia contained questions on attitudes to domestic violence. But the rise of participatory approaches, particularly Participatory Poverty Assessments, in recent years has highlighted the importance of more qualitative data.[4] Participatory approaches can play several important roles in a poverty-monitoring system, not least of which is defining the parameters of the monitoring system itself by broadening understanding of poverty and identifying the priority concerns of the poor.

Both quantitative and qualitative data should be collected in ways that may be disaggregated in analytically useful ways. When the welfare of population subgroups is changing in different ways, then aggregate figures can give a misleading picture. Most socioeconomic data lend themselves to gender disaggregation. Analysis can also be made on the basis of region and ethnicity, and for other marginal or vulnerable groups. There can be a difficulty here of the sample size required to give reliable results at the desired level of disaggregation. Given the importance of geographical patterns in poverty, and the demand that should be generated for such data by decentralization, there are good grounds for supporting surveys of the necessary size. More problematic is the continuing difficulty of disaggregation of data collected at the level of the household. Alternative survey techniques are being developed to handle the biases that may result from, for example, asking a man about tasks performed by women.

Despite the progress that has been made, the development of poverty-monitoring systems is at an early stage

---

Box 14.2 Getting poverty data quickly: the CWIQ

The CWIQ is a survey tool that complements other surveys by quickly making available information: results can be presented within one or two months of the fieldwork. Rapid processing is made possible by reliance on high-tech methods, though the procedures are not technically demanding of the users. The standard questionnaire includes data on household characteristics and welfare matters such as health, nutrition, and employment. The data may be broken down by poverty quintiles (based on a few normative questions on household income and expenditure), rural/urban, socioeconomic groups, and geographic region.

The focus is on simple indicators, such as usage (school enrollment, for instance), access (to clean water, for example) and satisfaction, but also includes some "output" indicators such as illness. For example, CWIQ in Lagos State (Nigeria) revealed that 42 percent of urban households are within 15 minutes of a school, whereas none of the rural households sampled were—less than 10 percent of urban households were more than an hour away, compared to nearly one-third of rural ones.

CWIQ was piloted in Kenya in 1996 with a sample of 700 households, followed by one in Ghana later that year. Both countries then carried out national surveys (covering 15,000 households in Ghana) the following year, and in Ghana some of the technology is being adopted for the year 2000 census. Other countries are now adopting the questionnaire.

in many countries. Units responsible for these activities are now being established in the context of national programs to eradicate poverty. Just as for poverty-reduction policies in general, poverty monitoring need not imply new activities. The surveys that constitute a poverty-monitoring system may well be in place but not conceived of as such. Hence existing activities need to be drawn together into a coherent program consistent with a government conceived strategy for poverty reduction. A poverty-monitoring unit will thus act primarily as an umbrella, which coordinates information flows, bringing together data producers and users and producing publicly available information so that government can be held accountable for its record of progress toward meeting its poverty-reduction goals. Ideally, such units should be associated with, or be a part of, the coordinating body for poverty-reduction activities, as is the case with, for example, Uganda's poverty planning and eradication unit in the Ministry of Finance, Planning and Economic Development. In the Ugandan case, poverty-reduction targets are an integral part of the medium-term expenditure framework, laying a basis for reporting progress in poverty reduction. To date, systems for response to the information collected are less well established.

Given government budget constraints, donor support is likely to be vital for poverty-monitoring systems. Such support should not, of course, undermine domestic control ("ownership" in donor parlance) of the system. But the problem with the EWS is that donors have been reluctant to trust government information as a basis for action. A balance is clearly required between external quality control and development of a domestically based system.

Donors may support the development of the poverty-monitoring systems in similar ways to previous support for the collection and processing of statistics. Such support has followed three models. The traditional model has been technical support to the statistics office through training and the provision of expatriate assistance. Within this context support could be given to initiate or sustain specific survey activities. A second model is to provide the expertise to undertake and process specific surveys. The DHSs have come closest to this model, where a standardized questionnaire and report format are used across countries, produced by Macro International in Maryland. Finally, support may be given for a specific survey though the responsibility for the survey rests with the local institution; the Social Dimensions of Adjustment (SDA) and subsequent assistance to household income and expenditure surveys have been of this form. The LSMS

questionnaire is a prototype, but there have been far more variations between countries than has been the case for the DHS. These three approaches can be characterized as (i) support to institutional development, (ii) doing the survey, and (iii) survey-specific institutional development, although this characterization is a bit extreme, as in practice the second model has involved local institutions.

Two trade-offs are at work in determining the appropriate form of support: institutional development versus getting the job done and adapting to local circumstances versus maintaining intercountry comparability. With respect to the first of these, the completion of surveys in most African countries has tilted the balance in favor of developing local capacity. The position with respect to the second depends upon the nature of the data being collected. However the trade-off may not be as great as imagined, since adaptation to local circumstances may make data more comparable rather than less; modifying questionnaires to embrace diversity in systems of production and consumption will result in overall welfare indicators (such as consumption) that are comparable in a way they would not be if important elements of local livelihood strategies were missed by surveys.

Although poverty-monitoring systems should be adapted to local circumstances, the following principles can be proposed:

- Clear identification of existing data products and producers, and uses and users.

  Though data may be widely available, much of these data are not well used. The starting point for a poverty-monitoring system is an audit of what is available. Equally important is to identify current and potential users of data. The current situation suggests that the challenge is not so much to meet demand as to generate demand, which implies facilitating a process of dialogue in which potential data users are persuaded of its benefits and so become committed to data collection and dissemination.

- Assessment of data products against international standards and local circumstances.

  There is a need to develop international trust in locally produced data, which means that international standards should be applied, and the donors have a window on data collection processes, which will be provided by their continuing support for activities in this area. But these needs have to be weighed against not only the importance of local ownership but also of adapting to country-specific circumstances: "one size fits all" is not a rule that applies to surveys of poverty-related issues in Africa. A further consideration is domestic continuity. Although many more data are now available, there are still few countries for which reliable time series data on poverty measures can be compiled. Changes in survey design and sampling have compounded this problem. Panel data are virtually unavailable.[5]

- Mapping of data needs for reporting, research and response, and identification of data. gaps

The beginning of this chapter outlined the main functions of a poverty-monitoring system. Despite the quantity of data available, it is possible that there are gaps in the nature of data collected, so that additional collection work should be scheduled. Some of these gaps will be the result of emerging data needs as poverty-reduction policies are put in place, such as data allowing analysis of the targeting of public expenditures.

- Listing of priority poverty indicators through a consultative process, with public commitment by government to meeting agreed upon goals.

The importance of political commitment to poverty reduction has been a major theme of this report, a part of which is government commitment to poverty-reduction targets. But these targets should be domestically determined with the government held accountable to the local population for progress toward them. Target setting should thus be part of a national consultative process, which sets requirements and public interest in data collection.

- Identify and establish links between reporting data and channels for accountability, research data and local researchers, and response data and policymakers.

Establishing links between producers and users has been stressed, as has generating demand among potential users. But such measures are only the starting point for providing a basis for action on what the data show. Public accountability is important here, pointing to the need for the timely provision of publicly available data. In Ghana the most recently available published income-poverty data are from 1992, although results from the 1998 survey are being processed (Booth 1999), and the nonavailability of more recent data casts doubt on government's willingness to have its record exposed to public scrutiny.

- Creating the umbrella for the poverty-monitoring system, with an appropriate mix of input, process, and outcome indicators based on both quantitative and qualitative approaches.

Most surveys are oriented toward outcomes (such as income and mortality), though data are also collected with relevance to analyzing causes (such as asset distribution and access to services). But there are areas of data collection that can play a valuable part in monitoring processes that may be overlooked as a part of poverty monitoring. For example, line ministries have, or are developing, Management Information Systems (MISs) that provide timely data covering all three of input, process, and outcome.

- A balance between rapidly available information and more traditional data gathering.

The timely provision of data, as can be provided by MISs and CWIQs, is important in providing information on which policymakers can act. In particular, if poverty-monitoring systems are to develop an EWS, so that the vulnerable can be protected before they cross the line into destitution, then the process indicators of MISs and the intermediate ones collected in a CWIQ will be particularly valuable. However, the importance of these should not undermine continued collection of quality data by traditional large-scale surveys.

Notes

1. Bamberger (1996) suggests that the data and expertise are not available in Africa for the sort of targeted approaches used in Latin America. But poverty data are improving rapidly: in Mozambique, for example, a central database is being compiled of its various safety net programs (Greeley and Jenkins 1999).

2. Since maternal mortality data are notoriously poor, this may seem an unfair example. But it is one of the indicators used for the IDTs (box 13.1, chapter 13), raising the question of whether changes reflect actual changes or improved data quality.

3. In Benin the poverty monitoring unit (*Cellule Technique pour la DSD, CTDSD*) was placed in the influential National Monitoring Commission for the Structural Adjustment Program, giving poverty matters a central position in policy debates.

4. Speed of collection and processing has been a main advantage of qualitative approaches. But first LSMS, and now the CWIQ surveys, have overseen major strides in more rapid processing of quantitative data.

5. The LSMS sampling methodology is an unsatisfactory compromise between repeated random samples and a panel. It would probably be more satisfactory to use random samples for major household surveys while conducting a panel survey as a separate exercise.

CHAPTER 15

Donor Countries Need to Do More, Too

The Gap between Donor Aspirations and Practices

If all aid could be targeted successfully and without cost at the extreme poor, it would be possible to rapidly eliminate extreme poverty, nearly doubling the mean income of the poorest (White 1996). Of course, there is a multitude of reasons why such a transformation is not feasible, but this fact provides a dramatic yardstick against which actual achievements can be assessed. This is all the more relevant because at the 1995 World Social Summit, donor governments committed themselves to devote at least 20 percent of their aid budgets to basic services that benefit the poor, and in the following year donors adopted the target to halve extreme poverty in developing countries by 2015. Various of them state that they pursue poverty reduction as the overarching goal of their development cooperation policies, or as one of two or three central goals, with France and the United States the only major exceptions. How well do actual donor records match up to these aspirations?

It is a sign of the low priority that has been placed on the poverty-reduction goal in the past that until very recently there was little systematic information with which to answer this question. Evidence of this low priority for poverty reduction can be taken from a number of sources, of which four examples are given here. First, an evaluation of the poverty impact of Danish aid found "there was neither ubiquitous nor explicit poverty orientation reflected in most of the project designs or documentation of the selected interventions assessed" (DANIDA (Danish International Development Agency) 1996, p. viii). Second, a World Bank review of their own poverty-reduction strategy in Africa found that "poverty reduction is rarely a central or motivating theme in the business plan or country assistance strategy [and] even though the

operational cycle begins correctly with a poverty assessment, the poverty focus is often lost by the time a lending program is implemented" (World Bank 1997b, p. 15). Third, a review of the treatment of poverty by the Swedish International Development Agency (SIDA) found that "a large number of projects and programs supported by SIDA do not specify poverty reduction as an explicit objective. Swedish development cooperation is largely driven by objectives other than (direct) poverty reduction" (Tobisson and de Vylder 1997, pp. 21–22). Finally, a study of a number of European donors (Cox and Healey 1998) analyzed 90 projects, which were designated by the donors concerned as their most poverty-oriented projects. However, when classified according to objective criteria, less than one-third of the projects could be said to have a direct poverty orientation, and 23 percent did not even have an indirect one (see table 15.1a).

But as donors' policy statements renew their commitment to poverty reduction, more evidence is now becoming available, and a picture is beginning to develop. The following is a highly condensed statement of the main results of recent research:

- Real aid flows to poor countries have declined quite sharply in recent years, as indicated in figure 5.6, chapter 5. This shows net aid to Africa to have fallen in real terms by a one-fifth between 1994 and 1997. Other Development Assistance Committee data show that, contrary to the international commitments just

Table 15.1a Little aid is directly targeted at the poor

	Direct	*Indirect*	*Other*
Poverty orientation (n = 90)	29	48	23

Source: Cox and Healey (1998).

117

cited, a declining share of total aid is going to the least developed countries, with the proportion falling between 1986/87 and 1996/97, from 38.1 percent to 31.5 percent.[1]

- Donors have apparently not used recipient governments' revealed commitment to tackling poverty as a basis for country aid allocations. Econometric analysis of aid allocations shows that "donor interest varables," capturing commercial and political considerations, are a major determining factor for bilateral aid allocations.

- Until a few years ago, only a small proportion of aid deliveries was explicitly designed as poverty reducing. For example, as recently as 1993 none of the OECD bilateral donors nor the World Bank allocated aid to basic health and education at a rate significantly different from zero.

- Donor policy statements have shifted toward a stronger emphasis on poverty in the 1990s, but much of the policy remains poorly articulated, with little or no clear idea how to achieve pro-poor growth and a reluctance to embrace land reform.

- Along with the shift toward a stronger poverty emphasis, the donor agenda is converging around a consensus on common issues such as partnership, sector programs, and the need for a comprehensive approach.

There is general agreement, however, that the situation is changing quite fast, so that the proportions for 1996 (latest available) equivalent to those quoted in the last paragraph were a little under 6 percent for the DAC donors and 7 percent for the World Bank. About 28 percent of all International Development Association commitments were stated to be poverty targeted in 1995, although that proportion had not been rising, and the labeling of funds in this manner is somewhat problematic (see White 1996). Among European donors, proportions of total aid portfolios with a specific poverty focus in the mid-1990s ranged from a high of 19 percent (Netherlands) to approximately zero (European Community, France, Spain). As of the mid-1990s, estimates of the overall average share of poverty-focused aid were 10 to 15 percent; a comparable figure for today is probably on the order of 20 percent.

But even if the share of aid directed to the poor is increasing, that does not mean that the benefits end up in the hands of the poor. Vested interests and entrenched bureaucracy on the side of both African governments and donors can result in inappropriate use of aid resources. Too much is spent on studies and salaries, consultants and conferences, expatriates and expertise, and too little on the drugs, school books, and rural infrastructure that will make a direct difference to the lives of the poor.

Change is also apparent with respect to process. Donors now place great stress on partnership. But thus far there has been far more donor rhetoric than action on this front, to the extent that donors continue to subvert accountability by making governments responsive more to donor needs than those of the local population. The proper role for donors is to facilitate domestic platforms for policy debate and create space for the pro-poor political coalitions. These processes will generate systems of accountability onto which donors will have a window, rather than requiring separate channels of accountability to donors. Difficulties also exist here in the partnership concept that deserve explicit recognition. One is the tension between donors' desire for influence and genuine partnership. Second is the fundamental inequality in the partnership, particularly when donors appear reluctant to relinquish the power afforded them by being the ones giving the money.[2] Related to this inequality is the extent to which donors are willing to enter contractual obligations. Finally, difficulties lie in identifying appropriate partners who share donor objectives, and what to do if they don't (or don't fully), or they change their mind.

A part of the move to partnership is a supposed increased reliance on a sector approach in which aid is provided as budget support. However, donors have retained a high degree of earmarking of funds to specific activities, thus impeding the intended government-led nature of the process and creating potential distortions in resource allocations. Finally donors are also embracing the need for a comprehensive approach, referred to in this report mostly as an integrated approach. These is no detracting from the importance of this approach, but once again the government should have the lead in this process. Preparation of individual donor strategies, including even those of the World Bank, do not take precedence over local initiatives and should not be allowed to dominate them.

Despite these changes donors are still struggling to some extent with putting poverty reduction into practice. Many donors have not developed a clearly defined conceptualization of the poverty problem and few donors utilize country assistance strategies as a mechanism for mainstreaming poverty reduction and for engaging with recipient governments and civil societies on poverty reduction. Some have moved in this direction, however, resulting in a large gap between best donor practices and the average.[3] Poverty concerns, although not entirely absent, have not formed an important part of the policy dialogue with

African governments.[4] Understanding the causes of poverty is not an easy task, and not one that all Poverty Assessments have been up to, partly because they appear constrained to have neglected political aspects (Hanmer, Pyatt, and White 1997). An analysis of country strategy papers prepared by the U.K. aid agency Department for International Development revealed the problem of the "missing middle," a failure to identify how planned interventions rooted in weak analysis would reduce poverty of the causes of poverty or prioritization of either major causes of poverty or major groups of the poor (Booth and White 1999).

Although the situation is improving over time among several of the leading aid agencies, there is still far to go in mainstreaming poverty reduction in their operational policies and modalities. Despite the pressures in this direction, success is not assured. Incentive structures within agencies are not specifically designed to encourage staff to prioritize poverty reduction in practice; and often little training and operational guidance has been provided to them in the poverty area. Monitoring systems that could provide accountability against poverty reduction objectives, and stimulate lesson learning and feedback, although improving, are still deficient. But there are also vested interests, such as commercial pressures on aid programs, and the interests of aid workers and consultants, that resist too great a change in the way aid works.

So far as the weak available evidence permits a judgement: it appears that more than 70 percent of projects nominated by donors as having an explicit poverty focus brought positive benefits to the poor, and a 25 percent had a large impact (table 15.1b). However only a one-fifth of these poverty-focused projects had actually been closely targeted on poor groups, and only about the same proportion were judged very likely to be sustainable when the time came for donors to withdraw.

Table 15.1b Poverty effects are often not large (results of survey of poverty-oriented projects of European donors)

		High	Moderate	Negligible
Targeting	(n = 82)	21	41	38
Degree of participation	(n = 89)	17	48	35
Integration of gender	(n = 75)	28	35	37
Sustainability	(n = 67)	19	45	36
Poverty impact	(n = 73)	25	48	27

Notes: n is sample size, and figures are a percentage of sample.
Source: Cox and Healey (1998).

It is clear from the above account that, although the situation is an improving one, there remains a gulf between the aspirations or rhetoric of the donors and their actual practices in the poverty-reduction area. At present, it is doubtful whether donors' explicitly poverty-related work has made a significant difference to the overall extent of poverty. Many of the more important ways in which donors need to improve their records are the mirror image of the facts just reported. The following points require particular emphasis:

- The importance of exercising greater *selectivity* in aid allocations, to enhance the support given to governments pursuing vigorous antipoverty strategies and to exclude support for governments hostile to this objective. Engaging with recipient governments and civil society in a dialogue on poverty-related policy topics and utilizing country assistance strategy processes as a means of building a consensus on an antipoverty strategy.

- Alongside selectivity goes the notion of *partnership*, which means placing more reliance on government to take the lead, both in defining the poverty-reduction strategy and in managing the role of aid in this process.[5] However, the caveats with respect to partnership in practice mentioned above should be borne in mind.

- Improved *project identification and design*, including a less top-down approach and involvement of the poor at the outset; more systematic integration of gender equality aspects; supporting more locally initiated projects and programs; and adopting project designs that maximize visible benefits to the poor. Where countries have well-functioning systems of accountability, these define government's spending priorities, and aid funds should be subsumed into this system.

- *Reduced biases* towards urban interventions and projects located in the more prosperous parts of the rural economy; more effective targeting of poor beneficiaries.

- Following from the previous point, donors can *invest more in agriculture* and *prioritize activities that transfer resources to the poor*, such as labor-intensive works.

- Actions to *mainstream* the poverty-reduction goal within agencies' internal management systems, including stronger incentives and guidance for agency staff; better poverty monitoring of country programs; broadening the range of skills available to agencies and increasing the training provided for staff; and greater decentralization of expertise and authority.

The discussion in chapter 6 of the influence of economic reforms supported by the International Monetary Fund (IMF) and the World Bank argued that more could be done to reduce programs' ill effects on vulnerable people. More specifically, the following is recommended:

- Reforms should be consciously designed so as to minimize the costs and maximize the benefits to poor groups—a principle the IMF was slow to accept (arguably doing so following the results of the Extended Structural Adjustment Facility (ESAF) evaluation, and more recently with the adoption of Poverty Reduction Strategy Papers (PRSPs), which are discussed below)—and pro-poor measures should be integral to the design of programs.[6] Particular care should be taken with measures changing government spending patterns, and with other fiscal measures.
- Positive measures are better than ameliorative responses: strengthening the rural infrastructure, provision of primary health and education, and of treated water. Export promotion also has a good pro-poor record.
- Safety net provisions should continue to be improved in the light of emerging experience, particularly to improve participation of, and accessibility to, targeted groups.

Finally, donors can play a role, albeit a limited one, in building consensus toward poverty reduction. One useful way in which they can do this is by sponsoring (but not setting) the research agenda to fill the gaps in knowledge mentioned above.

Responding to Conflict and Postconflict Situations

This report has illustrated the various ways in which warfare and other forms of violent conflict are a potent source of poverty in Africa. Indeed, some have suggested that it has become the largest single determinant of poverty on the continent, with a high proportion of all states having experienced substantial levels of violence in recent decades. Donor agencies affect this situation both negatively and positively.

Negatively, there is the ever present danger that the resources they provide may be diverted, through fungibility, into fueling the conflict, or that donor governments may explicitly aggravate the situation by engaging in, and providing arms for, proxy wars in pursuit of wider geopolitical policy objectives. Positively, and particularly when they are seen as standing outside the conflict, donors may be in a position to use their influence and resources to help defuse potentially violent situations, to help bring conflicts to an end, to protect those most at risk, and to aid postconflict recovery. It is only relatively recently that donors have begun to bring their responses to conflict situations within the mainstream of their activities. They should accelerate this trend. More specific suggestions include the following:

- Starting with conflict assessments—these should be historically sensitive and should recognize the tendency for violence to become embedded in social and political structures.
- Giving greater priority to finding ways to encourage conflict prevention.
- Recognizing that conflict is often not exogenous to the wider economic and social situation and integrating it into their broader relief development aid planning.
- Giving more attention to the macroeconomic framework for recovery from conflict, particularly in determining how to deal with hyperinflation, capital flight, and urban bias, and the effects of these on the poor.
- Seeking to ensure that any peace dividend resulting from ending a conflict should benefit most those who have suffered worst from the violence in question.
- Giving explicit dimension to the gender dimensions of conflict and also to the special vulnerability of children.
- Official and nongovernmental organization donors should more fully recognize the potentially perverse consequences of their aid and take active steps to minimize this risk. They should be more proactive and strategic in their relations with local parties to conflicts, to avoid cooptation by them and to moderate their excesses.

While the role of the international community in conflict situations is a difficult one, since their actions, even if benign, may extend the conflict, they have a clearer, and important, part to play in postconflict reconstruction. It is easy to respond to the most obvious and pressing need, such as refugees or rebuilding hospitals and bridges. But the reconstruction effort is also social and institutional. During prolonged conflict particularly, government capacity to provide normal services will be undermined (Haughton 1998). If further conflict is to be avoided, then development must go hand in hand with reconstruction. As several studies have shown (see, for example, Collier 1999), poor economic performance is a significant determinant of the probability of conflict. Hence, as emphasized by Haughton (1998), the international community must not focus only on the obvious "immediate needs," but also on addressing long-term development needs. In the first instance this can be done fairly quickly through a wide range of projects, with few conditions imposed on the government; more normal donor relations can resume after two to three years of successful reconstruction and growth.

The Way Ahead

The talk among aid workers is that the way they do business is changing radically—ideas are more important than money, and influence matters more than investment. These changes took root with the adoption of sector programs, discussed above, which, partly on account of the Strategic Partnership with Africa, are most advanced in Africa. Sector programs fit well with the World Bank's advocacy for a Comprehensive Development Framework, and better still with the notion of PRSPs, which have been given an added impetus by the enhanced Highly Indebted Poor Country (HIPC) initiative for accelerated debt reduction (see below). Current thinking suggests that conditionality is going to change; the main requirement to be placed on governments will be that they prepare and implement a PRSP; that is, government, on the basis of available data, defines a poverty reduction strategy and thus sets an expenditure program that responds to the needs of that strategy. Government's own priorities will therefore determine the areas of focus for the various donors operating in that country.

While these developments are certainly to be welcomed as a step in the right direction, the record of past failures must certainly raise doubt as to whether "the answer" has now been discovered. Indeed, there are good reasons to exercise some caution as to both the concept and how it will work in practice. It is possible to question the need for "a strategy," most now industrial countries (and indeed those of East Asia) have achieved poverty reduction without an umbrella strategy. What matters most is that adequate resources flow to the right sectors (such as education) that ensure both growth and poverty reduction. That said, a PRSP may play a useful political role in shifting the center of political gravity in a poverty-oriented manner, as the New Deal did in the United States and the 1945 Labour government did in the United Kingdom. To work, however, PRSPs must be rooted in the domestic political scene, and this will take time. There is a very real danger that donors will rush through PRSPs, governments will make the necessary verbal commitments, and donors will come up with the funds to pay consultants to write the plans, which government will adopt. Although it is

true that donors are paying attention to process, it is conceivable that the consultative process will involve donor-friendly nongovernmental organizations the donors see as representing civil society rather than addressing genuine political groupings. But nothing will change, for there will be no domestic constituency. The track record of donors being able to take a hands-off approach to allow the necessary time and institutional and political processes to take place is not encouraging.

There is a widespread consensus among academics that formal policy conditionality failed to bring about many of the desired policy changes in a timely manner (see, for example, Killick, Carlsson, and Kierkegaard 1998). But this is not to say that the international community is irrelevant to the policy debate; they can and do have a role to play. But a more deep rooted and longer lasting effect is more likely if the focus is on facilitating policy debate on key issues, perhaps influencing the agenda, but only informing debate rather than trying to preempt the outcome. It is in any case far from obvious that the donor community has all the answers; this report has highlighted some key gaps in knowledge, such as the impact of land liberalization.

These comments apply equally to donor attempts to influence governance. Reviews of political conditionality conclude that it has had, at best, mixed effects (see, for instance, Stokke 1995 and Crawford 1997). Donors have also funded projects to promote democratic institutions (anticorruption commissions, for example), but these can only be as good as the overall environment, so the question comes back to how that may be influenced. But despite the importance placed in this report on the political context, it would be wrong to see "getting governance right" as the panacea to poverty reduction. There is no single quick fix (no big idea waiting to be discovered), a fact with which the donor community needs to reconcile itself.

Using debt relief for the poor

It may be right to say that influence matters more than investment, but aid is still money, so the question remains of how aid funds should be spent. Presently, more funds are to be directed to give debt relief to HIPC, but provided there is a demonstrable link with poverty reduction. Chapter 6 argued that the large overhang of external debt in many of the poor countries of Africa represents a serious obstacle to effective antipoverty programs, by diverting resources from public investment and social services, and by discouraging private saving and investment through increasing uncertainties and reducing prospective rates of return. Hence at the macro level a link between debt relief and poverty reduction is to be expected. But can a stronger link be forged?

Chapter 6 cautioned against erecting too close a connection between external debt relief and poverty reduction, not least because of the opportunity cost of much of the relief provided, the associated risk that poor countries without large debts may lose out, and because of the difficulties of ensuring that resources released through debt relief schemes actually benefit poor people. The creation of more or less elaborate mechanisms for channeling the proceeds of debt relief into social spending may yield poor results, partly because of fungibility but also because previous attempts to micromanage what are essentially free resources have slowed down disbursements and created allocative inefficiencies.[7] The ideal is where the indebted governments are themselves politically committed to the poverty-reduction objective, in which case mechanisms to earmark the funds are redundant in any case.

However, there are things that can be done. Without going into the complexities of the debt situation, four points may be made:

- Greater debt relief is still needed. Because they must move at the pace of the most reluctant creditors, successive debt relief arrangements have proved inadequate. The HIPC initiative, targeted specifically on low-income countries, while marking a major advance on previous schemes, is no exception to this generalization. Even after the further improvements agreed at the 1999 G-8 summit in Cologne, the indications remain that further broadening and deepening of its coverage will be required. In the meantime, various governments of poor countries will continue to be hamstrung by an unsustainable and draining debt burden.[8]
- There is a strong case for using debt relief to encourage recipient governments to adopt a poverty-reduction goal. Governments judged to have demonstrated a strong commitment to poverty reduction should be eligible for exceptional treatment in debt relief. Governments actively hostile to poverty reduction should, as a consequence, be disbarred from debt relief.
- Provided that there is sufficient government commitment to make such arrangements meaningful, creditor governments and their aid agencies should encourage creation of special fiscal mechanisms for channeling the "debt relief dividend" into expenditure programs

targeted at poverty groups, along lines similar to arrangements introduced by the Ugandan authorities.
- However, such spending should not necessarily be confined to the social sector. For example, this report has at a number of points stressed the value for many poor people, as well as for the economy as a whole, of improving rural infrastructure.

Conclusion

It is clear from the above that responsibility for acting against the scourge of poverty is far from being a matter for African governments alone. Donor governments are only now beginning to address the problem seriously, and there is still far to go in improving their policies and practices. African governments need to change their approaches. But so do OECD governments, as creditors and as donors. For too long vested interests have prevented aid budgets from benefiting the poorest. New trends in the use of aid and in aid management are encouraging, but not without problems. Most of these problems revolve around the design of effective poverty-reducing aid programs and allowing African governments a lead role in partnership arrangements. The current moves toward the Comprehensive Development Framework and the PRSP are certainly steps in the right direction, though past donor practice does not inspire confidence that donors will allow the time and space for the emergence of domestic constituencies for poverty reduction. The answer to the reduction of African poverty lies in Africa, and the biggest contribution donors can make is to recognize that fact.

Notes

1. *Source:* OECD (Organization for Economic Cooperation and Development) (1999, table 26). These proportions related to all least developed countries, not just African ones.

2. By contrast, the United States was only one equal member of the OEED (forerunner of the OECD) which oversaw the Marshall Plan. The Colombo Plan had an element of self-administration. But Africa has not enjoyed the same right to play a part in management of aid to the continent.

3. There is a movement now to have "participatory" country assistance strategies, with the World Bank having perhaps moved furthest in this direction with the piloting of the Comprehensive Development Framework. There is a real danger of swamping government and some civil society organizations if each donor engages in such participatory exercises on an individual basis. The

ideal is for a government-led process involving all major donors, which is a generalization of the Sector Program approach.

4. This state of affairs will change, at least in form, if the Policy Framework Paper is replaced with a poverty reduction strategy.

5. African governments have generally left aid management to the donors, whereas they should take a more active stance on such issues (which of course requires that the donors give them the space to do so). One area to start this process would be for government to assume responsibility for evaluation, with some mechanism for donor quality control.

6. A currently fashionable notion is that adjustment should "do no harm," but it is not clear how the process of adjustment, requiring fundamental shifts in the structure of production, can achieve this end. A more realistic conception is to focus on "winners" and "losers," with systems of compensation, or safety nets, as required.

7. The experience of import support was that donor attempts to channel funds to particular uses resulted in cumbersome procedures that weighed down government and donor bureaucracies and slowed procurement, with little or no discernible benefits (see White 1999a).

8. Under both the original HIPC and in its enhanced form governments are required to commit more resources to poverty reduction some time in advance of receiving additional debt relief.

Appendix

Selected Statistical Data

Table A.1 Poverty indices at PPP$/day, selected African countries

| Countries | Year | PPP$1/day | | PPP$2/day | |
		Headcount	Poverty gap	Headcount	Poverty gap
Botswana	1985–86	33.0	12.4	61.0	30.4
Côte d'Ivoire	1988	17.7	4.3	54.8	20.4
Ethiopia	1981–82	46.0	12.4	89.0	42.7
Kenya	1992	50.2	22.2	78.1	44.4
Madagascar	1993	72.3	33.2	93.2	59.6
Niger	1992	61.5	22.2	92.0	51.8
Nigeria	1992–93	31.1	12.9	59.9	29.8
Rwanda	1983–85	45.7	11.3	88.7	42.9
Senegal	1991–92	54.0	25.5	79.6	47.2
South Africa	1993	23.7	6.6	50.2	22.5
Uganda	1989–90	69.3	29.1	92.2	56.6
Zambia	1993	84.6	53.8	98.1	73.4
Zimbabwe	1990–91	41.0	14.3	68.2	35.5

Source: World Bank, *World Development Indicators 1999.*

Table A.2 Poverty headcounts based on national poverty lines

	Year	National	Urban	Rural
Benin	1995	33		
Burkina Faso[a]	1994–1995	56	13	65
Burundi	1990	36		
Cameroon	1984	40	44	32
CAR	1993	61	33	77
Chad	1995–1996	64	63	67
Côte d'Ivoire[a]	1995	42	29	51
Djibouti[a]	1996	41	38	84
Ethiopia[a]	1995–1996	46	21	50
Gambia[a]	1992	50	21	73
Ghana	1992	31	27	34
Guinea[a]	1994–1995	44	18	57
Guinea–Bissau	1991	49	24	61
Kenya	1992	42	29	46
Malawi	1990–91	54		

(Table continued on next page)

Table A.2 continued

	Year	National	Urban	Rural
Mali[a]	1994	55	8	64
Mauritania[a]	1995	39	18	56
Niger	1989–93	63	52	66
Nigeria	1985	43	32	50
Rwanda	1993	51	...	...
Senegal[a]	1991	33	16	40
Sierra Leone	1989	68	53	76
South Africa[a]	1993	44	40	86
Swaziland[a]	1994	63	36	70
Tanzania[a]	1993	42	20	51
Togo	1987–89	32	...	...
Uganda	1993	55	...	...
Zambia	1991	68	46	88
Zimbabwe	1990–91	26	...	...

... Not available.

a. Source data is from African Development Indicators (ADI); remaining data from *World Development Indicators* (WDI).

Table A.3 Mortality indicators in Sub-Saharan Africa

	Infant mortality rate (per 1,000)			Under-five mortality (per 1,000)			Life expectancy at birth (years)	
	1970	1980	1997	1970	1980	1997	1980	1997
Angola	178	154	125	301	261	209	41	46
Benin	146	116	88	...	214	149	48	53
Botswana	95	71	58	139	94	88	58	47
Burkina Faso	141	121	99	278	...	169	44	44
Burundi	138	122	119	228	193	200	47	42
Cameroon	126	94	52	215	173	78	50	57
CAR	139	117	98	248	...	169	46	45
Chad	171	123	100	252	235	182	42	49
Congo Dem. Rep.	131	112	92	245	210	148	49	51
Congo Rep.	101	89	90	160	125	145	50	48
Côte d'Ivoire	135	108	87	240	170	140	49	47
Eritrea		91	62		...	95	44	51
Ethiopia	158	155	107	239	213	175	42	43
Gabon	138	116	87	232	194	136	48	52
Gambia	185	159	78	319	216	110	40	53
Ghana	112	94	66	186	157	102	53	60
Guinea	181	185	120	345	299	182	40	46
Guinea–Bissau	185	169	130	316	290	220	39	44
Kenya	102	75	74	156	115	112	55	52
Lesotho	134	119	93	190	168	137	53	56
Madagascar	153	119	94	285	216	158	51	57
Malawi	193	169	133	330	265	224	44	43
Mali	204	184	118	391	...	235	42	50
Mauritania	148	120	92	250	175	149	47	53
Niger	170	150	118	320	320	...	42	47
Nigeria	139	99	77	201	196	122	46	54
Rwanda	142	128	124	210	...	209	46	40
Senegal	135	117	70	279	190	110	45	52
Sierra Leone	197	190	170	363	336	286	35	37
South Africa	79	67	48	108	91	65	57	65
Tanzania	129	108	85	218	176	136	50	48
Uganda	109	116	99	185	180	162	48	42
Zambia	106	90	113	181	149	189	50	43
Zimbabwe	96	80	69	138	108	108	55	52

Source: World Bank, *World Development Indicators.*

Table A.4 Nutrition and water access indicators in Sub-Saharan Africa

	Access to safe water 1996	Underweight[a] 1992–97	Stunted[b] 1992–97
Angola	32	35	...
Benin	72	29	25
Botswana	70	27	...
Burkina Faso	...	33	29
Burundi	58	38	...
Cameroon	41	...	...
CAR	23	23	28
Chad	24	39	40
Congo Dem. Rep.		34	45
Congo Rep.		24	45
Côte d'Ivoire	72	24	24
Eritrea	7	44	38
Ethiopia	26	48	64
Gabon	67	...	...
Gambia	50	26	30
Ghana	65	27	26
Guinea	55	24	...
Guinea–Bissau	53	23	...
Kenya	45	23	34
Lesotho	62	16	44
Madagascar	16	34	50
Malawi	60	30	48
Mali	48	40	30
Mauritania	64	23	44
Niger	48	43	40
Nigeria	50	39	38
Rwanda	...	29	49
Senegal	50	22	23
Sierra Leone	34	...	...
South Africa	59	9	23
Tanzania	49	31	43
Uganda	42	26	38
Zambia	53	24	42
Zimbabwe	77	16	21

... Not available.

a. Percentage of children with weight less than two standard deviations below that of the reference population of that height.

b. Percentage of children with height less than two standard deviations below that of the reference population of that age.

Source: World Bank, *World Development Indicators 1999.*

Table A.5 Nutrition indicators for eight African countries

	Height for age			Weight for height			Weight for age		
	First year	*Second year*	*Change*	*First year*	*Second year*	*Change*	*First year*	*Second year*	*Change*
National									
Ghana (1988–93)	29.5	26.2	–3.3	8.0	12.0	4.0 [1]	30.8	29.6	–1.2
Madagascar (1992–97)	49.3	48.6	–0.7	5.7	7.8	2.0 [1]	39.2	40.2	1.0
Mali (1987–95)	24.0	33.0	9.0 [1]	10.8	24.6	13.8 [1]	30.9	43.7	12.8 [1]
Senegal (1986–92)	23.0	22.1	–0.9	6.0	10.4	4.4 [1]	22.0	26.9	4.9 [1]
Tanzania (1991–96)	43.6	43.7	0.2	6.4	7.3	1.0 [1]	29.5	30.9	1.4
Uganda (1988–95)	43.2	38.7	–4.5 [1]	1.9	5.3	3.4 [1]	23.3	26.1	2.9 [1]
Zambia (1992–96)	40.0	42.6	2.5 [1]	5.2	4.2	–0.9 [1]	23.4	23.8	0.4
Zimbabwe (1988–94)	30.0	23.5	–6.6 [1]	1.2	5.8	4.6 [1]	12.8	17.2	4.4 [1]
Rural									
Ghana (1988–93)	31.4	32.3	0.9	8.5	13.1	4.6 [1]	33.0	33.6	0.7
Madagascar (1992–97)	50.6	49.5	–1.1	6.0	8.3	2.3 [1]	40.3	41.3	1.0
Mali (1987–95)	26.2	36.2	10.0 [1]	12.3	24.4	12.2 [1]	33.6	46.6	13.0 [1]
Senegal (1986–92)	26.5	32.7	6.3	7.1	13.4	6.4 [1]	25.9	33.0	7.1 [1]
Tanzania (1991–96)	44.9	46.1	1.3	6.4	7.3	0.9	30.4	33.2	2.8 [1]
Uganda (1988–95)	45.2	40.7	–4.5 [1]	2.0	3.2	1.3 [1]	24.2	27.5	3.2 [1]
Zambia (1992–96)	46.5	48.9	2.4	5.0	4.9	–0.1	29.3	28.4	–0.9
Zimbabwe (1988–94)	34.3	25.0	–9.3 [1]	1.1	5.6	4.5 [1]	14.6	18.5	3.9 [1]
Urban									
Ghana (1988–93)	24.6	17.0	–7.6 [1]	7.3	9.1	1.8	25.2	19.5	–5.7 [1]
Madagascar (1992–97)	40.5	44.8	4.3	3.8	5.3	1.5	32.0	35.6	3.6
Mali (1987–95)	19.6	23.9	4.3	9.9	24.9	15.0 [1]	25.7	35.4	9.7 [1]
Senegal (1986–92)	17.5	15.2	–2.3	3.5	8.8	5.3 [1]	15.3	16.5	1.2
Tanzania (1991–96)	38.0	32.6	–5.5 [1]	5.1	8.1	3.0 [1]	26.0	20.1	–5.9 [1]
Uganda (1988–95)	24.8	22.7	–2.1	0.6	1.4	0.7 [1]	13.4	15.3	2.0
Zambia (1992–96)	32.8	32.9	0.1	5.4	3.3	–2.1 [1]	20.9	16.7	–4.2
Zimbabwe (1988–94)	16.0	19.0	3.0	1.4	6.5	5.0 [1]	6.9	13.5	6.6 [1]

Note: Superscript "1" indicates significant at the 5 percent level.
Source: Sahn, Stifel, and Younger (1999), tables 3 and 4.

Table A.6 Level and change in poverty of asset index (and decomposition)

	First period	*Second period*	*Change*	*Growth*	*Redistribution*	*Residual*
Ghana (1988–93)	25.0	8.5	–16.4	–38.7	8.5	13.7
Kenya (1988–93)	24.9	23.2	–1.7	–2.8	5.5	–4.3
Madagascar (1992–97)	25.5	12.5	–13.0	–18.4	–13.0	18.4
Mali (1987–95)	23.0	16.0	–7.0	–43.0	16.0	20.0
Senegal (1986–92)	24.6	28.8	4.2	–1.9	4.2	1.9
Senegal (1992–97)	28.8	24.7	–4.1	–13.2	1.0	8.1
Tanzania (1991–96)	22.6	19.1	–3.5	–11.9	1.1	7.3
Uganda (1988–95)	26.8	24.4	–2.4	–9.3	7.5	–0.6
Zambia (1992–96)	24.9	18.2	–6.7	2.0	–11.7	3.0
Zimbabwe (1988–94)	23.3	30.1	6.8	8.1	–2.0	0.8

Source: Sahn, Stifel, and Younger (1999).

Table A.7 Net primary school enrollment rates by consumption quintile, region, and gender

| | | Rural areas | | | | | Urban areas | | | | | |
| | | Poorest quintile | | Richest quintile | | | Poorest quintile | | Richest quintile | | | |
Year	Countries	Male	Female	Male	Female	All	Male	Female	Male	Female	All	All
1994–95	Burkina Faso	22	12	45	42	27	58	48	87	74	69	33
1993	CAR	39	19	58	38	37	50	42	78	74	65	48
1995	Côte d'Ivoire	20	13	45	31	30	43	35	75	42	50	38
1996	Djibouti	64	32	87	73	64	59	48	82	74	68	68
1995–96	Ethiopia	14	8	23	13	13	62	56	75	74	67	21
1992	Gambia	13	6	38	28	19	42	26	53	68	49	31
1997	Ghana	60	53	71	70	61	60	65	71	76	68	63
1994–95	Guinea	21	5	31	24	18	46	29	77	65	56	29
1994	Kenya	67	64	80	81	75	71	76	98	91	84	76
1993–94	Madagascar	10	13	44	41	26	38	37	66	70	57	31
1994	Mali	24	9	38	23	21	62	51	64	63	57	23
1995	Mauritania	25	18	52	38	34	48	51	71	58	58	44
1995	Niger	14	8	20	9	15	42	29	65	60	50	21
1992	Nigeria	48	47	71	62	51	56	55	74	73	63	56
1994–95	Senegal	21	22	32	25	22	47	50	84	82	63	37
1996	Zambia	54	50	68	72	60	69	72	84	83	78	67

Source: World Bank, *African Development Indicators* (1998–99).

Table A.8 Net primary school enrollment rates by consumption quintile, region, and gender

| | | Rural areas | | | | | Urban areas | | | | | |
| | | Poorest quintile | | Richest quintile | | | Poorest quintile | | Richest quintile | | | |
Year	Countries	Male	Female	Male	Female	All	Male	Female	Male	Female	All	All
1994/95	Burkina Faso	22	12	45	42	27	58	48	87	74	69	33
1993	CAR	39	19	58	38	37	50	42	78	74	65	48
1995	Côte d'Ivoire	20	13	45	31	30	43	35	75	42	50	38
1996	Djibouti	64	32	87	73	64	59	48	82	74	68	68
1995/96	Ethiopia	14	8	23	13	13	62	56	75	74	67	21
1992	Gambia	13	6	38	28	19	42	26	53	68	49	31
1997	Ghana	60	53	71	70	61	60	65	71	76	68	63
1994/95	Guinea	21	5	31	24	18	46	29	77	65	56	29
1994	Kenya	67	64	80	81	75	71	76	98	91	84	76
1993/94	Madagascar	10	13	44	41	26	38	37	66	70	57	31
1994	Mali	24	9	38	23	21	62	51	64	63	57	23
1995	Mauritania	25	18	52	38	34	48	51	71	58	58	44
1995	Niger	14	8	20	9	15	42	29	65	60	50	21
1992	Nigeria	48	47	71	62	51	56	55	74	73	63	56
1994/95	Senegal	21	22	32	25	22	47	50	84	82	63	37
1996	Zambia	54	50	68	72	60	69	72	84	83	78	67

Source: World Bank, *African Development Indicators* (1998–99).

Table A.9 Net secondary school enrollment rates by consumption quintile and region

| Year | Countries | Rural areas | | | Urban areas | | | National |
		Lowest quintile	Upper quintile	All	Lowest quintile	Upper quintile	All	All
1994–95	Burkina Faso	2	14	6	18	57	36	12
1993	Central African Republic	21	22	23	42	62	52	36
1995	Côte d'Ivoire	3	11	9	20	38	28	18
1996	Djibouti	3	9	7	10	52	31	30
1995–96	Ethiopia	0	1	1	20	34	30	6
1992	Gambia	3	11	8	19	26	25	16
1997	Ghana	32	40	35	40	49	45	38
1994–95	Guinea	1	3	3	16	34	25	12
1994	Kenya	3	16	9	15	44	27	11
1993–94	Madagascar	1	23	8	15	64	41	15
1994	Mali	2	8	4	12	23	18	5
1995	Mauritania	1	11	6	17	33	26	15
1995	Niger	1	3	3	13	29	24	7
1992	Nigeria	26	46	38	41	61	58	46
1994–95	Senegal	1	6	3	11	52	25	13
1996	Zambia	8	17	12	23	46	33	20

Source: World Bank, *African Development Indicators* (1998–99).

Table A.10 Benefit incidence of public spending on health in selected countries

| | Quintile shares of: | | | | | | | | Total subsidy as percentage of per capita expenditure | |
| | Primary facilities | | Hospital outpatient[a] | | Hospital inpatient | | All health | | | |
	Poorest	Richest	Poorest	Richest	Poorest	Richest	Poorest	Richest	Poorest	Richest
Africa										
Côte d'Ivoire (1995)	14	22	8	39	...	...	11	32	2.0	1.3
Ghana (1992)	10	31	13	35	11	32	12	33	3.5	2.3
Guinea (1994)	10	36	1	55	...	...	4	48	...	...
Kenya (1992)[b]	22	14	13	26	...	...	14	24	6.0	1.1
Madagascar (1993)	10	29	14	30	...	...	12	30	4.5	0.5
Tanzania (1992/93)	18	21	11	37	20	36	17	29	...	...
South Africa (1994)	18	10	15	17	...	...	16	17	28.2	1.5

... Not available.
a. Hospital subsidies combine inpatient and outpatient spending in Côte d'Ivoire, Guinea, Kenya, Madagascar, and South Africa.
b. Rural only.
Source: Castro-Leal and others (1999).

Table A.11 Primary enrollments and literacy

Country[a]	Primary GER		Adult literacy
	1985	1995	
Somalia	11.5	8.7	...
Niger	25.5	29.0	13.6
Liberia	36.9	33.4	...
Mali	22.7	34.2	31.0
Ethiopia	37.4	37.5	35.5
Djibouti	40.0	38.5	46.3
Burkina Faso	27.0	39.5	19.2
Guinea	34.5	48.4	35.9
Burundi	52.5	50.6	35.4
Sudan	50.0	51.8	46.1
Sierra Leone	62.7	53.0	31.4
Eritrea	...	56.6	...
Chad	43.5	57.7	48.1
Central African Republic	75.0	58.9	60.0
Mozambique	87.3	60.3	40.1
Senegal	56.4	64.8	33.1
Tanzania	74.9	67.0	67.8
Guinea–Bissau	63.4	67.9	54.9
Côte d'Ivoire	71.6	68.7	40.2
Democratic Rep. of Congo	86.5	71.7	77.3
Benin	67.7	72.0	37.0
Madagascar	103.6	72.5	...
Uganda	73.0	73.0	61.8
Comoros	83.7	74.4	57.3
Ghana	75.7	76.1	64.5
Angola	106.3	76.7	...
Gambia	68.1	77.0	38.6
Mauritania	48.3	78.5	37.7
Kenya	98.8	85.2	...
Nigeria	95.8	88.0	57.1
Cameroon	...	88.0	...
Zambia	104.2	89.3	78.2
Seychelles	...	96.0	79.0
Rwanda	62.9	96.5	...
Lesotho	110.1	99.8	71.4
Mauritius	109.5	106.6	82.9
Botswana	105.2	112.2	69.8
Democratic Republic of Congo	147.2	113.9	74.9
Zimbabwe	135.6	115.5	85.1
South Africa	91.8	116.7	81.8
Togo	92.7	118.5	...
Swaziland	101.9	125.6	76.7
Namibia	132.5	132.7	...
Malawi	59.9	135.0	56.4
Cape Verde	117.0	135.0	71.6
Gabon	...	142.0[b]	48.0

... Not available.

a. Data are not available for Equatorial Guinea and São Tomé and Principé.

b. 1993–95 average.

Sources: UNESCO Yearbook, 1998; *World Development Indicators 1998.*

Table A.12 Net primary enrollments by expenditure quintiles, urban/rural, and gender[a] (percentages) country expenditure quintiles

		1			*2*			*3*			*4*			*5*		
		T	M	F	T	M	F	T	M	F	T	M	F	T	M	F
Burkina	urban	53	58	48	66	69	62	73	78	68	79	85	74	80	87	74
Faso	rural	17	22	12	20	27	12	24	31	15	33	39	26	44	45	42
Central	urban	46	50	42	65	70	59	69	71	66	73	74	71	76	78	74
African Rep.	rural	29	39	19	35	42	27	37	46	27	40	48	33	48	58	38
Côte d'Ivoire	urban	40	43	35	41	43	40	50	51	50	69	78	60	53	75	42
	rural	17	20	13	33	36	30	30	24	37	34	38	25	39	45	31
Djibouti	urban	54	59	48	70	74	65	70	77	64	75	78	71	79	82	74
	rural	48	64	32	65	79	52	74	82	62	65	78	53	82	87	73
Ethiopia	urban	59	62	56	66	66	67	68	66	70	71	74	69	74	75	74
	rural	11	14	8	12	15	9	14	17	10	14	18	10	18	23	13
Gambia	urban	34	42	26	49	58	41	54	58	41	49	45	52	60	53	68
	rural	9	13	6	15	18	11	16	19	14	25	30	19	33	38	28
Ghana	urban	62	60	65	67	71	63	71	73	68	70	72	68	73	71	76
	rural	57	60	53	55	56	54	62	60	63	66	67	65	71	71	70
Guinea	urban	38	46	29	55	63	47	57	69	46	66	74	58	71	77	65
	rural	13	21	5	14	17	9	15	18	12	22	34	12	28	31	24
Kenya	urban	73	71	76	85	82	90	83	88	80	92	94	89	95	98	91
	rural	66	67	64	73	75	72	78	79	78	80	82	78	80	80	81
Madagascar	urban	38	38	37	51	50	53	68	69	67	68	69	67	68	66	70
	rural	12	10	13	21	22	19	28	26	31	36	31	42	43	44	41
Mali	urban	57	62	51	55	57	53	51	50	52	58	61	55	64	64	63
	rural	17	24	9	13	14	11	20	26	14	21	28	13	31	38	23
Mauritania	urban	49	48	51	59	55	62	62	65	59	57	62	52	65	71	58
	rural	22	25	18	33	32	35	36	35	37	39	42	35	46	52	38
Niger	urban	36	42	29	45	50	42	55	59	50	54	57	50	63	65	60
	rural	11	14	8	15	22	8	19	26	14	14	17	12	14	20	9
Nigeria	urban	55	56	55	63	62	65	69	71	66	69	72	67	74	74	73
	rural	48	48	47	50	51	49	55	54	56	58	59	56	67	71	62
Senegal	urban	49	47	50	60	64	57	55	60	51	72	76	68	83	84	82
	rural	21	21	22	18	20	17	21	27	15	23	27	19	28	32	25
Sierra Leone	urban	62	65	59	55	61	50	77	78	75	68	71	65	75	81	66
	rural	63	66	59	66	70	61	66	67	64	29	34	23	23	24	22
Zambia	urban	70	69	72	78	81	76	80	82	78	82	83	82	83	84	83
	rural	52	54	50	58	55	60	62	62	62	65	64	65	70	68	72

a. The data are for various years from 1989/90 to 1997, the majority of which are for 1992–96.
Source: African Development Indicators, 1998/99, tables 15–1 to 15–22.

Table A.13 1996 gender gaps in primary gross enrollment ratios (GER), 1996

Low primary GER countries	Gender gap (female-male enrollment)	Moderate primary GER countries	Gender gap (female-male enrollment)	High primary GER countries	Gender gap (female-male enrollment)
Chad	–40.8	Benin	–40.7	Togo	–40.1
Guinea	–29.9	Guinea–Bissau	–37.2	Malawi	–12.9
Central African Rep.	–25.1	Congo, Dem. Rep.	–26.2	Congo, Rep	–10.8
Ethiopia	–23.3	Côte d'Ivoire	–21.2	Swaziland	–6.5
Mozambique	–20.4	Gambia	–20.3	Zimbabwe	–3.5
Sierra Leone	–19.1	Nigeria	–20.2	Rwanda	–2.6
Burkina Faso	–16.9	Uganda	–13.0	South Africa	–2.1
Mali	–16.2	Ghana	–12.8	Mauritius	–0.9
Niger	–14.0	Comoros	–10.8	Cape Verde	+0.5
Senegal	–13.8	Mauritania	–9.6	Botswana	+1
Djibouti	–12	Cameroon	–8.6	Namibia	+1.8
Liberia	–11.9	Angola	–5.9	Lesotho	+10.6
Eritrea	10.6	Zambia	–5.7	Seychelles	…
Burundi	–9.4	Madagascar	–2.3	Gabon	…
Sudan	–9.1	Tanzania	–1.2		
Somalia	–5.3	Kenya	0		

… Not available.
Sources: UNESCO Yearbook (1998); UNDP (1998).

References and Bibliography

Background Papers

Appiah, Kweku. 1999. "Poverty and Education in Sub-Saharan Africa." Background paper 10.

Baulch, Bob, and Ursula Grant. 1999. "Poverty, Inequality and Growth in Sub-Saharan Africa." Background paper 3c.

Bloom, Gerry, and Henry Lucas. 1999. "Poverty and Health in Sub-Saharan Africa." Background paper 7.

Booth, David, Melissa Leach, and Alison Tierney. 1999. "Experiencing Poverty in Africa: Perspectives from Anthropology." Background Paper 1b.

Cherel-Robson, Mila, and Bob Baulch. 1999. "Growth, Inequality and Poverty in Mauritania." 1987–96. Background paper 3d.

Cortijo, Marie-Jo, and Nathalie LeBrun. 1999. "Policy Reforms and Poverty in Tanzania." Background paper 3b.

de Haan, Arjan. 1999. "Migration and Poverty in Africa: Is there a Link?" Background paper 6a.

de Haan, Arjan, Simon Maxwell, Michael Lipton, and Frederic Martin. 1999. "Poverty Monitoring in Sub-Saharan Africa." Background paper 2.

Harper, Caroline, and Rachel Marcus. 1999. "Child Poverty in Sub-Saharan Africa." Background paper 4.

Kabeer, Naila, and Ann Whitehead. 1999. "From Uncertainty to Risk: Poverty, Growth and Gender in the Rural African Context." Background paper 5.

Larivière, Sylvain, Frédéric Martin, and Aliou Diagne. 1999. "Agricultural Production, Rural Livelihood and Poverty Reduction in Sub-Saharan Africa." Background paper 8.

Lariviere, Sylvain, Frédéric Martin, Boilly Martin, and Marie-Helene. 1999. "How the Poor Perceive Poverty in Sub-Saharan Africa." Background paper 1a.

Lipton, Michael. 1999. "Grounds for Hope and Action: Poverty Reduction and Fertility Transition in Sub-Saharan Africa." Background paper 6b.

Luckham, Robin, Ismail Ahmed, and Robert Muggah. 1999. "The Impact of Conflict on Poverty." Background paper 9.

McCulloch, Neil, and Bob Baulch. 1999. "Poverty, Inequality, and Growth in Zambia." Background paper 3a.

References and Bibliography

Ablo, Emmanuel, and Ritva Reinikka. 1998. "Do Budgets Really Matter? Evidence from Public Spending on Education and Health in Uganda." Policy Research Paper No. 1926. World Bank, Washington D.C.

ADB (African Development Bank). 1999. *African Development Report 1999*. Abidjan, Ivory Coast.

Adelman, I., and S.J. Vogel. 1992. "The Relevance of ADLI for Sub-Saharan Africa." In *African Development Perspectives Yearbook, 1990/91*, vol. II. Münster, Lit: 258–279.

Addison, Tony. 1993. "A Review of the World Bank's Efforts to Assist African Governments in Reducing Poverty." ESP Discussion Paper No 10. World Bank, Washington, D.C.

Aggarwal, Bina. 1997. "Bargaining and Gender Relations Within and Beyond the Household." *Feminist Economics* 3(1): 1–51.

Aird, Sarah. 1999. "Ghana's Slaves to the Gods." *Human Rights Brief* 7(1): 6–8.

Alderman, H., and M. Garcia. 1993. "Poverty, Household Food Security and Nutrition in Rural Pakistan." International Food Policy Research Institute (IFPRI) Research Report No. 96, Washington, D.C.

Ali, Ali A. G. 1999. "Poverty, Inequality and Growth: Issues and Facts." Paper presented at AERC/AFDB/GCA/UNECA/ World Bank Collaborative Project conference "Can Africa Claim the 21st Century?" July 6–11, Abidjan, Ivory Coast.

Ali, Ali A.G., and Erik Thorbecke. 1998. "The Magnitude of Poverty in Sub-Saharan Africa: Some Preliminary Results." Cornell University. Processed.

Appleton, Simon, T. Emwanu, J. Kagugube, and J. Muwonge. 1999. "Changes in Poverty in Uganda, 1992–97." Oxford: Centre for the Study of African Economies. May. Processed.

Ascher, W. 1984. *Scheming for the Poor: The Politics of Redistribution in Latin America.* Cambridge, Mass.: Harvard University Press.

Ayittey, George B. N. 1998. *Africa in Chaos.* Basingstoke, U.K.: Macmillan.

Bamberger, Michael. 1996. "Key Issues in the Design and Management of Targeted Poverty Alleviation Programs." In Michael Bamberger, Abdullahi M. Yahie, and George Matovu, eds. *The Design and Management of Poverty Reduction Programs and Projects in Anglophone Africa.* Washington, D.C.: Economic Development Institute, World Bank.

Baulch, Robert. 1996. "The New Poverty Agenda—A Disputed Consensus." *IDS Bulletin* 27(1): 1–10.

Baulch, Robert, and John Hoddinot. 1999. "Economic Mobility and Poverty Dynamics in Developing Countries." Brighton: Institute of Development Studies and Washington, D.C.: IFPRI. Processed.

Bayart, Jean-Francois, Stephen Ellis, and Beatrice Hibou, eds. 1999. *The Criminalisation of the State in Africa.* Oxford: James Currey.

Benneh, G. 1996. *Toward Sustainable Smallholder Agriculture in Sub-Saharan Africa.* IFPRI, Washington, D.C.

Besley, Timothy, and Ravi Kanbur. 1994. "The Principles of Targeting." In Michael Lipton and Jacques van der Graag, eds. *Including the Poor.* Washington, D.C.: World Bank.

Bigsten, A., and Kayizzi-Mugerwa, S. 1999. *Crisis, Adjustment and Growth in Uganda: A Study of Adaptation in an African Economy.* London: Macmillan.

Blackden, Mark, and Chitra Bhanu. 1999. "Gender, Growth and Poverty Reduction." 1998. *Africa: Poverty Status Report.* World Bank, Washington, D.C.

Bloom, David, and David Canning. 1999. "Economic Development and the Demographic Transition." Harvard Institute for International Development (HIID), Cambridge, Mass. Processed.

Bonte, P. 1999. "Ethnicity and Land Tenure in Sahel." In S. P. Reyna and R. E. Downs, eds. *Deadly Developments: Capitalism, States and War.* University of New Hampshire, Durham: Gorden Breach Publishers.

Booth, David. 1999. "Ghana Country Report." Report for Department for International Development/Swedish International Development Authority (SIDA) project "Creating a Framework for Reducing Poverty: Institutional and Process Issues in National Poverty Policy." London: Overseas Development Institute (ODI). Processed.

Booth, David, and Howard White. 1999. "How Can Country Strategies be a More Effective Tool for Poverty Reduction? Issues from a Review of the 'New' CSPs." London: ODI. Processed.

Bourguignon, Francoise, and Christian Morrisson. 1992. *Adjustment and Equity in Developing Countries: A New Approach.* Organization for Economic Cooperation and Development, Development Assistance Committee (OECD-DAC), Paris.

Bouton, L., C. Jones, and M. Kiguel. 1994. "Macroeconomic Reform and Growth in Africa: Adjustment in Africa Revisited." Policy Research Working Paper No. WPS 1394. World Bank, Washington, D.C. December.

Bredenkamp, Hugh, and Susan Schadler, eds. 1999. *Economic Reforms and Adjustment in Low-Income Countries.* Washington, D.C.: International Monetary Fund.

Broch-Due, Vigdis. 1995. "Poverty and Prosperity: Local and Global Perspectives." Occasional Paper No. 1. Uppsala: Nordiska Afikainstitutet.

Brocklesby, Mary Ann, and Jeremy Holland. 1998. "Participatory Poverty Assessments and Public Sector Improvements: Key Messages from the Poor." Centre for Development Studies, University of Swansea. Processed.

Bruce, John W. 1998. *Country Profiles of Land Tenure: Africa, 1996* Land Tenure Center Research Paper No. 130. Madison: Land Tenure Center, University of Wisconsin.

Bruno, Michael, Martin Ravallion, and Lyn Squire. 1996. "Equity and Growth in Developing Countries: Old and New Perspectives on the Policy Issues." Policy Research Working Paper 1563. World Bank, Washington, D.C.

Buchanan-Smith, Margaret, and Susanna Davies. 1995. *Famine Early Warning and Response: The Missing Link.* London: Intermediate Technology Publications.

Calamitsis, Evangelos, Anupam Basu, and Dhaneshwar Ghura. 1999. "Adjustment and Growth in Sub-Saharan Africa." Working Paper WP/99/51. International Monetary Fund (IMF), Washington, D.C.

Callaghy, Thomas M. 1991. "Lost Between State and Market: The Politics of Economic Adjustment in Ghana, Zambia and Nigeria." In Joan Nelson, ed. *Economic Crisis and Policy Choice: The Politics of Adjustment in the Third World.* Princeton University Press, 257–320.

Carrin, G., and C. Politi. 1995. "Exploring the Health Impact of Economic Growth, Poverty Reduction and Public Health Expenditure." *Tijdschrift voor Economie en Management* 40: 227–46.

Castro-Leal, Florencia, Julia Dayton, Lionel Demery, and Kalpana Mehra. 1999. "Public Social Spending in Africa: Do the Poor Benefit?" *World Bank Research Observer* 14(1). February.

Chabal, Patrick, and Jean-Pascal Daloz. 1999. *Africa Works.* Oxford: James Currey.

Clapham, Christopher. 1991. "The African State." In Douglas Rimmer, ed. *Africa 30 Years On.* London: James Currey, 91–104.

————. 1996. *Africa and the International System: The Politics of State Survival.* Cambridge University Press.

Cohen, Barry. 1998. "The Emerging Fertility Transition in Sub-Saharan Africa." *World Development* 26(8): 1431–61.

Colclough, Christopher, and Keith Lewin. 1993. *Educating All the Children: Strategies for Primary Schooling in the South.* Oxford: Clarendon Press.

Collier, Paul. 1999. "Doing Well out of War." World Bank, Washington, D.C. www.worldbank/research/conflict/papers.

Collier, Paul, and Anke Hoeffler. 1999. "On Economic Causes of Civil War." World Bank, Washington, D.C. www.worldbank/research/conflict/papers.

Collier, Paul, and Jan Willem Gunning. 1999a. "Why Has Africa Grown Slowly?" *Journal of Economic Perspectives* 13(3): 3-22.

————. 1999b. "Explaining African Economic Performance" *Journal of Economic Literature* 37: 64–111.

Coquery-Vidrovitch, Catherine. 1997. *African Women: A Modern History.* Boulder, Colo.: Westview Press.

Coulson, Andrew. 1979. *African Socialism in Practice: The Tanzanian Experience.* Nottingham: Spokesman.

Cox, Aidan, ed. 1999. *Donor Poverty Reduction Policies and Practices.* Development Assistance Committee Scoping Study. Revised draft. March. OECD-DAC, Paris.

Cox, Aidan, and John Healey. 1998. "Promises to the Poor: The Record of European Development Agencies." Poverty Briefing No. 1. November. London: Overseas Development Institute.

Cox, Aidan., John Healey, and P. Hoebink. Forthcoming. *Promises to the Poor: The Poverty Reduction Policies of European Development Cooperation Agencies and Their Effectiveness.* London: Macmillan.

Crawford. 1997. Foreign Aid and Political Conditionality: Issues of Effectiveness and Consistency. *Democratization* 4(3): 69–108.

Crehan, Kate. 1997. *The Fractured Community: Landscapes of Power and Gender in Rural Zambia.* Berkeley: University of California Press.

Crewe, Emma, and Elizabeth Harrison. 1998. *Whose Development? An Ethnography of Aid.* London: Zed Books.

Crook, Richard, and A. S. Sverrisson. 1999. "To What Extent Can Decentralized Forms of Government Enhance the Development of Pro-Poor Policies and Improve Poverty-Alleviation Outcomes." Brighton: Institute of Development Studies, University of Sussex. Processed.

DANIDA (Danish International Development Agency). 1996. *Poverty Reduction in Danish Development Assistance.* Evaluation Report 1996/14. Copenhagen: DANIDA.

Deininger, Klaus, and Lyn Squire. 1996. "Measuring Income Inequality: A New Database." World Bank, Washington, D.C. Processed.

Delgado, Christopher L. 1995. "Africa's Changing Agricultural Development Strategies: Past and Present Paradigms as a Guide to the Future." International Food Policy Research Institute, Food, Agriculture and the Environment Discussion Papers 3. Washington, D.C.: IFPRI.

Delgado, Christopher, Jane Hopkins, and Valerie A Kelly. 1998. *Agricultural Growth Linkages in Sub-Saharan Africa.* International Food Policy Research Institute Research Reports 107. Washington, D.C.: IFPRI.

Demery, Lionel. 1999. "Poverty Dynamics in Africa: An Update." World Bank, Washington, D.C. October. Processed.

Demery, Lionel, Binayak Sen, and Tara Vishwanath. 1995. "Poverty, Inequality and Growth." Education and Social Policy Discussion Paper Series, number 70 (June). Washington D.C.: World Bank.

Demery, Lionel, and Lyn Squire. 1996. "Macroeconomic Adjustment and Poverty in Africa: An Emerging Picture." *World Bank Research Observer* 11(1) (February): 39–59.

Demographic Health Surveys. 1997. "DHS Maternal Mortality Indicators: An Assessment of Data Quality and Implications for Data Use." DHS Analytical Report No. 4. Calverton, Maryland: Macro International, Inc.

Deng, Lual. 1998. *Rethinking African Development: Toward a Framework for Social Integration and Ecological Harmony.* Trenton, N.J., and Asmara, Eritrea: Africa World Press.

Department for International Development. 1997. *Eliminating World Poverty: A Challenge for the 21st Century.* London: The Stationery Office.

Dercon, Stefan. 1997. "Wealth, Risk and Activity Choice: Cattle in Western Tanzania." *Journal of African Economies* 55(1): 1–42.

Devereux, Stephen. 1999. "Targeting Transfers: Innovative Solutions to Familiar Problems." *IDS Bulletin* 30(2): 61–74.

de Wal, Alex. 1997. *Famine Crisis: Politics and the Disaster Relief Industry in Africa.* Oxford: James Currey and Bloomington: Indiana University Press in association with African Rights and International African Institute.

Drangert, Jan-Olof. 1993. *Who Cares about Water? Household Water Development in Sukumaland, Tanzania.* Linköping: Linköping Studies in Arts and Science.

Easterly, William, and Ross Levine. 1997. "Africa's Growth Tragedy: A Retrospective, 1960–89." *Policy Research Working Paper 1503.* World Bank, Washington, D.C.

Eastwood, Robert, and Michael Lipton. Forthcoming. "The Impact of Changes in Human Fertility on Poverty."

Fairhead, James. 2000. "The Conflict over Natural and Environmental Resources." In E.W. Nafziger, F. Stewart, and R. Vayrynen, eds., *War, Hunger, and Displacement: The Origins of Humanitarian Emergencies.* Vol. 1, *Analysis.* Oxford: OUP.

Fairhead, James, and Melissa Leach. 1996. *Misreading the African Landscape: Society and Ecology in a Forest-Savanna Mosaic.* Cambridge University Press.

Fields, Gary. 1989. "Changes in Poverty and Inequality in Developing Countries." *World Bank Research Observer* 4(2): 167–85.

Fischer, S., E. Hernández-Catá, and M. Khan. 1998. "Africa: Is This the Turning Point?" Paper on Policy Analysis and Assessment, PPAA/98/6. May. IMF, Washington, D.C.

Food and Agriculture Organisation of the UN (FAO). 1999. *The State of Food Insecurity in the World, 1999*. Rome: FAO.

Francis, Paul A., S. P. I Agi, S. Ogoh Alubo, Hawa A. Biu, A. G. Daramola, Uchenna M. Nzewi, and D. J. Shehu. 1998. "Hard Lessons: Primary Schools, Community and Social Capital in Nigeria." World Bank, Washington D.C.

Franklin, Anita Shanta. 1995. *Land Law in Lesotho: Politics of the 1979 Land Act*. Aldershot, England: Avebury.

Frimpong-Ansah, Jonathan H. 1991. *The Vampire State in Africa: The Political Economy of Decline in Ghana*. London: James Currey.

Frischmuth, Christiane. 1997. "Gender Is Not a Sensitive Issue: Institutionalizing Gender-Oriented Participatory Approach in Saivonga, Zambia." IIED Gatekeeper Series 72. London: IIED.

Fuller, B. 1989. "Eroding Economy and Declining School Quality: The Case of Malawi." *IDS Bulletin* 20(1): 11–16.

Gabre-Madhin, E., and Bruce Johnson. 1999. "Accelerating Africa's Structural Transformation: Lessons from East Asia." IFPRI Markets and Structural Studies Division Discussion Paper 34. Washington, D.C.: IFPRI.

Ghura, Dhaneshwar. 1995. "Macro Policies, External Forces, and Economic Growth in Sub-Saharan Africa." *Economic Development and Cultural Change*, 43(4), July.

Glewwe, P., and J. van der Gaag. 1990. "Identifying the Poor in Developing Countries: Do Different Definitions Matter?" *World Development* 24(6), June.

Govender, P. 1998. "Women's Budget in South Africa." In Steve Kayizzi-Mugerwa, Adebayo O. Olukoshi, and Lennart Wohlgemuth. *Towards a New Partnership with Africa, Challenges and Opportunities*. Nordiska Afrikainstitutet, Uppsala, Sweden.

Graham-Brown, Sarah. 1991. *Education in the Developing World: Conflict and Crisis*. London and New York: Longman.

Greeley, Martin, and Rob Jenkins. 1999. "Mainstreaming the Poverty-Reduction Agenda." Paper prepared for the Strategic Partnership with Africa Working Group on Poverty and Social Policy. October.

Grootaert, Christiaan, and Ravi Kanbur. 1995. "The Lucky Few Amidst Economic Decline: Distributional Change in Côte d'Ivoire as Seen through Panel Data Sets, 1985–88." *Journal of Development Studies* 31(4): 603–19.

Gupta, Sanjeev, Hamid Davoodi, and Rosa Alonso-Terme. 1998. "Does Corruption Affect Income Inequality and Poverty?" Working Paper 98/76. IMF, Washington, D.C.

Haddad, Lawrence, Marie Ruel, and James Garrett. 1998. "Growing Urban Poverty and Undernutrition and Some Urban Facts of Life: Implications for Research and Policy." IFPRI, Washington, D.C. Processed.

Hanmer, Lucia, Graham Pyatt, and Howard White. 1997. *Poverty in Sub-Saharan Africa: What Do We Learn from World Bank Poverty Assessments?* Institute of Social Studies, The Hague.

Hanmer, Lucia, and Felix Naschold. 1999. "Are the International Development Targets Attainable?" London: Overseas Development Institute. May. Processed.

Hanmer, Lucia, and Howard White. 1999. *Human Development in Sub-Saharan Africa: The Determinants of Under-Five Mortality with Case Studies of Zambia and Zimbabwe*. Report for SIDA. ISS, The Hague.

Hansungule, Michelo, Patricia Feeney, and Robin Palmer. 1998. "Report on Land Tenure Insecurity on the Zambian Copperbelt." Lusaka, Zambia: Oxfam GB.

Haughton, Jonathan. 1998. "The Reconstruction of War-Torn Economies." HIID, Cambridge, Mass. Processed.

Hayami, Yujiro. 1997. *Development Economics: From Poverty to the Wealth of Nations*. Oxford: Clarendon Press.

Healey, John, and Tony Killick. Forthcoming. "Using Aid to Reduce Poverty." In Finn Tarp, ed., and Peter Hjertholm, ed. assistant, *Foreign Aid and Development: Lessons Learnt and Directions for the Future*. London: Routledge.

HelpAge International. 1999. *The Ageing and Development Report: Poverty, Independence and the World's Older People*. London: Earthscan.

Hoppers, W. 1989. "The Responses from the Grassroots: Self-reliance in Zambian Education." IDS Bulletin 20(1) 17–23.

Howard, Mary, and Ann Millard. 1997. *Hunger and Shame: Child Malnutrition and Poverty on Mount Kilimanjaro*. London: Routledge.

Hulme, David, and Paul Mosley. 1997. "Microenterprise Finance: Is there a Conflict between Growth and Poverty Alleviation?" *World Development* 26(5): 783–90.

Hunt, Diane. 1984. *The Impending Crisis in Kenya: The Case for Land Reform*. Guildford: Gower.

Illiffe, John. 1987. *The African Poor*. Cambridge University Press.

ILO (International Labor Organization). 1999. *World Employment Report, 1998-99*. Geneva.

IMF (International Monetary Fund). Various years. *World Economic Outlook*. IMF, Washington, D.C.

Jackson, Robert H., and Carl G. Rosberg. 1984. "Personal Rule: Theory and Practice in Africa." *Comparative Politics* 421–42. Reprinted in Peter Lewis, ed. 1998. *Africa: Dilemmas of Development and Change*. Boulder, Colo.: Westview Press.

Jodha, N. S. 1988. "Poverty Debate in India: A Minority View." *Economic and Political Weekly* 22(45–47): 2421–28.

Kayizzi-Mugerwa, S. 1998. "A Review of Macroeconomic Impediments to Technology Adoption in African Agriculture." *African Development Review* 10(1), June.

Killick, Tony. 1995a. *The Flexible Economy: Causes and Consequences of the Adaptability of National Economies.* London: Routledge, chapter 6.

———. 1995b. "Structural Adjustment and Poverty Alleviation." *Development and Change* 26(2) 305–331.

———. 1997. "Adjustment, Income Distribution and Poverty in Africa: A Research Guide." ODI, London. Processed.

———. 1998. "Have Africa's Economies Turned the Corner?" Paper presented at the Enterprise for Africa conference, University of Edinburgh. ODI, London (revised draft), June.

———. Forthcoming. "Adjustment, Income Distribution and Poverty in Africa: A Research Guide." AERC Special Paper. Nairobi: African Economic Research Consortium.

Killick, Tony, Jerker Carlsson, and Anna Kierkegaard. 1998. "European Aid and the Reduction of Poverty in Zimbabwe." Working Paper 109. ODI, London.

Lambert, Rachel. 1994. "Monitoring Food Security and Coping Strategies: Lessons Learnt from the SADS Project, Mopti Region, Mali." Save the Children, London.

Levin, Richard, Ian Solomon, and Daniel Weiner. 1997. "Class, Gender and the Politics of Rural Land Reform." In Richard Levin and Daniel Weiner, eds. *No More Tears: Struggles for Land in Mpumalanga, South Africa.* Trenton, N.J.: Africa World Press.

Lipton, Michael, and Jacques van der Gaag, eds. 1993. *Including the Poor.* World Bank, Washington, D.C., chapter 1.

MacGaffey, Janet. 1988. "Economic Disengagement and Class Formation in Zaire." In D. Rothchild and N. Chaza, eds. *The Precarious Balance: State and Society in Africa.* Boulder, Colo.: Westview Press, chapter 7

MacKenzie, A. Fiona. 1998. *Land, Ecology and Resistance in Kenya, 1880–1952.* Portsmouth: Heinemann.

MAP (Monitoring the AIDS Pandemic). 1998. *The Status and Trends of the HIV/AIDS Epidemics in the World.* Boston.

Mauldin, W. Parker. 1994. "Maternal Mortality in Developing Countries: A Comparison of Rates from Two International Compendia." *Population and Development Review* 20(4): 413–21.

Maxwell, Daniel. 1999. "The Political Economy of Urban Food Security in Sub-Saharan Africa." *World Development* 27(11), November.

McKay, Andrew, Chris Milner, Abbi Kedir, and Susana Franco. 1999. "Trade, Technology and Poverty: The Linkages. A Review of the Literature." CREDIT, University of Nottingham. February. Processed.

Meagher, Kate. 1995. "Crisis, Informalization and the Urban Informal Sector in Sub-Saharan Africa." *Development and Change*, 26(2), April.

Mkandawire, Thandika. 1998. "Thinking about Developmental States in Africa" *African Development in a Comparative Perspective Study No. 9.* United Nations Conference on Trade and Development (UNCTAD), Geneva.

Moore, Mick, and James Putzel. 1999. "Politics and Poverty: A Background Paper for the *World Development Report 2000/1.*" Brighton: IDS, University of Sussex. Processed.

Moore, Mick, Jennifer Leavy, Peter Houtzager, and Howard White. 1999. "Polity Qualities: How Governance Affects Poverty." Brighton: IDS, University of Sussex. Processed.

Moser, Caroline. 1996. *Confronting Crisis: A Comparative Study of Household Response to Poverty and Vulnerability in Four Poor Urban Communities.* Environmentally Sustainable Development Studies and Monographs Series No. 8. World Bank, Washington, D.C.

Mosley, Paul. 1999. "The Performance of the Research System and the African Green Revolution: Maize, Sorghum and Cassava." Paper presented at the DSA Conference, University of Bath, England, September 12–14.

Mosley, Paul, Turan Subasat, and John Weeks. 1995. "Assessing Adjustment in Africa." *World Development* 23(9): 1459–73.

Narayan, Deepa, and Lant Pritchett. 1997. "Cents and Sociability: Household Income and Social Capital in Rural Tanzania." Policy Research Working Paper 1796. World Bank, Washington, D.C.

Nelson, Joan. 1996. "Household Equivalence Scales: Theory versus Policy." In *Feminism, Objectivity and Economics.* London: Routledge.

ODI (Overseas Development Institute). 1999. "Making Adjustment Work for the Poor." Poverty Briefing No. 5. London.

OECD-DAC (Organization for Economic Cooperation and Development, Development Assistance Committee). *Development Cooperation.* Various years. OECD, Paris.

———. 1999. *Scoping Study of Donor Poverty Reduction Policies and Practices.* Synthesis Report. Revised draft, March. OECD, Paris.

Oshikoya, Ojo and Temitope Oshikoya. 1995. "Determinants of Long-Run Growth: Some African Results." *Journal of African Economies* 4(2): 163–91.

Quisumbing, Agnes, Lawrence Haddad, and Christine Peña. 1995. "Gender and Poverty: New Evidence from Ten Countries." FCND Discussion Paper No. 9. IFPRI, Washington, D.C.

Ranis, Gustav, and Frances Stewart. 1999. "Strategies for Success in Human Development." Paper presented at the Development Studies Association Annual Conference, Bath, England, September 12–14. Processed.

Reddy, Sanjay, and Jan Vandemoortele. 1996. "User Financing of Basic Services." United Nations Children's Fund Staff Working Paper, Evaluation, Policy and Planning Series. New York.

Rodrik, Dani. 1999. "The New Global Economy and Developing Countries: Making Openness Work." ODC Policy Essay 24. Washington, D.C.

Roemer, M., and M. K. Gugerty. 1997. "Does Economic Growth Reduce Poverty?" Technical Paper. CAER Discussion Paper No. 5. HIID, Cambridge, Mass.

Rosen, Sydney, and Jeffrey Vincent. 1999. "Household Water Resources and Rural Productivity in Sub-Saharan Africa: A Review of the Evidence." HIID Discussion Paper 673. Cambridge, Mass.

Sachs, J., and A. Warner. 1995. "Economic Convergence and Economic Policies." Development Discussion Paper 502. HIID, Cambridge, Mass.

Sahn, David, Paul Dorosh, and Stephen Younger. 1996. *Economic Reform and the Poor in Africa.* Oxford: Clarendon Press.

Sahn, David, David Stifel, and Stephen Younger. 1999. "Inter-temporal Changes in Welfare: Preliminary Results From Nine African Countries." Cornell University. Processed.

Savvides, Andreas. 1995. "Economic Growth in Africa." *World Development* 23(3): 449–58.

Scoones, Ian, ed. 1995. *Living with Uncertainty: New Directions in Pastoral Development.* London: Intermediate Technology Publications.

Sen, Amartya. 1990. "Individual Freedom as a Social Commitment." *New York Review of Books,* 14 June.

Sharma, Narendra, Torbjorn Damhaug, Edeltraut Gilgan-Hunt, David Grey, Valentina Okaru, and Daniel Rothberg. 1996. "African Water Resources: Challenges and Opportunities for Sustainable Development." Technical Paper No. 331. World Bank, Washington, D.C.

Silla, Eric. 1998. *People Are Not the Same: Leprosy and Identity in Twentieth-Century Mali.* Portsmouth: Heinemann.

Stevens, Christopher. 1999. "Liberalization and Poverty: An Oxfam–IDS Research Project." August.

Stewart, F. 1995. *Adjustment and Poverty: Options and Choices.* London: Routledge.

Stiglitz, Joseph. 1998. "Towards a New Paradigm for Development: Strategies, Policies, and Processes." 1998. Prebisch Lecture. Processed.

Stokke. 1995. *Aid and Political Conditionality.* EADI book series 16, European Association of Development Research and Training Institutions. London: Frank Cass.

Tiffen, Mary, Michael Mortimore, and Francis Gichuki. 1994. *More People, Less Erosion: Environmental Recovery in Kenya.* Chichester, England: John Wiley and Sons.

Tobisson, Eva, and Stefan de Vylder. 1997. "Poverty Reduction and Gender Equality: An Assessment of Sida's Country Reports and Evaluations in 1995–96." *Sida Studies in Evaluation 97/2.* Swedish International Development Authority, Stockholm.

Toye, John. 1999. "Nationalizing the Anti-Poverty Agenda." *IDS Bulletin* 30(2): 6–12.

Tripp, Aili Mari. 1998. "Gender, Political Participation, and the Transformation of Associational Life in Uganda and Tanzania." In Peter Lewis, ed. *Africa: Dilemmas of Development and Change.* Boulder, Colo.: Westview Press.

Turnbull, Colin. 1973. *The Mountain People.* London: Cape.

UNAIDS. 1998. *AIDS Epidemic Update.* Geneva.

———. 1999. *Acting Early to Prevent AIDS: The Case of Senegal.* Geneva.

UNIP (United National Independence Party). 1963. "When UNIP Becomes Government." Election Manifesto, Lusaka, Zambia.

United Nations. 1998. *World Economic and Social Survey, 1998.* New York.

UNDP (United Nations Development Program). 1998. *Human Development Report.* Oxford and New York: Oxford University Press.

van de Walle, Dominique. 1998. "Targeting Revisited." World Bank Research Observer. 13(2): 231–48.

von Braun, Joachim, Tesfaye Teklu, and Patrick Webb. 1999. *Famine in Africa: Causes, Responses and Prevention.* Baltimore: Johns Hopkins University Press.

WDR (World Development Report). 1990. New York: Oxford University Press.

White, Howard. 1996. "How Much Aid Is Used for Poverty Reduction?" *IDS Bulletin,* 27(1), January.

———. 1997. "The Economic and Social Impact of Adjustment in Africa: Further Empirical Analysis." Working Paper No. 245. April. Institute of Social Studies, The Hague.

———. 1999a. *Dollars, Dialogue and Development.* SIDA, Stockholm.

———. 1999b. "Global Poverty Reduction: Are We Heading in the Right Direction?" *Journal of International Development* 4: 503–19.

White, Howard, and Jennifer Leavy. 1999. "The Impact of Adjustment Policies: A Literature Review." GESPA Working Paper No. 11. SIDA, Stockholm.

WHO (World Health Organization). 1997. *Third Report on the World Nutritional Situation 1997.* Geneva.

———. 1999. *World Health Report.* Geneva.

Wood, Adrian, and Jörg Mayer. 1999. "Africa's Export Structure in a Comparative Perspective." Brighton: IDS and Geneva: UNCTAD. Processed.

Working Group on Factors Affecting Contraceptive Use. 1993. *Factors Affecting Contraceptive Use in Sub-Saharan Africa.* Washington, D.C.: National Academy Press.

World Bank. 1990. "World Bank–Tanzania Relations, 1961–87." Report No. 8329. Washington, D.C.

———. 1994. *Adjustment in Africa: Reforms, Results and the Road Ahead.* New York: Oxford University Press.

————. 1995a. *Social Impact of Adjustment Operations.* Operations Evaluation Department (OED) Report No. 14776. Washington, D.C.

————. 1995b. "Rural Women in the Sahel and Their Access to Agricultural Extension: Senegal Country Study." Washington, D.C.

————. 1996. *Taking Action for Poverty Reduction in Sub-Saharan Africa: Report of an Africa Region Task Force.* Washington, D.C.

————. 1997a. *Listening to Farmers: Participatory Assessment of Policy Reform in Zambia's Agriculture Sector.* Washington, D.C.

————. 1997b. *Taking Action to Reduce Poverty in Sub-Saharan Africa.* Washington, D.C.

————. 1998. *World Development Indicators.* Washington, D.C.

————. 1999. *World Development Indicators.* Washington, D.C.

————. 1999. *Global Development Finance, 1999.* Washington, D.C.